当代西方文化学入门（第二版）

INTRODUCTION TO WESTERN CULTURAL STUDIES

彭保良　刘岩　编著

WUHAN UNIVERSITY PRESS
武汉大学出版社

图书在版编目(CIP)数据

当代西方文化学入门:英文、汉文/彭保良,刘岩编著.—2 版.—武汉:武汉大学出版社,2022.8(2025.7 重印)
ISBN 978-7-307-23146-7

Ⅰ.当… Ⅱ.①彭… ②刘… Ⅲ. 西方文化—教材—英、汉 Ⅳ.G11

中国版本图书馆 CIP 数据核字(2022)第 113305 号

责任编辑:罗晓华　　责任校对:李孟潇　　版式设计:韩闻锦

出版发行:**武汉大学出版社**　(430072　武昌　珞珈山)
(电子邮箱:cbs22@ whu.edu.cn 网址:www.wdp.com.cn)
印刷:湖北云景数字印刷有限公司
开本:787×1092　1/16　印张:12.25　字数:257 千字　插页:1
版次:2008 年 1 月第 1 版　2022 年 8 月第 2 版
2025 年 7 月第 2 版第 2 次印刷
ISBN 978-7-307-23146-7　定价:35.00 元

第二版前言

一本教材要保持它应有的活力，就要适时不断更新。作为一本文科教材，《当代西方文化学入门》出版已有十多个年头。仅从时间上看，它已经到了一个非更新不可的节点。另一方面，经过十几年的使用，我们对该教材积累了大量的第一手课堂经验，对课本的内容、知识衔接、段落编排和彼此的联系，有了来自实践中的新的认识。课堂外，随着通信技术的迅猛发展，大众社会向视觉文化①的转向，知识传播途径的变化，所带来的不仅是信息爆炸的时代，而且孕育了一个人文和个性张扬的时代。但是，无论时代怎样变迁，教育还要始终如一地遵循它自身的规律：传承经典，塑造社会精英，培养国家栋梁。在此前提下，教材的编写既要注重文化知识的积淀，又要关注社会现实和时代命脉，让学生学有所用，学有所成。因此，无论是课堂所学，还是社会所需，都使我们意识到，更新教材势在必行。

其次，响应国家"课程思政建设"的号召，也是本次教材修订的主要原因之一。"教书育人"是我们中华民族文化传统的一个重要方面。其实，这句教育箴言所涵盖的内容，有一半内容可以从"思政"的方面来理解，即教育是为什么人、怎样培养人才的问题。只不过在当今世界经济全球化的大形势下，我们有必要更加明确这一目的，那就是我国的高等教育是为社会主义建设培养人才。因此，本次教材修订，不仅注重所选文本的文化内容，而且更需要明确知识在意识形态构建中的作用。

另外，由于我国外语学习不断注重对学生应用能力的培养，以及学分制在不少院校的推广，本次教材修订增加了大量的阅读材料和自学练习，以便增加学生学习的主动性和自主性，并希望通过练习对学生的学习质量和方法有所监控。

最后，编者在此感谢广东外语外贸大学，没有校方对此次教材修订所给予的经济方面的资助，新书就不能如愿付梓出版。同时，我还要感谢我的六位研究生，他们不辞辛苦，在寒假期间帮我审校教材中文字和格式等方面的问题。尽管如此，本书仍难免有纰漏之处，欢迎广大读者批评指正。

编　者

2022 年 2 月 16 日

---

① 周宪．视觉文化的转向[M]．北京：北京大学出版社，2008.

第一版前言

广东外语外贸大学英文学院本科生开设的“文化研究概论”(又名“比较文化”, 1998 年由毛思慧教授设计)课程已有近十个年头。虽然该课程自从开设以来广受学生的欢迎, 在院(校)内形成了一定的影响(既是我院英美文化与传播专业学生的专业必修课, 又是其他学院学生的选修课), 但有一个问题亟待解决: 我们需要一部英文版的文化研究教材。因为一方面, 学生阅读西方文化研究的原著感觉比较吃力, 需要背景知识和有关专业知识方面的辅导; 另一方面, 我们需要加强教材建设、完善教学方法以及不断扩大文化研究课程的影响, 而一本难易适中的英文教材是至关重要的。因此, 出于现实的需要, 我们(编者)在教学之余开始收集相关的材料。经过一年多的筹备, 这本小书终于可以付梓出版了。

本书有六个篇章(单元), 每章(单元)以介绍引进西方文化研究的理论为主。而每章又分为若干节, 每节包含主课文(用于课堂教学)和补充阅读段落(用于学生自学)。主课文的每个段落后附有两项练习: 理解问题、缺词填空。前者考查学生对课文及知识的理解和应用, 后者则是帮助学生梳理并加深理解课文的重点、要点和难点。而每个补充阅读段落后都附有数量不等的对错判断题。这部分材料可作为副课文使用。编辑这部分内容主要出于以下考虑: 增加相关内容的信息量; 提供更深程度的理论知识, 扩大学生相关领域的知识面; 调动学生的学习主动性。补充阅读材料相对于主课文而言, 其深度、广度和长度都有所增加, 有些理论的阐述甚至是英语原文。本教材的适用对象是英语专业的本科学生, 也可作为自学文化研究理论的入门材料。由于时间仓促, 加之编者水平有限, 书中难免存在不足之处, 敬请广大读者批评指正。

本书第五章的主课文由刘岩编写, 其余各章均由彭保良编写。由于种种原因, 我们并未如愿联系到所有原材料的作者。在此谨对所有作者表示由衷的感谢。

编　者

2008 年于白云山麓

目　　录

第一章　基本概念

当今世界，社会结构、制度框架、经济方式、交往媒介、生活状况、心理需求都发生了巨大的变化，现实向文化、学术、观念提出了重新解释的需求。“文化研究”(Cultural Studies，又可称“文化学”)的兴起是对这个世界社会生活的巨大变革向传统学术、传统学科提出的巨大挑战的回应。① 作为一门学问，它在西方已存在半个世纪之多。随着文化研究的发展，文化研究中心、文化研究科系在英美大学里如雨后春笋般涌现，文化研究的成果给高校课堂教学注入了新的内容和活力。在西方，文化研究发展迅速、影响广泛，大有超越传统文学批评之势。

尽管如此，文化研究却是一门新兴的学科。这是因为，它的出现标志着西方人文思想进入了一个多样、多变、复杂、兼容和反叛的时代。首先，文化研究以一个不是流派而胜似流派的科别风靡学界和知识界。虽然它常被人指责没有纲领、缺乏系统和过于宽泛，但是，它解决当今复杂多变的社会和国际问题的能力是有目共睹的。比如说，国际恐怖主义的出现，不可能是哪一个传统的单一学科所能够解释清楚的，而需要历史、文化、宗教、经济、政治甚至是哲学知识的综合运用才可能找出令人比较信服的答案。显而易见，正是文化研究的这种跨学科性才使它本身具备了传统学科无法比拟的功能。其次，文化研究挑战传统学科及其学术思想。比如，传统的文学是属于少数(识字)人的特权，而文学批评也只关注文字文本的阅读和研究。文化研究的出现，既打破了传统文科学科的界限(比如，文字、声、影、文本都是它研究的对象)，又消解了不同文化形式的优劣(比如，精英文化与通俗文化和大众文化之间的转换等)。

文化是一个宽泛复杂的概念，一章的篇幅不足以涵盖所有有关的基本概念和术语，因此本章根据本教材内容的需要进行取舍。第一章将着重讨论“文化”“文化的类型”“文化研究”等概念。

---

① 金元浦．文化研究：理论与实践[M]．郑州：河南大学出版社，2004.

第一节 文化的定义与作用

导 读

学习文化研究，当然应该从了解文化的基本概念开始。比如，什么是文化？根据学者的研究，中西方有关“文化”的定义达两百多种。但是，广为人们所接受的定义在东西方有两种。在中国，文化被分为“广义文化”和“狭义文化”，而在西方，文化被分为大写“C”(Culture)和小写“c”(culture)的文化。比较东西方对文化的界定，人们发现广义的文化和大写“C”所表示的文化类似，而狭义的文化和小写“c”的文化定义接近。即文化一方面可定义为人类社会历史实践过程中所创造的物质财富和精神财富的总和，包括文学、艺术、音乐、建筑、哲学、科学技术成就等；另一方面，文化又可定义为社会意识形态以及与之相适应的制度和组织机构，包括人们的风俗习惯、生活方式、行为准则、社会组织和相互关系等。然而，在文化研究者看来，这些传统的有关文化的定义，都毫无例外地忽略了人和文化的关系(人和文化的互动关系)，它是一种静态的精英模式文化观。文化研究者认为，(对人来说)文化做什么远比文化是什么重要得多。

Passage One: Definitions of Culture

1. There are hundreds of definitions of culture. It is difficult to define because it is a large and inclusive concept. A culture is not usually discussed by the members who share it. Edward Hall, a key researcher into cultures, writes that culture is those deep, common, unstated experiences which members of a given culture share, which they communicate without knowing, and which form the backdrop against which all other events are judged. Some people also argue that culture is like the water fish swim in—a reality that is taken for granted, rarely examined. It is in the air we breathe and as necessary to our understanding of who we are as air is to our physical life.

2. Culture contains three characteristics and does three things. Culture is the **coherent**, **learned**, **shared** view of a group of people about life's concerns that **ranks** what is important, **furnishes** attitudes about what things are appropriate, and **dictates** behavior. Each culture, past

or present, is coherent and complete with itself. Regardless of how peculiar a fragment of a culture seems, when it is placed within the whole tapestry of the culture, it makes sense. Culture is not something we are born with, but rather it is learned. This is not to say people can talk objectively about their own culture. Much of what is learned about one's own culture is stored in mental categories that are recalled only when they are challenged by something different. We all have to be taught our culture. The process begins immediately after birth—even earlier, according to some. A culture is shared by a society. Members of the society agree about the meanings of things and about why. Members of a society probably agree without having to say so that something is necessary and important. Groups are motivated by common views, and these views are a dynamic force in enabling groups to achieve societal goals—protecting economic resources from unscrupulous outsider, for example.

3. Culture ranks what is important. But what is of paramount importance to one group may be virtually meaningless to another. This means that culture teaches people values, —which, according to some scholar, provide people with standards of competence and of morality guiding or determining attitudes, behavior, judgments, comparisons of self and others, rationalizations, exhortative attempts to influence on others, impression management and self-presentation. Culture furnishes attitudes. An attitude is learned, and it is a tendency to respond the same way to the same object or situation or idea. Attitudes are feelings about things, based on values. Attitudes can change, although change can be difficult. Attitudes are based on beliefs as well as values. Beliefs are convictions or certainties based on subjective and—often personal idea rather than on proof or fact. Culture dictates how to behave. Behavior comes directly from the attitudes about how significant something is—how it is valued. Values drive actions.

Exercises

A. Questions for Understanding

1. What is culture according to Edward Hall? What is your understanding of culture?
2. What are the three characteristics of culture? How do you interpret them?
3. According to this passage, how many things does a culture do?
4. How do people know what is more important and what is less important?
5. How do you like the idea that culture dictates people's behavior?

B. Gap Filling

Provide the missing words according to the paragraph you have just read.

1. Culture contains three characteristics and does three things. Culture is the coherent, learned, ______ view of a group of people about life's concerns that ranks what is important, ______ attitudes about what things are appropriate, and dictates behavior. Each culture, past or present, is coherent and complete with itself. Regardless of how peculiar a fragment of a ______ seems, when it is placed within the whole ______ of the culture, it makes sense. Culture is not something we are born with, but rather it is ______. This is not to say people can talk objectively about their own culture. Much of what is learned about one's own culture is stored in mental categories that are recalled only when they are challenged by something ______. We all have to be taught our culture. The ______ begins immediately after birth—even earlier, according to some. A culture is shared by a ______. Members of the society agree about the meanings of things and about why. Members of a society probably agree without having to say so that something is necessary and important. Groups are ______ by common views, and these views are a dynamic force in enabling groups to achieve societal goals—protecting economic resources from ______ outsider, for example.

Passage Two: Functions of Culture

1. How can we get the concept of culture to do more work for us? We might begin by reflecting on the fact that the concept gestures toward what appear to be opposite things: **constraint** and **mobility**①. The ensemble of beliefs and practices that form a given culture function as a pervasive technology of control, a set of limits within which social behavior must be contained, a repertoire of models to which individuals must conform. The limits need not be narrow—in certain societies, such as that of the United States, they—can seem quite vast—but they are not infinite, and the consequences for straying beyond them can be severe. The most effective disciplinary techniques practiced against those who stray beyond the limits of a given culture are probably not the spectacular punishments reserved for serious offenders—exile, imprisonment in an insane asylum, penal servitude, or execution—but seemingly innocuous responses: a condescending smile, laughter poised between the genial and the sarcastic, a small

① constraint: 抑; mobility: 扬(编者译), 是解释文化功能的两个概念。第一篇文章(Passage One)提到文化反作用于人。文化的反作用就可理解为“抑”和“扬”。

dose of indulgent pity laced with contempt, cool silence. And we should add that a cultured boundaries are enforced more positively as well: through the system of rewards that range again from the spectacular (grand public honors, glittering prizes) to the apparently modest (a gaze of admiration, a respectful nod, a few words of gratitude).

2. Art is an important agent then in the transmission of culture. It is one of the ways in which the roles by which men and women are expected to pattern their lives are communicated and passed from generation to generation. Certain artists have been highly self-conscious about this function. The purpose of his vast romance epic, ***The Faerie Queen***①, writes the Renaissance poet Edmund Spenser, is "to fashion a gentleman or noble person in virtuous and gentle discipline." The depth of our understanding of such a project, extended over a complex plot involving hundreds of allegorical figures, depends upon the extent of our grasp of Spenser's entire culture, from its nuanced Aristotelian conception of moral hierarchies to its apocalyptic fantasies, from exquisite refinement at court to colonial violence in Ireland. More precisely, we need to grasp the way in which this culture of mixed motives and conflicting desires seemed to Spenser to generate an interlocking series of models, a moral order, a set of ethical constraints ranged against the threat of anarchy, rebellion, and chaos.

3. To speak of *The Faerie Queen* only in terms of the constraints imposed by culture is obviously inadequate, since the poem itself, with its knights and ladies endlessly roaming an imaginary landscape, is so insistent upon mobility. We return to the paradox with which we started: if culture functions as a structure of limits, it also functions as the regulator and guarantor of movement. Indeed the limits are virtually meaningless without movement; it is only through improvisation, experiment, and exchange that cultural boundaries can be established. Obviously, among different cultures there will be a great diversity in the ratio between mobility and constraint. Some cultures dream of imposing an absolute order, a perfect stasis, but even these, if they are to reproduce themselves from one generation to the next, will have to commit themselves, however tentatively or unwillingly, to some minimal measure of movement; conversely, some cultures dream of an absolute mobility, a perfect freedom, but these too have always been compelled, in the interest of survival, to accept some limits. (From "Culture" by Stephen Greenblatt)

---

① *The Faerie Queen*《仙后》，长篇史诗。由英国文艺复兴时期的宫廷派诗人埃德蒙·斯宾塞于 1596 年所作，主要是为英国女王伊丽莎白一世歌功颂德。

Exercises

A. Questions for Understanding

1. According to Paragraph 1, what does a culture do to people? Name the two key concepts and explain them.

2. What are the examples given in the passage to illustrate the "function" of culture?

3. Why is Edmund Spenser quoted in Paragraph 2? Is it intended to justify "constraint" or "mobility" or both?

4. What does Paragraph 3 try to explicate? What is your attitude toward culture?

5. How does the author actually interpret the "mobility" and "restraint" in Paragraph 3? What hint is provided with regard to the understanding of culture?

B. Gap Filling

Provide the missing words according to the paragraph you have just read.

2. Art is an important ______ then in the transmission of culture. It is one of the ways in which the ______ by which men and women are expected to ______ their lives are communicated and passed from generation to generation. Certain artists have been highly ______ about this function. The purpose of his vast romance epic , *The Faerie Queen*, writes the Renaissance poet Edmund Spenser, is "to fashion a gentleman or noble person in virtuous and gentle discipline." The depth of our understanding of such a project, extended over a complex plot involving hundreds of ______ figures, depends upon the ______ of our grasp of Spenser's entire culture, from its Aristotelian conception of moral ______ to its ______ fantasies, from exquisite refinement at court to colonial violence in Ireland. More precisely, we need to grasp the way in which this culture of mixed motives and conflicting desires seemed to Spenser to generate an interlocking series of models, a moral order, a set of ethical ______ ranged against the threat of anarchy, rebellion, and chaos.

Supplementary Reading (1)

Passage A: Understanding Culture

1. The word "culture" has many different meanings. For some it refers to an appreciation of

good literature, music, art, and food. For a biologist, it is likely to be a colony of bacteria or other microorganisms growing in a nutrient medium in a laboratory Petri dish. However, for anthropologists and other behavioral scientists, culture is the full range of learned human behavior patterns. The term was first used in this way by the pioneer English anthropologist Edward B. Tylor in his book *Primitive Culture* published in 1871. Tylor said that culture is "that complex whole which includes knowledge, belief, art, law, morals, custom, and any other capabilities and habits acquired by man as a member of society". Of course, it is not limited to men. Women possess and create it as well. Since Tylor's time, the concept of culture has become the central focus of anthropology.

2. Culture is a powerful human tool for survival, but it is a fragile phenomenon. It is constantly changing and easily lost because it exists only in our minds. Our written languages, governments, buildings, and other man-made things are merely the products of culture. They are not culture in themselves. For this reason, archaeologists can not dig up culture directly in their excavations. The broken pots and other artifacts of ancient people that they uncover are only material remains that reflect cultural patterns—they are things that were made and used through cultural knowledge and skills.

Layers of Culture

3. There are very likely three layers or levels of culture that are part of your learned behavior patterns and perceptions. Most obviously is the body of cultural traditions that *distinguish* your specific society. When people speak of Italian, Samoan, or Japanese culture, they are referring to the shared language, traditions, and beliefs that set each of these peoples apart from others. In most cases, those who share your culture do so because they acquired it as they were raised by parents and other family members who have it.

4. The second layer of culture that may be part of your identity is a *subculture*. In complex, diverse societies in which people have come from many different parts of the world, they often retain much of their original cultural traditions. As a result, they are likely to be part of an identifiable subculture in their new society. The shared cultural traits of subcultures set them apart from the rest of their society. Examples of easily identifiable subcultures in the United States include ethnic groups such as Vietnamese Americans, African Americans, and Mexican Americans. Members of each of these subcultures share a common identity, food tradition, dialect or language, and other cultural traits that come from their common ancestral background and experience. As the cultural differences between members of a subculture and the dominant

national culture blur and eventually disappear, the subculture ceases to exist except as a group of people who claim a common ancestry. That is generally the case with German Americans and Irish Americans in the United States today—Most of them identify themselves as Americans first. They also see themselves as being part of the cultural mainstream of the nation,

5. The third layer of culture consists of *cultural universals*. These are learned behavior patterns that are shared by all of humanity collectively. No matter where people live in the world, they share these universal traits. Examples of such "human cultural traits" include:

(1) communication (via a verbal language consisting of a limited set of sounds and grammatical rules for constructing sentences)

(2) classification and categorization (via marriage, kinship, history, gender, race, class)

(3) ethics (distinguishing between good and bad behavior)

(4) social roles (leadership roles for the implementation of community decisions)

While all cultures have these and possibly many other universal traits, different cultures have developed their own specific ways of carrying out or expressing them. For instance, people in deaf subcultures frequently use their hands to communicate with sign language instead of verbal language. However, sign languages have grammatical rules just as verbal ones do.

Culture and Society

6. Culture and society are not the same thing. While cultures are complexes of learned behavior patterns and perceptions, societies are groups of interacting organisms. People are not the only animals that have societies. Schools of fish, flocks of birds, and hives of bees are societies. In the case of humans, however, societies are groups of people who directly or indirectly interact with each other. People in human societies also generally perceive that their society is distinct from other societies in terms of shared traditions and expectations.

7. While human societies and cultures are not the same thing, they are inextricably connected because culture is created and transmitted to others in a society. Cultures are not the product of lone individuals. They are the continuously evolving products of people interacting with each other. Cultural patterns such as language and politics make no sense except in terms of the interaction of people. If you were the only human on earth, there would be no need for language or government.

Is Culture Limited to Humans?

8. There is a difference of opinion in the behavioral sciences about whether or not we are

the only animal that creates and uses culture. The answer to this question depends on how narrow culture is defined. If it is used broadly to refer to a complex of learned behavior patterns, then it is clear that we are not alone in creating and using culture. Many other animal species teach their young what they themselves learned in order to survive. This is especially true of the chimpanzees and other relatively intelligent apes and monkeys. Wild chimpanzee mothers typically teach their children about several hundred food and medicinal plants. Their children also have to learn about the dominance hierarchy and the socialrules within their communities. As males become teenagers, they acquire hunting skills from adults. Females have to learn how to nurse and care for their babies. Chimpanzees even have to learn such basic skills as how to perform sexual intercourse. This knowledge is not hardwired into their brains at birth. They are all learned patterns of behavior just as they are for humans.

True or False Statements

(a1) From the opening sentence in Paragraph 1, we know that "culture" is easy to define.

(a2) For survival, human beings need culture, but it is easy to lose.

(a3) Culture can *only* be divided into three layers.

(a4) Every human society must have its culture. The two of which (society and culture) are the same thing.

(a5) According to the writer of this passage, only humans have their culture and society.

True or False: Matching Exercise

You have read Passage A ("Understanding Culture") in Supplementary Reading (1). Please judge if each of the explanations (numbered "a"... "n") matches with one of the words (numbered "1"... "21") in the word list. Write "T" for true and "F" for false.

1. society 2. piety 3. culture 4. aesthetics 5. subculture 6. real culture 7. ethnic group 8. ideal culture 9. ideology 10. acculturation 11. belief 12. assimilation 13. emotion 14. culture shock 15. attitude 16. ethnocentrism 17. values 18. cultural relativism 19. morality 20. super-organic 21. etiquette

(b1) a. the idea that culture is a system that is governed by rules that are not explainable in terms of human biology but that must be studied as aphenomenon in its own right to identify the lawful characteristics that govern cultural processes(9) (b2) b. feelings about what should be considered good, bad, moral, or immoral; the ideals that people long for but do not necessarily pursue(15)

(b3) c. the rules by which beauty is to be evaluated in a culture(2)

(b4) d. a group whose identity is based on shared customs especially of immigrants(7)

(b5) e. the attitude that one's own culture is the only good one and that the more other cultures differ from one's own, the more inferior: they are(16)

(b6) f. the ways people perceive their own customs and behaviors, often morea reflection of their feelings and ideals about what they should be than an accurate assessment of what they are(18)

(b7) g. cultural change that results from borrowing(10)

(b8) h. the process by which a society experiencing acculturation changes so much that it is hardly distinguishable from a more dominant one(12)

(b9) i. the consciously shared beliefs and feelings that members of a society consider characteristic of themselves(3)

(b10) j. values concerning proper and improper ways of treating other human beings(12)

(b11) k. the loneliness and depression that are often experienced when one is in a foreign cultural setting(14)

(b12) l. a pleasant or unpleasant subjective reaction to an experience, characterized by varying degrees of muscles tension and changes in respiration and heart rate(13)

(b13) m. values that govern manners and define what is considered courteous or civil ways of communicating with others(21)

(b14) n. principle that cultural traits are best understood in the context of the cultural system of which they are a part(17)

Passage B: Culture in Literature

1. The term "culture" has not always been used in literary studies, and indeed the very concept denoted by the term is fairly recent. "Culture or Civilization", wrote the influential anthropologist Edward B. Tylor in 1871, "taken in its wide ethnographic sense, is that complex whole which includes knowledge, belief, art, morals, law, custom, and any other capabilities and habits acquired by man as a member of society". Why should such a concept be useful to students of literature?

2. Here we can make our first tentative move toward the use of culture for the study of literature, for Western literature over a very long period of time has been one of the great

institutions for the enforcement of cultural boundaries through **praise and blame**①. This is most obvious in the kinds of literature that are explicitly engaged in attack and celebration; satire and panegyric. Works in these genres often seem immensely important when they first appear, but their power begins quickly to fade when the individuals to whom the works refer begin to fade, and the evaporation of literary power continues when the models and limits that the works articulated and enforced have themselves substantially changed. The footnotes in modern editions of these works can give us the names and dates that have been lost, but they cannot in themselves enable us to recover a sense of the stakes that once gave readers pleasure and pain. An awareness of culture as a complex whole can help us to recover that sense by leading us to reconstruct the boundaries upon whose existence the works were predicated.

3. We can begin to do so simply by a heightened attention to the beliefs and practices implicitly enforced by particular literary acts of praising or blaming. That is, we can ask ourselves a set of cultural questions about the work before us:

- What kinds of behavior, what models of practice, does this work seem to enforce?
- Why might readers at a particular time and place find this work compelling?
- Are there differences between my values and the values implicit in the work I am reading?
- Upon what social understandings does the work depend?
- Whose freedom of thought or movement might be constrained implicitly or explicitly by this work?
- What are the larger social structures with which these particular acts of praise or blame might be connected?

4. Such questions heighten our attention to features of the literary work that we might not have noticed, and, above all, to connections among elements within the work. Eventually, a full cultural analysis will need to push beyond the boundaries of the text, to establish links between the text and values, institutions, and practices elsewhere in the culture. But these links cannot be a substitute for close reading. Cultural analysis has much to learn from scrupulous formal analysis of literary texts because those texts are not merely cultural by virtue of reference to the world beyond themselves; they are cultural by virtue of social values and contexts that they have themselves successfully absorbed. The world is full of texts, most of which are virtually incomprehensible when they are removed from their immediate surroundings. To

① praise and blame：表扬和责备，与前面所提到的“扬”“抑”(mobility and constraint)作用相同。

recover the meaning of such texts, to make any sense of them at all, we need to reconstruct the situation in which they were produced-Works of art by contrast contain directly or by implication much of this situation within themselves, and it is this sustained absorption that enables many literary works to survive the collapse of the conditions that: led to their production.

5. Cultural analysis then is not by definition an extrinsic analysis, as opposed to an internal formal analysis of works of art. At the same time, cultural analysis must be opposed on principle to the rigid distinction between that which is within a text and that which lies outside. It is necessary to use whatever is available to construct a vision of the "complex whole" to which Tyior referred. And if an exploration of a particular culture will lead to a heightened understanding of a work of literature produced within that culture; so too a careful reading of a work of literature will lead to a heightened understanding of the culture within which it was produced.

6. The current structure of liberal arts education often places obstacles in the way of such an analysis by separating the study of history from the study of literature, as if the two were entirely distinct enterprises, but historians have become increasingly sensitive to the symbolic dimensions of social practice, while literary critics have in recent years turned with growing interest to the social and historical dimensions of symbolic practice. Hence it is more possible, both in terms of individual courses and of overall programs of study, for students to reach toward a sense of the complex whole of a particular culture. But there is much to be done in the way of cultural analysis even without an integrated structure of courses, much that depends primarily on asking fresh questions about the possible social functions of works of art. Indeed even if one begins to achieve a sophisticated historical sense of the cultural materials out of which a literary text is constructed, it remains essential to study the ways in which these materials arc formally put together and articulated in order to understand the cultural work that the text accomplishes.

7. For great works of art are not neutral relay stations in the circulation of cultural materials. Something happens to objects, beliefs, and practices when they are represented, reimagined, and performed in literary texts, something often unpredictable and disturbing. That "something" is the sign both of the power of art and of the embeddedness of culture in the contingencies of history. I have written at moments as if art always reinforces the dominant beliefs and social structures of its culture, as if culture is always harmonious rather than shifting and conflict-ridden, and as if there necessarily is a mutually affirmative relation between artistic production and the other modes of production and reproduction that make up a society. At times there is precisely such an easy and comfortable conjunction, but it is by no means necessary. Indeed in

our own time most students of literature reserve their highest admiration for those works that situate themselves on the very edges of what can be said at a particular place and time, that batter against the boundaries of their own culture. (From "Culture" by Stephen Greenblatt)

True or False Statements

(b15) The author quotes Edward Tylor in order to correct him.

(b16) We can infer from the first paragraph that literary criticism didn't take much interest in cultural studies before.

(b17) Paragraph 2 indicates that culture can help readers to gain the power that faded over time and recover a sense of stakes.

(b18) The way to revitalize a literary work is to ask cultural questions like "What kind ..." "Why ...".

(b19) The questions draw readers' attention to features, connections and elements used to be neglected.

(b20) According to Paragraph 5, cultural analysis of literary works breaks the literary boundaries.

(b21) In Paragraph 6 the author implies that literature ends up in culture.

(b22) A cross-disciplinary perspective is not advocated as to literary studies.

(b23) In Paragraph 6, the author is not satisfied with the on-going educational system of liberal art, but what is actually happening among individual scholars somehow consoles him.

第二节 通俗、大众与高雅文化

导 读

文化研究看待文化的视角是变化的、动态的。文化既发展变化又多种多样，文化既是时代的产物又是时代的标志。文化发展到今天，经历了不同的历史时期和阶段，演变出了高雅文化、精英文化、大众文化和通俗文化等不同类型。这些不同形式的文化既相互区别又彼此联系。当然，精英文化长期以来占据着主导地位，是精英阶层、统治阶层和主流社会的价值观和意识形态的反映。而通俗文化则是指属于普通大众的但处于从属地位的族群的文化。尽管在汉语里有时人们把通俗文化和大众文化等同起来看，但是，严格说来，二者是有区别的，不可恣意混淆。至于高雅文化，它主要是指文化作品以及与之相应的传统解读方法。下面的几段文字从人和文化的作用和反作用论述几种不同形式的文化。

Passage: Types of Culture

1. "Popular" is a more elusive term even than "culture", and one meaning of the word, a widespread but debased one, is statistical—what is most popular is what appeals to the most people. Another, a more productive one, is that "the popular" serves the interests of "the people". "The people" as we use the term here, is not a class or social category, but rather a shifting set of social interests and positions that are defined by their subordinate relations to the dominant society. In this definition, the "**complaint wives**"① were not behaving as members of "the people" for they (the people) were promoting the power relations and maintaining the norms of the dominant society—they were performing the roles and identities provided for them, they were making sense of their experience in a predetermined way, using the provided value system to evaluate their experience and to enjoy only the pleasure that culture legitimates.

2. "The people", then, are better recognized by what they *do* than by who they *are*, and popular culture, by analogy, is better recognized by what it *does* than by what it *is*. Popular culture is more a culture of process than of products. This understanding of the word "popular" is both recent and a reversal of its earlier uses in cultural theory. As Europe and America industrialized themselves during the nineteenth century, their populations moved from rural areas to the cities that were built at high speed to house the workforce needed by the new mills and factories. This urbanized, highly concentrated mass of people was a new social phenomenon that traditional concepts of the people as rural peasantry or folk could not describe. As the development of a society's language and its ways of thinking is shaped primarily by its ruling classes (though this is less the case in today's multicultural, market driven societies), so the ways of talking and thinking about this new "people" reflected ruling class interests—they were either elitist and anxious, or patronizing and nostalgic.

3. Mass culture, like high culture and like **Brechts**② putative popular culture, is a culture

① "complaint wives"："不甘做男人附庸的"家庭主妇们。本文是节选，作者已在其上文讨论过"complaint"的具体含义。

② 布莱希特(Bertolt Brecht, 1898—1956)，德国戏剧家兼诗人，提出"史诗戏剧"理论和"间离效果"的演出方法，强调作品的理性分析和教育作用。

of products for products are readily sold. Mass culture produces cultural commodities, high culture produces artworks or texts, The cultural commodities of mass culture—films, TV shows, CDs, etc. —are produced and distributed by an industrialized system whose aim is to maximize profit for the producers and distributors by appealing to as many consumers as possible. This industrialized mass culture is not popular culture, though it does produce many of the resources out of which popular culture is made, and its market centered approach means that it is often more effective in producing texts that the people can use for their progressive purposes than was Brecht with his explicit progressive intentions. The marketplace has always been a site of negotiation rather than one of economic exploitation, and the market places of capitalism are, in this respect, no different from those of other economic systems. In industrialized societies the people make their culture out of resources that are not of their making and ate not under their control. Popular culture typically involves the art of making do with what is available.

4. Popular culture, then, is not mass culture, though it is typically made from it. The relationship between the commercial interests of mass culture and popular interests is always antagonistic and unstable. The people constantly scan the repertoire produced by the cultural industries to find resources that they can use for their own cultural purposes. The industry similarly constantly scans the tastes and interests of the people to discover ones that it can commodify and turn to its own profit. The same may be said of the relations between high culture and popular culture, for popular culture is also defined in part by its difference from the high brow. High culture is recognized better by its texts or artworks than by its processes, though the cultural processes performed by these texts are now much more central in literary studies than at times they have been. Many argue that in postmodernity the distinctions among high mass, and popular culture are rapidly disappearing, I think that this is overstating the case, though there is evidence that the boundaries are blurring and becoming more permeable. But some differences remain.

5. Many of these differences are clustered around the status and use of the text. In popular culture the text is a cultural resource to be plundered or used in ways that are determined by the social interests of the reader/user not by the structure of the text itself, nor by the intentions (however we may discern them) of its author. Indeed, the text typically originates from a social position that differs markedly from that of its popular readers/users. To the extent that its conditions of origin are inscribed more or less explicitly within its structure, the text works in ways that can oppose the interests of its readers? The relations between reader and text contain strong elements of antagonism. In this light the text may be compared to the terrain of a

landowner and the reader to a poacher: so the reader poaches meanings that promote his/her interests while avoiding capture by an ideological gamekeeper who controls the overall structure of the text itself. The reading relations of high culture are not typically seen as antagonistic. (From "Popular Culture" by John Fiske)

Exercises

A. Questions for Understanding

1. What are the two "slippery words" the author intends to discuss?

2. How many ways are there in defining word "popular" according to Paragraph 1? Which one do you like better? Why?

3. What are supposed to be the differences between "what they do" and "who they are" in recognizing popular culture?

4. According to Paragraph 2, who may be "the people" (referred to in Paragraph 1) in the process of industrialization in Europe and America?

5. What similarities do "mass culture" and "high culture" share according to Paragraph 3 ?

6. According to Paragraphs 4 and 5, how can people tell apart popular culture, mass culture and high culture?

7. What relationship does the metaphor (landowner and poacher) reveal between the author and the reader? Do you agree?

8. How many cultural concepts altogether do you think the author discusses in this passage?

B. Gap Filling

Provide the missing words according to the paragraph you have just read.

3. "The people", then, are better recognized by what they ______ than by who they ______, and popular culture, by analogy, is better recognized by what it *does* than by what it *is*. Popular culture is more a culture of ______ than of products. This understanding of the word "______" is both recent and a ______ of its earlier uses in cultural theory. As Europe and America industrialized themselves during the nineteenth century, their populations moved from rural areas to the cities that were built at high speed to ______ the workforce needed by the new mills and factories. This urbanized, highly ______ mass of people was a new social phenomenon that traditional concepts of the people as rural peasantry or folk could not describe. As the development of a society's language and its ways of thinking is ______ primarily by its ruling

classes (though this is less the case in today's multicultural, market driven societies), so the ways of talking and thinking about this new "______" reflected ruling class interests—they were either elitist and anxious, or patronizing and ______.

Supplementary Reading(2)

Passage A: Simulating Transparency

1. How do mass media simulate and subvert political transparency? The basic idea is simple. Sometimes the most effective strategy for hiding something may be to leave it out in the open, and merely alter the context in which people view it. Instead of hiding facts, one should instead seek to change background realities. Large law firms in the United States have long understood this point. When faced with requests for discovery in civil cases, they understand that simply stonewalling to avoid the disclosure of sensitive information is not always the most effective strategy. Instead they can adopt a dual strategy of aggressive over compliance coupled with strategic manoeuvre. They flood the other side with so much information and so many documents—most of them extraneous—that the other side lacks the time or ability to find the relevant information. At the same time, the law firm can raise continual technical objections to the progress of discovery, without ever ultimately withholding anything. These tactics are most useful against a weaker, smaller opponent with less information processing and filtering resources. They are designed to demoralise the other side, raise the costs of litigation, and divert time and energy from the most important substantive questions in the lawsuit. In this way one can use the discovery process—which is, after all, designed to achieve a certain kind of informational transparency—to undermine the values of transparency. One can use the form of transparency to achieve substantial obscurity. This example demonstrates the two basic strategies for simulating transparency: *diversion of attention* and *supplementation of reality*. The goal is to consume the opponent's time and attention. Equally important, one tries to shift the ground of battle to issues of information management and technical questions of procedure. In short, one creates a new practical legal reality for the opponent. This new reality competes with and displaces the substantive issues that originally motivated the lawsuit. In other words, the skillfully played discovery battle creates new objects of contention: it produces ever new things to be concerned about, to become angry about, and to fight about. In the public arena,

simulation of transparency also uses diversion and supplementation. But although the public is trying to obtain information, it is not in the same position as a litigant. Politicians and the mass media do not necessarily regard the public as an adversary. Rather politicians seek to shape and benefit from public opinion, and mass media seek to entertain the public and maintain public attention and influence. Nevertheless, in achieving these ends politicians and the media, both collectively and agonistically, divert audience attention and supplement politics with new political realities.

2. Many different kinds of mass media can simulate transparency. But the dominant medium of political communication in our age—and hence the dominant medium of political transparency—is television. To understand how television simulates transparency, we must understand how television shapes what we see through it. When we use television to understand politics, we see things in the way that television allows them to be seen. At the same time, television creates new forms of political reality that exist because they are seen on television. Television tends to emphasise entertainment value. It subjects culture to a Darwinian process: The less entertaining is weeded out, the more entertaining survives to be broadcast. Hence coverage of public events, politics, and even law must eventually conform to the requirements of "good television", that is, the kind of television that grabs and keeps viewers' attention by absorbing and entertaining them. Television encourages coverage that focuses on the personal celebrity of participants and on the sporting elements of political conflict. Over time, television coverage of politics tends to focus less on substantive policy issues than on the techniques of securing political advantage and political viability. The question of "who's winning" and how are they achieving this victory tends to dominate television coverage. In one sense stories about backstage political manoeuvring and spin control offer a kind of transparency, because they purport to give viewers an "inside" account of the strategic considerations of politicians and public officials. But in another sense they divert attention from substantive policy debates. Given the limited time available for broadcast and the limited attention of audiences, "inside" stories about strategy and jockeying for political advantage tend to crowd out stories about substantive policy questions. Moreover, because politicians understand how important mass media have become to retaining power and influencing citizens, television helps create a new reality populated by spin doctors, pollsters, pundits and media consultants. Thus eventually political life begins to conform more closely to the image of politics that television portrays it to be. Television portrays a world of image manipulation and spin control largely devoid of substantive debate or reasoned analysis. Because television is so central to successful mass politics, it

eventually helps produce the very elements that it portrays. We might call this a self-fulfilling representation.

True or False Statements

Paragraph 1：

(a6) Mass media is not in the control of those in control.
(a7) Law firm in this paragraph can be viewed as an example of mass culture.
(a8) Politicians and mass media are not complices.
(a9) The transparency is made untransparent through simulation of the mass media.

Paragraph 2：

(a10) Television is the major tool to create the political reality through pleasure principle.
(a11) The author seems to dislike television which serves the interest of those in power.
(a12) Television is still welcome by the majority of people.

第三节　文化研究

导　读

根据权威人士的比较研究，世界文化研究呈现“三足鼎立”格局：(1)以法国为中心的比较文学“欧洲学派”：其特征是注重对实际存在的文学影响与接受进行实证的、经验的研究。其理论背景是实证主义社会学、符号学和接受美学。(2)以美国为中心的北美学派：注重平行比较和理论分析。其理论背景是阐释学传统以及“二战”以来的一些新理论。(3)以印度、中国和日本为中心的东方学派。其特征是跨越东西方文化传统的平行比较和诗学对话，同时也兼顾影响研究和超学科研究以及同各民族之间的文学比较研究。其理论背景是一种通过东西方诗学对话而求得既可以用于西方又可以用于东方的文学阐释理论。

本节的重点是介绍后殖民主义和性别研究。虽然文化研究的派别林立，但后殖民主义和性别研究是两个具有普遍意义的文化批评模式。后殖民主义关注前殖民地国家和人民生存状况以及当今殖民主义怎样继续存在的问题。而性别研究则关注在社会性别化的过程中所谓“男”和“女”所负载的文化含义。总之，本节想告诉人们的是，文化研究是一种后现代的解构主义思潮和实践活动。即反传统、反权威、反定性、反所谓真理等殖民主义和父权意识形态所构建的知识模式，力争在当今世界上创造一个多极、平等、自由的人与人、民族与民族之间的对话渠道。

Passage One: Historical Development of Cultural Studies

1. The 1960s saw a revolution in literary theory. Until this decade New Criticism dominated literary theory and practiced with its insistence that one ultimately correct interpretation of a text could be discovered if the critical reader followed the methodology prescribed by the New Critics, believing that a text contained its meaning within itself. New Critics paid little attention to a text's historical context or to the feelings, beliefs, and ideas of a text's reader. For the New Critics, a text's meaning was inextricably bound to ambiguity, irony, and paradox found within the structure of the text. By analyzing the text alone, New Critics believed that an astute critic would be able to identify a text's central paradox and be able to explain how the text ultimately resolved that paradox while at the same time supporting the text's overarching theme.

2. **Jacques Derrida, Stanley Fish, J. Hillis Miller, Michel Foucault**①, and many others—these philosopher-critics questioned the language of texts and of literary analysis. Unlike the New Critics, who believed that the language of literature was somehow different from the language of science and everyday conversation, these postmodernists insisted that the language of texts is not distinct from the language used to analyze such writings. For these critics, all language is discourse. In other words, the discourse or language used in literary analysis helps shape and form the text being analyzed. We cannot separate the text and the language used to critique it. Language, then, helps create what we call objective reality,

3. Believing that objective reality can be created by language many post-modernists posit that all reality is a social construct. From this point of view, there is no objective reality, but many subjective understandings of that reality—as many realities as there are people. How, then, do we come to agree on public and social concerns such as values/ethics/and the common good? According to many **postmodern**② thinkers, each society or culture contains within itself a

---

① Jacques Derrida, Stanley Fish, J. Hillis Miller, Michel Foucault：雅克·德里达，斯坦利·费斯，希利斯·米勒，米歇尔·福柯。四位为后现代主义/后解构主义学家，文化研究的重要学者。

② postmodern：后现代的；指后现代性（postmodernity）或后现代主义（postmodernism）。前者是一种思想：怀疑所谓的“真理、理性、客观真理”等传统概念，反对启蒙主义的行为规范；认为世界是不确定的、偶然的、多样的、不稳定的和非理性的。后者指一种文化：它指通过自省的、游戏的、派生的、肤浅的和消解中心的艺术来打破高雅和通俗文化的界限以及冲破艺术和日常生活经验之间的藩篱。

dominant cultural group who determines that culture's ideology or its **hegemony**①—its dominant values, its sense of right and wrong, and its sense of personal self-worth. All people in a given culture are consciously and unconsciously asked to conform to the prescribed hegemony. The message sent to them by the dominant culture has been clear: Conform and be quiet; deny yourself and all will be well.

4. But many have not been quiet. Writers and thinkers such as Toni Morrison, Alice Walker, Gabriel Garcfa Marquez, Carlos Fuentes, Gayatri Spivak, Edward Said, and Frantz Fanon have dared and continue to challenge the dominant cultures and the dictates such cultures decree. They have not been silenced. Defying the dominant culture, they believe that an individual's view of life, values, and ethics does matter. Not one culture but many; not one cultural perspective, but a host; not one interpretation of life, but countless numbers is their cry.

5. Joined by postmodern literary theorists and philosophers, Africans, Australians, Native Americans, women and many other writers are finding their voices among the cacophony of dominant and overpowering cultural voices. Believing that they can effect cultural change, these new voices refuse to conform and be shaped by their cultured hegemony. These newly heard but long-existent voices can now be overheard at the discussions taking place at the literary table, where they present their understanding of reality, society, and personal self-worth.

6. Known as cultural studies, an analysis and an understanding of these voices can be grouped into several principal approaches two of which are: postcolonialism, and gender studies. Although each group has its own concerns, all seek after the same thing: to be heard and understood as valuable and contributing members of society. Their individual and public histories, they assert, do matter. They believe that their past and their present are intricately interwoven. By denying and suppressing their past, they declare that they will be denying themselves. Their desire is to be able to articulate their feelings, concerns, and assumptions about the nature of reality in their particular cultures without becoming marginalized. Often called **subaltern**② writers—a term used by Marxist critic **Antonio Gramsci**③ to refer to the

① hegemony：霸权，指统治阶级通过知识滥觞和意识形态控制（不使用强制或威胁的办法）使被统治者心甘情愿地接受自己的从属地位。该词发端于安东尼奥·葛兰西（Antonio Gramsci，见脚注③）1971 年的著作《狱中日记选》（*Selection from the Prison Notebook*）。

② subaltern：下属的，从属的。该词因印度裔的美国后殖民主义学者盖亚特莉·斯皮瓦克（Gayatri G. Spivak）的《下属能说话吗?》（"Can the Subaltern Speak?"）一文而在文化研究界更加流行。它指的是在一个社会或文化里处于从属地位的人，比如父权社会里的妇女、全球化过程中处于劣势的发展中的民族和国家等。

③ Antonio Gramsci：安东尼奥·葛兰西（1891—1937），作家、政治家、意大利马克思主义的奠基人；因反法西斯于 1926 年在罗马被捕入狱，在狱中写了大量的日记，后被整理出版，成为其霸权理论的重要基础。

classes who are not in control of a cultured ideology or hegemony—these writers provide new ways to see and understand cultural forces at work in literature and in ourselves, Although each approach's literary theory and accompanying methodology are still developing, a brief overview of the central tenets of the two known approaches will enable us to catch a glimpse of their diverse visions of literature purposes and functions in today's world.

Exercises

A. Questions for Understanding

1. Is New Criticism in Paragraph 1 refuted or supported? Why?
2. Why does it (New Criticism) incur acute criticism from Jacques Derrida and his like?
3. Why is there no such objective reality as some people may traditionally uphold?
4. According to Paragraph 5, why are there so many people keen on the discussions "at the literary table"?
5. Is "cultural studies" pursued only by the literary criticism as it (this passage) may indicate?

B. Gap Filling

Provide the missing words according to the paragraph you have just read.

4. Believing that ______ reality can be created by language many post-modernists ______ that all reality is a ______ construct. From this point of view, there is no objective ______, but many ______ understandings of that reality—as many realities as there are people. How, then, do we come to agree on public and social concerns such as values/ethics/and the common ______? According to many ______ thinkers, each society or culture contains within itself a dominant cultural group who determines that culture's ______ or its ______—its dominant values, its sense of right and wrong, and its sense of personal self-worth. All people in a given culture are consciously and unconsciously asked to conform to the ______ hegemony. The message sent to them by the dominant culture has been clear: Conform and be quiet; deny yourself and all will be well.

Passage Two: Two Trends of Cultural Studies

1. The terms *post-colonialism* and *postcolonialism* first appear in the late 1980s in many

scholarly journal articles and as a subtitle in Bill Ashcroft, Gareth Griffiths/and Helen Tiffin's text "The Empire Writes Back"; "Theory and Practice in Post-Colonial Literatures" (1989) and again in 1990 Adam and Helen Tiffin's *Past the Last Post*: *Theorizing Post-Colonialism and Post-Modernism*. By the mid-1990s, the terms had become firmly established in scholarly writing.

2. Like **deconstruction**① and other postmodern approaches to textual analysis, postcolonialism is a heterogeneous field of study where even its spelling provides several alternatives. Some argue that it should be spelled postcolonialism with no hyphen between post and colonialism, whereas others insist on using the hyphen as in post-colonialism. Many of its adherents suggest there are two branches: those who view postcolonialism as a set of diverse methodologies that possess no unitary quality, as suggested by Homi Bhabha and Arun P. Murkejee, and those who see postcolonialism as a set of cultural strategies centered in history. Even this latter group however, can be subdivided into two branches: those who believe postcolonialism refers to the period after the colonized societies or countries have become independent and those who regard postcolonialism as referring to all the characteristics of a society or culture from the time of colonization to the present.

3. However postcolonialism is defined, that it concerns itself with diverse and numerous issues becomes evident when we examine the various topics discussed in one of its most prominent texts, Ashcroft, Griffiths and Tiffins' *The Post-colonial Studies Reader* (1995). Such subjects include universality, difference, nationalism, postmodernism, representation and resistance, ethnicity, feminism, language education, history, place, and production. As diverse as these topics appear, all of them draw attention to one postcolonialism's major concerns: highlighting the struggle that occurs when one culture is dominated by another. As postcolonial critics are ever ready to point out, to be colonized is to be removed from history. In its interaction with the conquering culture, the colonized or indigenous culture is forced to go

---

① deconstruction：解构，又称解构主义(deconstructionism)。解构(主义)源于雅克·德里达 1966 年在约翰·霍普金斯大学的一篇学术论文：《结构、符号及其在人文学科话语中的作用》(*Structure*, *Sign*, *and Play in the Discourse of Human Sciences*)。他认为，结构主义理论(structuralist theory)总是预设意义上的一个中心，这个中心主导着整个结构(structure)而(又通过结构)和其他无数个中心相连。解构主义的实质是质疑西方柏拉图之后的形而上的哲学论断。解构主义的代表作是德里达的《论语法》(*Of Granunatology*. 1967)；在德里达的影响下，美国(洲)掀起了"解构"浪潮。加拿大原型(神化)批评理论家诺斯洛普·弗雷(Northrop Frye)，黑格尔式的马克思主义者格奥·卢卡奇(Georg Lukacs)，把解构思想引入诗歌批评的保罗·德曼(Paul de Man)都不约而同地向"新批评"(见本节 Passage One，脚注①)发起了挑战，因此形成了所谓的"美洲解构主义"(American Deconstruction)。

underground or to be obliterated. Only after colonization occurs and the colonized people have had time to think and then to write about their oppression and loss of cultural identity does postcolonial theory come into existence.

4. Although a number of postcolonial theorists and critics such as Frantz Fanon, Homi K. Bhabha, and Gayatri Chakravorty Spivak have contributed to postcolonialism's ever-growing body of theory and its practical methodology, the key text in the establishment of postcolonial theory is Edward W. Said's ***Orientalism***①(1978). In this text, Said chastises the literary world for not investigating and taking seriously the study of colonization or imperialism. According to Said, nineteenth-century Europeans tried to justify their territorial conquests by propagating a manufactured belief called Orientalism—the creation of non-European stereotypes that suggested "Orientals" were indolent, thoughtless, sexually immoral, unreliable, and demented. The European conquerors, Said notes, believed that they were accurately describing the inhabitants of their newly conquered land. What they failed to realize, maintains Said, is that all human knowledge can be viewed only through one's political, cultural, and ideological framework. No theory, either political or literary, can be totally objective.

5. Concerned primarily with feminist theories of literature and criticism and sometimes used synonymously with feminism or feminist theories, *Gender Studies* broadens traditional feminist criticism to include an investigation not only of femaleness but also maleness. What does it mean, it asks, to be a woman or a man? Like traditional feminist theory, gender studies continues to investigate how women and men view such terms as ethics, definitions of truth, personal identity, and society. Is it possible, gender specialists question, that women view each of these differently than men?

6. Into the multivoiced feminist theories, gender studies adds the ever-growing and ever-diverse voices of black feminists, the ongoing concerns of French feminism, and the impact of poststructural theories on customary feminist issues. Its authors include the almost canonical status of writers such as Adrienne Rich, Bonnie Zimmerman, Gayatri Spivak, and Toril Moi. Striving to develop a philosophical basis of feminist literary theory, gender studies re-examine the canon and question the traditional definitions of the family, sexuality, and female reproduction. In addition, it continues to articulate and investigate the nature of feminine writing

① *Orientalism*：《东方主义》，由美籍巴勒斯坦人爱德华·赛义德(Edward Said[za:'i: d])著。本书主要是通过福柯的话语权力说和葛兰西的霸权理论来解读西方(英法等前殖民主义国家)的历史、文学、法律、哲学等书籍或文献(话语)，指出所谓"东方"只不过是殖民主义和帝国主义通过想象所构建的一个和"西方"这个概念相对立的"他者"形象。

itself. And it joins feminist scholarship with postcolonial discourses, noting that postcolonial literature and feminist writings share many characteristics, the chief being that both are examples of oppressed peoples.

7. As with feminist theory, the goal of gender studies is to analyze and challenge the established canon in literature, art and other areas of knowledge. Women themselves, gender specialists assert, must challenge the hegemony and free themselves from the false assumptions and the long held prejudices that have prevented them from defining themselves. By involving themselves in cultural theory and its accompanying practices, gender specialists believe women and men alike can redefine who they are, what they want to be, and where they want to go.

Exercises

A. Questions for Understanding

1. Why are there two different spellings (post-colonialism and postcolonialism) about the same concept?

2. What are the concerns or the interests of postcolonial theories?

3. In what way(s) does gender studies benefit feminism according to Paragraph 6?

4. What is the goal of gender studies? Who do you think might be interested in gender studies?

5. In what way (s) might postcolonialism and gender studies support each other?

B. Gap Filling

Provide the missing words according to the paragraph you have just read.

5. Like ______ and other postmodern approaches to ______ analysis, postcolonialism is a ______ field of study where even its spelling provides several ______. Some argue that it should be spelled postcolonialism with no ______ between post and colonialism, whereas others insist on using the hyphen as in post-colonialism. Many of its ______ suggest there are two branches: those who view postcolonialism as a set ______ methodologies that possess no unitary quality, as suggested by Homi Bhabha and Arun P. Murkejee, and those who see postcolonialism as a set of cultural ______ centered in history. Even this latter group however, can be subdivided into two branches: those who believe postcolonialism refers to the period after the colonized societies or countries have become ______ and those who regard postcolonialism as referring to all the ______ of a society or culture from the time of colonization to the present.

Supplementary Reading(3)

Passage A: Some Foci for Cultural Studies

Representation

1. At its most general level, cultural studies frames culture as a system of representation. This approach to culture is based in part on a branch of linguistics called semiotics, the study of signs and the processes by which signs communicate meaning. In semiotics, signs express or convey meaning by uniting signifiers (i. e., forms) and signifieds (i. e., concepts). Cultural studies extends the semiotic approach to language to the study of culture. Culture is constituted by images, sounds, objects, and activities (i. e., signifiers) that convey or signify concepts (i. e., signifieds). Because the study of culture is framed by a language-based approach to representation, cultural artifacts, images, sounds, and activities are viewed or analyzed as texts and signifying practices.

2. A signifying practice is the creation of a sign that produces meaning that must be interpreted according to a shared set of social and cultural codes. For example, an individual's choice as to the vehicle he or she drives can be understood as a signifying practice if we consider that cars mean more than simply the sum of their mechanical parts. Aside from their functional purpose, automobiles represent extensions of identity and thereby communicate lifestyles: A jeep represents a rugged, outdoorsy lifestyle; a convertible represents the carefree fun of youth; a hybrid represents environmental consciousness; a sports car represents wealth and status. Advertising helps produce and reinforce the attachment of these social meanings (i. e., signifieds) to automobiles as things (i. e., signifiers). Because cultural practices such as driving a car communicate meaning only to the extent that they can be interpreted within a shared set of social codes, culture provides the symbolic resources by which we come to define, understand, and express ourselves as individuals.

3. The various social meanings we draw upon and internalize in order to define for ourselves and others who and what we are as individuals is a function of the representational systems to which we have access and the meaning that is attached by self and others to the symbols that circulate within that system. Thus, the power to determine the horizons of what

counts as meaningful can be achieved by controlling the images, symbols, and social codes that make up cultural life, and this power is equivalent to the power to legitimate and naturalize a particular worldview as common sense, thereby determining the horizons within which self-definition and social meaning are achieved. This process of controlling and fixing the horizons of common sense is often referred to as hegemony.

The Politics of Representation

4. The word "representation" refers to the struggle to control the symbols, discourses, images, practices, and representations that define who, what, and how we are, should be, and can be. Rooted as they were in Marxist social analysis, early cultural studies scholars focused on social class as the essential category for subjective identification. However, as the cultural studies field matured and its theoretical contexts changed, some cultural studies scholars began to challenge the centrality of social class by noting its marginalization of other forms of subjective experience, most notably the experience of race and gender. Rather than being reducible to a class-based subject position determined by the economic and social arrangements of capitalism, identity was constituted by multiplicity, heterogeneity, and contradiction. Insights provided by the work of French philosopher Michel Foucault encouraged cultural studies scholars to turn toward a discursive theory of identity.

5. A *discursive* theory of identity argues that as objects of knowledge, identity and its attendant social markers such as race, ethnicity, or gender are products of discourse, constituted by the very language we use to talk about them and therefore do not lie outside language as essential, noncontingent objects or concepts to which language refers. They come to be defined as meaningful concepts only within the horizons of how we conceptualize, talk about, and act on that meaning. As a product of discourse rather than determinate social structures, identity can be understood as a crucial resource for the exercise of critical social agency. The multiplicity of signifying cultural practices made available to individuals offers possibilities for resisting and countering oppressive social structures and narratives through the strategic and contingent expression of cross-boundary social affiliation and rearticulation. In this sense, linking identity and the politics of representation highlights the discursive and historically contingent nature of identity formation and thus opens up spaces for counterhegemonic practice to act and be in ways that confront and challenge power and offer possibilities for more equitable, just social realities.

Hegemony and Ideology

6. Hegemony is a concept associated with Italian political theorist Antonio Gramsci that

describes how social authority is exercised not through direct force or the brute display of power, but through the subtle and hidden arrangements that structure social and cultural life and that shape the beliefs, values, and ideas to which we have access. Thus, existing social formations seem quite normal and natural, as do the commonsense horizons for thinking about alternative social arrangements. Hegemony is asserted through the validation and circulation of images and representations. Hegemony does not tell us what to think so much as it defines the parameters within which our acts and ideas have meaning. Coupled with insights provided by other cultural theorists, Gramsci's work helped cultural studies scholars bridge key formulations of ideological reproduction. Early critical theorists had generally approached ideology as a form of distorted consciousness. In this formulation, ideology is a set of false beliefs expressed at the level of culture that obscures oppressive social structures. Later formulations of ideology took a more complex view in suggesting that ideology structures our consciousness and constitutes our subjectivity. In this way, ideology is defined as a lived experience rather than as a set of false beliefs that obscures a real or authentic state of affairs. A key Gramscian insight developed by cultural studies scholarship is that hegemony is never totalizing. Subordinate groups are not simply passively positioned subjects upon whom power is encoded. Rather, power is resisted and contested on the symbolic field of culture. Resistance to the imposition of dominant, hegemonic social values and beliefs is often referred to as counterhegemonic practice.

7. Counterhegemonic practices are performed or expressed through a variety of oppositional social and cultural forms that critique, subvert, or offer alternatives to hegemonic worldviews. It is important to note that a cultural studies approach to cultural analysis assumes an explicit political stance through its critical exploration of the power-culture nexus. Cultural studies is a theoretically informed way to explain that nexus and challenge it as well in the interest of emancipatory and counterhegemonic goals.

Identity

8. The concepts of representation and hegemony help frame one of the primary aims of cultural studies scholarship, which is to understand and critique how social identities are articulated in relation to hegemonic discourses. Broadly speaking, individuals define themselves and are defined by others via the social codes and meaning systems to which they have access. For example, common-sense notions about what it means to be masculine or feminine are shaped at least partially by the images of men and women we see on billboard advertisements, on television, and in magazines. In addition, individuals signify these gender norms through the

choices they make, among many others, about the clothes they wear, the music they listen to, the automobiles they drive, the way they interact with others. In reading these symbols as texts, individuals are encouraged or positioned to identify with these images. Sometimes, dominant, hegemonic representations can define identities in ways that are limiting and oppressive, for example, media messages that suggest in subtle and overt ways that passivity is a desirable feminine trait.

True or False Statements

(a13) Culture includes representation although the latter expresses the former.

(a14) Language plays an important role in studying cultural meaning.

(a15) A jeep representing an outdoor lifestyle is cultural practice.

(a16) Various social meanings reside in individuals.

(a17) In the struggle to control symbols capital has the say.

(a18) Identity can be understood as the multiplicity of signifying cultural practices which include representation, discourse, social agency, etc.

(a19) Ideology is a set of false beliefs expressed at the level of culture that obscures oppressive social structures.

(a20) Wearing one's clothes can be counterhegemonic.

第二章　符号与文化

在日常生活中，最司空见惯的往往也是最容易为人们所忽略的。文化研究关注的是人和人的创造(精神和物质财富)。但如果没有语言和符号，文化就不大可能存在，文化研究也就无从谈起。所以，我们所说的文化实际上是符号和语言负载的文化，研究文化必然涉及语言和符号。符号学家罗兰·巴特(Roland Barthes)对符号、文化和人的关系有一个形象的比喻。人好比驾驶汽车的司机，而语言或符号好比车窗透明的玻璃，人们要看到车外面风景如画的大自然(文化)，就要透过车窗透明的玻璃。在认识文化的过程中，人们对语言和符号常常视而不见，因为它们像透明的物质，人们下意识地忽略其存在。但是，符号(语言)和文化的关系是一种互为关系。就像不通过玻璃人们无法看到车外风景一样，只有语言和符号才能保证文化的可知性，符号表达文化，文化靠符号存在。

符号指“所有在某种形式上或在其他方面能为知觉揭示出意义的一切现象”(卡西勒)。符号的应用始自远古，比如原始社会就已广泛使用符号或象征。美国哲学家、符号学的奠基人之一皮尔斯(Sanders Pierce)把符号分为三类：符象(icon)、符标(index)、符记或象征(symbol)。这三类符号的抽象层次越来越高。符象与所指对象具有外形的相似性的特征，而符记或象征的任意性和约定俗成性最为突出，是符号的最高层次。符号学对很多人来说是一个比较新的概念，大约从20世纪60年代开始兴起。语言学家把符号学定义为“研究社会中符号生命的科学”(索绪尔)，“处理的是构成所有符号的任何结构基础的那些原理”(雅各布森)。符号学的出现极大地促进了文化研究的发展，使文化研究更加系统化、深入化。符号学是个非常宽泛的概念，包罗所有表义系统，也包括语言学。但由于语言学的先入为主，人们往往把语言学和其他类型的符号体系分而论之。所以，符号学习惯上指除语言之外的表义系统。在文化研究的视域中，符号可分为音(听觉符号)、像(视觉符号)、语(口头、书面语言)。文化既千差万别又丰富多彩。但是，文化在许多方面也存在“共性”，比如文化认知上的“刻板印象”(stereotype)。刻板印象是指人们用普遍规律来概括某一个体或集体的人或物。比如英国人怎么样，南方人爱吃什么之类的问题，都要用一种归纳总结的方法来回答。但和归纳总结不同的是，刻板印象往往无视客观事实、忽略他人意识，明显带有否定、负面的观点，特别是殖民主义、帝国主义和欧洲中心主义等意识形态下的刻板印象，都不可避免地带有歧视、排斥和丑化“他”民族的特征。因此，从事文化研究要了解“刻板印象”的特征和作用。

第一节 表征、对话、话语

导 读

在本节里，表征、对话、话语等都是符号学的概念。表征(representation)是一个古老的符号学概念。指在表义系统(符号体系)中，人们使用一个物体或符号代表另外一个客观存在的东西，使其(被代表的对象)进入文化层面。比如，有人把在海边捡到的卵石或贝壳放在家中供自己欣赏。那么，这时的物实际上已经不仅仅是物体的概念，而是代表某种东西，比如大自然、海洋或其他联想。表征可大可小，大到一部作品或一个体系，小到一个符号或一个手势等。对话和话语也是符号概念，是符号系统里不同的表义形式。如果说表征强调符号本身，那么，对话强调意义产生的过程和渠道：双(多)方(人)的活动，重点在交流主体的反应；而话语是一个比较宽泛和复杂的概念，既包括符号体系又包括各种各样的表义形式，还涉及意义产生的主体：人。话语强调意义产生的效果。文化学中的话语有别于传统语言学的话语，是一个相对较为开放的体系，强调符号的政治性。“话语”的使用打破或模糊了很多传统的概念，比如文学和非文学话语的区别、媒介的不同(无论什么媒介表义都可称为话语)和体裁的优劣。

Passage: Representation, Discourse and Dialogue

(1) Representation

1. Representation is the most traditional term used to refer to symbols (words, pictures, musical notes) invented by humans to stand for or represent real-world things. It is a classical construct derived from aesthetics—the criticism of art objects. Aristotle applied the term to the symbol systems of verbal (and, by implication, musical and visual) art, considered the repository of determinate or finite meaning. The values of accuracy (Aristotle's "imitation of life"), fixed meaning, and universally correct comprehension stem from the classical assumption that human superiority resides in the ability to devise, manipulate, and understand

symbols. Aristotle praised symbol-creation as the characteristic that distinguishes humans from lower animals: "From childhood, men have an instinct for representation, and in this respect man differs from the other animals in that he is far more imitative and learns his first lessons by representing things." (***Poetics***[①], Ⅳ: 2) From classical times to the modern era, the language of representation dominated the scientific tradition of rationalism, which presumes that accurate representation gives rise to universal and singular meaning. Modern literary criticism, notably that of the American New Critics and the Russian **formalists**[②], follows this tradition.

2. The time-honored legacy of representation as a foundational concept facilitates its adaptation to disciplines other than aesthetics, including semiotics and political theory. In the latter, the notion of symbolicrep resentation (things that stand for other things) is extended to political representation (people who act for other people). Although representation is "an extremely elastic notion which extends all the way from a stone representing a man to a novel representing a day in the life of several Dubliners", its use is often limited to language.

(2) Discourse

1. Discourse is fundamentally antithetical to "representation". Whereas the latter treats a verbal outcome as a closed product (a "work" or "object"), the former treats it as an open process. Since the 1970s, when "discourse analysis" became influential in the social sciences, the term has been used to refer to language, as an open-ended dynamic interaction among speakers (or writers) and listeners (or readers) in situation-specific contexts. However, **poststructuralists**[③] use "discourse" more broadly as a generic referent to *all communicative events* in life and art rather than more narrowly as a specific referent to spoken interchanges between literary characters. Generalized usage rests on the postmodern blurring of boundaries between literature and non-literature, between one medium and another, and between one set of genre conventions and another. Blurring challenges such modernist hierarchies as the superiority of art versus science, of literary discourse versus non-literary discourse, and of poetry versus

① Poetics:《诗学》，亚里士多德著。

② formalism：形式主义，和"新批评"一脉相承，强调文本至高无上的地位，避免作品批评的审美化和道德化，其代表人物是俄国的谢克罗夫斯基(Shklovsky)、穆卡洛夫斯基(Mukarovsky)和雅各布森(Jacobson)。

③ poststructuralism：后结构主义，和结构主义分庭抗礼，认为"结构"本身并没有"中心""稳固"之类的东西，而是意识形态在语言中的反映。后结构主义强调交际主体的主观能动性，交际者是知识的源泉，所有知识都先于主体的经验而存在。

prose.

2. Postmodern critics expose the *implicit empowerment* in hierarchical ranking and use "discourse" as a synonym for the power struggle encapsulated in the fluidity of language-in-use. Language is viewed as the expression of "*linkages between power, knowledge, institutions, intellectuals, the control of populations, and the modem state as these intersect in the functions of systems of thought*". These linkages are arenas of conflict among various parties jockeying for power, which is always being negotiated and renegotiated. In postmodern work, "discourse" is the term of choice to describe communication that is fluidrather than fixed—an ensemble of voices, attitudes, and values activated by participants in the process.

(3) Dialogue

1. Dialogue is a related concept, originally referring to verbal interchanges among literary characters (as did discourse)—that is, characters spoken words, given written form in a dramatic script or a novel. The term acquired a postmodern flavor via the dialogic criticism of **Mikhail Bakhtin**①, a Russian formalist whose major works were written in the inter-war period, but were not influential in English until the 1980s. Bakhtin defined dialogue as a *polyphonic* interchange among divergent voices, with each individual voice taking "shape and character in response to and in anticipation of other voices". He conceived of the "dialogic" novel as the opposite of the "monologic" one. In monologic novels such as Tolstoy's, the author attempts to subordinate the characters' voices to his controlling purpose, whereas in dialogic novels such as Dostoevsky's, the author relinquishes control, allowing a multiplicity of independent and unmerged voices—his term is "polyphony"—to be heard.

2. Bakhtin extended the concept of dialogic interaction from the novel to all language, viewed as a polyphonic conversation rather than as a series of univocally pronounced propositions. As such, "dialogue" has now come to mean an open-ended exchange among numerous voices (often called "polyvocality in the social science literature"), each having its own characteristic manner of expression. Although Bakhtin's theory elevates "dialogue" as the primary socio-verbal component of a work, the totality is not a determinate product of the medley of voices, social attitudes, and values that are articulated. Rather, the various voices and modes of communication are oppositional, contradictory, and irreconcilable.

3. To sum up so far, representation refers to the existence of a finished product in any media whose ostensibly "correct" meaning is accessible to all. Discourseand "dialogue" refer

---

① Mikhail Bakhtin：米卡尤·巴赫金，俄国符号学家、批评家，以"复调理论""狂欢理论"而闻名。

more narrowly to the transactive process in language whereby meaning is socially constructed by readers, writers, and those written about.

Exercises

A. Questions for Understanding

1. According to Aristotle what marks off human beings from animals?

2. In Paragraph 1 of "Representation", for what has language been charged from the classical times to the modern era?

3. What is the poststructuralists' definition of discourse?

4. What is the "generalized usage" of discourse?

5. According to a quote (Paragraph 2, "Discourse") what does discourse do?

6. In what way(s) does Tolstoy (托尔斯泰) differ from Dostoevsky(陀思妥耶夫斯基)in literary creation?

B. Gap Filling

Provide the missing words according to the paragraph you have just read.

6. ______ is fundamentally ______ to "representation". Whereas the latter treats a ______ outcome as a closed ______ (a "work" or "object"), the former treats it as an open ______. Since the 1970s, when "discourse analysis" became influential in the social sciences, the ______ has been used to refer to language, as an ______ dynamic interaction among speakers (or writers) and listeners (or readers) in situation-specific contexts. However, poststructuralists use "discourse" more broadly as a ______ referent to all ______ events in life and art rather than more narrowly as a specific referent to spoken interchanges between literary characters. Generalized usage rests on the postmodern blurring of ______ between literature and non-literature, between one medium and another, and between one set of genre conventions and another. Blurring challenges such modernist hierarchies as the superiority of art versus science, of literary discourse versus non-literary discourse, and of poetry versus prose.

Supplementary Reading(4)

Passage A: Understanding Discourse

1. The prevailing sense of "discourse" is defined by the OED as "A spoken or written

treatment of a subject, in which it is handled or discussed at length; a dissertation, treatise, homily, sermon, or the like". "While previous, archaic definitions of discourse have been process or succession of time, events, actions, etc. or the act of understanding", discourse is most simply understood today as a sort of unit of language organized around a particular subject matter and meaning. This can be contrasted to other ways in which language has been broken down into much smaller units of analysis, such as into individual words or sentences in studies of semantics and syntax. Furthermore, as opposed to the linguistic conception of language as a generally stable, unified, abstract symbolic system, discourse denotes real manifestations of language—actual speech or writing.

2. Because the form that discourse takes cannot be solely the product of individual choice, the word entails a meaningful ambiguity between generality and specificity. Discourse can refer either to what is conventionally said or written in a general context, or to what is said or written on a particular occasion of that context. One example of discourse in our culture is one that posits that being cold and wet can cause a person to develop a cold—a belief which doctors reject as unscientific. Yet if I specifically were to say, "have a cold because I got caught in the rain last night," this would also be an example of discourse. My words would reflect my own particularity by stating the fact that I, as an individual, had been caught in the rain last night—yet at the same time my words are determined by a social commonplace. The ambiguity exists between generality and specificity because the idea of discourse implies that the specific is also always general.

3. Yet while discourse most often denotes an instance of language, it is also important to note that in other frameworks, discourse is not necessarily a linguistic phenomenon; it can also be conceptualized as inhabiting a variety of other forms, such as visual and spatial. For example, in his analysis of the development of the modern penal system **Foucault**① cites the medical and juridical discourse about the necessity of rehabilitating criminals—but he also cites the actual structure of prisons, designed to maximize surveillance, as contributing to the discourse of this conceptualization of criminality.

4. The idea of discourse thus emphasizes that language is a social and communal practice, never external to or prior to society (as some conceptualizations of linguistics, such as

---

① Michel Foucault 米歇尔·福柯(1926—1984),法国哲学家和"思想系统的历史学家"。他对文学评论及其理论、哲学(尤其在法语国家中)、批评理论、历史学、科学史(尤其医学史)、批评教育学和知识社会学有很大的影响。福柯通过考古学和谱系学研究,以后结构的散落性—来源论—差异性—断裂性来代替古典历史书写的总体化—起源论—同质化—连续性原则,进而揭示了身体、知识、权力之间的辩证关系,为后结构式的重写历史开辟了道路。他的"话语的权力说"在文化研究界极具影响力。

Saussure's, may seem to assume). In semiotics, one way to conceptualize discourse, then, is to see it as a reflection of its particular context in a particular part of society. According to linguist **Michael Halliday**①, discourse is "a unit of language larger than a sentence and which is firmly rooted in a specific context. There are many different types of discourse under this heading, such as academic discourse, legal discourse, media discourse, etc. Each discourse type possesses its own characteristic linguistic features". This definition of discourse emphasizes the way in which social context—who is speaking, who is listening, and when and where the instance of language occurs—determines the nature of enunciations. It is clear how legal discourse and media discourse, will demonstrate fundamentally different conventions of style, wording, and other "linguistic features".

5. A more complex understanding of discourse emphasizes that formal conventions of the mode of expression are not the only aspect of language. Underlying beliefs and worldviews, specific to the social context, are seen to be mediated by discourse. According to the Dictionary of Semiotics, discourse, "in strictly semiotic terms", does not refer to the literal or "narrative" level of language but to the interaction between "the figurative dimension, relating to the representation of the natural world" and "the thematic dimension, relating to the abstract values actualized in an utterance". As evident in the previous example of the discourse that states that coldness and wetness can cause a cold, discourse entails underlying assumptions about the nature of the world and of particular social values and beliefs. In contemporary **continental philosophy**②, this understanding of discourse as the covert embodiment of social values is taken on a more critical, political level—discourse is seen by some philosophers as a means of the legitimization of social and political practices. The Italian Marxist Antonio Gramsci wrote about ideology as "a conception of the world that is implicitly manifest in art, in law, in economic activity and in all manifestations of individual and collective life". For him, discourse mediates ideological justifications of the status quo that come to be accepted as "common sense". Similarly, anthropologist **Pierre Bourdieu**③ wrote that the ultimate objective of a discourse is

① Michael Halliday：米歇尔·韩礼德(1925—2018)，悉尼大学教授，功能语言学派创始人。其语言学理论不仅应用于对英语语言的分析，也广泛应用于印欧语系和非印欧语系语言的分析。

② continental philosophy：欧陆哲学，一个颇具争议的概念，主要指于欧洲大陆产生的哲学及其派别。比如现象学、存在主义、阐释学、解构主义以及其他批评理论等。

③ Pierre Bourdieu：皮埃尔·布迪厄(1930—2002)，当代法国最具国际性影响的思想大师之一，任巴黎高等研究学校教授，法兰西学院院士。早在1972年布迪厄就已出版了经典的社会学著作《实践理论概要》。1975年布迪厄创办了《社会科学的研究行为》杂志。1980年布迪厄出版了另一部重要著作《实践的逻辑》，这部著作的英译本出版于1990年。布迪厄20世纪80年代末在美国芝加哥大学的讲座内容《反观社会学的邀请》则发表于1992年。

the "recognition of legitimacy through the misrecognition of arbitrariness". Through the proliferation of discourse, beliefs and ideas that are actually socially and historically specific are legitimized by their seemingly universal and natural appearance. An example of this sort of discourse might be advertising discourse in capitalist society. Advertisements may portray luxury products as naturalized needs; this discourse thereby reinforces a consumption-driven culture.

6. Using a similar theory of discourse as ideology, **Louis Althusser**① sees discourse as naturalizing "subject-positions", or social roles. Althusser writes, "Like all obviousnesses, including those that make a word name a thing or have a meaning...the obviousness that you and I are subjects...is an ideological effect, the elementary ideological effect". If subject positions are an ideological effect, then individuals are given social identities that are established by discourse, a discourse that at the same time naturalizes such subject positions and conceals this very process.

7. The discursive production of the subject has been theorized in other ways that do not utilize the concept of ideology. For Foucault, discourse is a medium through which power and norms function. Foucault describes how, in modernity, scientific discourses such as the "human sciences" which claim to reveal human nature actually establish norms and prescribe optimum modes of conduct. These discourses also establish ways of identifying, understanding, and managing "deviant" subjects. By describing and categorizing individuals in detail, these discourses exert an unprecedented amount of power over the individual's comportment and relationship to herself. For example, in *The History of Sexuality*, Foucault describes how psychological discourses actually produced a new understanding of personhood by creating the concept of sexuality as a fundamental marker of identity. Whereas previously, non-heterosexual acts were simply seen as against nature, under the new discourse they became psychologically deviant, indicating of a whole array of other psychological disturbances. The idea of the homosexual, the invert, and the **sadomasochist**② developed, thereby constituting a new experience of the individual as a sexual being and, through its most minute descriptions of the meanings of sexuality, a tighter control over the subjective experiences of individuals.

① Louis Althusser：路易斯·阿尔都塞(1918—1990)，法国著名哲学家，出生于阿尔及利亚。从20世纪60年代初开始接受结构主义思潮影响，运用结构主义方法解释马克思的著作，对经验主义、历史主义和人道主义进行批判，构成了有别于正统马克思的“结构主义马克思主义”思想体系。

② sadomasochist：施虐受虐狂者。

8. While borrowing the Foucauldian concepts of power, **Judith Butler**① takes a slightly different stance on the way in which discourse produces the subject. Butler is particularly interested in the embodiment of gender—a process that she calls **performativity**②. Butler claims that gender identity is actually an ongoing process of "citing" gender norms that permeate society, mediated by a heterononnative discourse that describes masculinity and femininity as stable, natural, and mutually exclusive. In fact, a gender identity only seems to naturally emanate from the subject, while what is actually occurring is an ongoing reiteration and performance of gendered comportment that never fully achieves the gender ideal. If one fails even to approximate gender norms, one fails to be socially recognized as fully human. For Butler, discourse actually demarcates the necessary conditions for the embodiment of personhood.

9. Understood as a medium, then, discourse functions as a powerful tool through which linguistic conventions, social and political beliefs andpractices, ideologies, subject positions, and norms can all be mediated. Yet as we have seen, discourse does not simply serve as a connecting link between a stable, exterior society and the individual. All of these social values emanate from individuals who enunciate a discourse that is at the same time not completely their own, a discourse which in turn implants and reinforces the notions it contains. Discourse always consists of both input and output, and is always at once an extension of our culture and of ourselves.

True or False Statements

(a21) Discourse, judging from the above passage, can mean language in use, values loaded in the language and communicative activities.

(a22) Different people have different understandings and explications of the term

---

① Judith Butler：朱迪斯·巴特勒(1956—)，被誉为后结构女性主义的开山之人，后结构主义哲学家。她的学术涉猎主要集中在政治学、女性主义批评以及酷儿理论(queertheory)等领域。从 1987 年 20 世纪末，她已出版了十部学术专著。其中最有影响的是 *Gender Trouble* 一书。此书至 1999 年已再版十次。

② performativity：表演性(编者暂译)，朱迪斯·巴特勒有关性别研究(酷儿理论)的创造性术语。受语用学语言行为理论(speech-act)的影响，巴特勒认为人们接受对所谓"现实"的(传统)概念，实际上就会用行为把它们给做(表现)出来(落实到行动上)。就性别而言，所谓阴阳、男女等性别概念是要通过行为体现出来的。她的原话是这样表述的："As performance which is performative, gender is an act, broadly construed, which constructs the social fiction of its own psychological interiority."更为重要的是，巴特勒对性别的解读是为了让人们了解所谓性别的实质，即文化构建，从而强调作为个体的人在这种文化构建中的主观性和主动性。

(discourse) for different purposes.

(a23) The author in Paragraph 1 doesn't really explain clearly the concept "discourse" although he/she tries to.

(a24) The idea conveyed in Paragraph 2 is "ambiguity" of discourse.

(a25) The different interpretations per se about the term discourse prove the supposition that discourse is power.

(a26) The idea that "discourse" emphasizes language's social and communal practice better explains the concept.

(a27) According to Halliday discourse is a unit of language larger than a sentence and which is not rooted in a context.

(a28) Scholars except Foucault and Halliday mentioned in the passage seem to be keener on the political connotations of discourse.

(a29) It's possible to study culture without reference to discourse.

Passage B: The Flexibility of Discourse

1. The term discourse has several definitions. In the study of language, discourse often refers to the speech patterns and usage of language, dialects, and acceptable statements, within a community. It is a subject of study in peoples who live in secluded areas and share similar speech conventions.

2. Sociologists and philosophers tend to use the term discourse to describe the conversations and the meaning behind them by a group of people who hold certain ideas in common. Such is the definitions by philosopher Michel Foucault, who holds discourse to be the acceptable statements made by a certain type of discourse community. This explanation will primarily consider the definition pertaining to sociology.

3. A discourse community can be defined as people who share similar thoughts and ideas. The fan base of the Rolling Stones for example, might constitute a discourse community. Within this fan base, certain attitudes would be considered unacceptable and outside of the community. For example, someone who did not hold the song Brown Sugar in the same high esteem as other members of the discourse community might be summarily tossed out on his ear. Ideology defines what can be discussed.

4. Discourse in this manner can exist over time and represents the total of all written/spoken/recorded thoughts that the community claims. Thus early analysis of the Rolling Stones is as valid as opinions held today by modem fans. When discourse applies to a larger

philosophical ideal, like Marxism, discourse explaining Marxism, predating Marxism, and applying Marxism to today would all be part of the community, and some study the history of such discourse.

5. Discourse is flexible to the degree to which a discourse community allows such. For example the discourse of the post-structuralists tends to be wide open to new interpretations and ideas, as well as vehement attacks on the contribution of others. As long as some members of the community accept new discourse, then it forms part of the community and thus exists without a time line.

6. Rhetoricians and philosophers often speak of competing discourses. We can see such an example in the Christian right movement and the liberal left. Each group has a discourse that competes with other thoughts and beliefs and each has a history. Some study the times when certain competing discourses begin to emerge and become more popular. For example, a philosopher or political scientist might look at the predominant religious right and question how this discourse influenced presidential elections.

7. The same analysis of competing discourses might be applied to approaches to literature or art. For example, for a while, post-modernist discourse tended to be most influential in the study and interpretation of art. This has led to a backlash from formalist critics and their discourse community. Philosophers like Foucault see competing discourses as something akin to war. In fact, real war can be often attributed to competing discourses.

8. Others liken discourse and its communities to an essential need for humans to express belonging and share beliefs. The variety of discourse communities is essential because of a person's individual needs. Evaluation of discourse helps us to discover trends in all discourse communities.

9. Studies may also exist to determine how words within discourse can express viewpoints. The words couch potato has negative connotations and is primarily employed by those who view watching television as an inferior activity. Contrasting this to the words avid television fan shows how feelings about a subject are often expressed in words. A liberal person might employ the term bible thumper, where a person belonging to the religious right might employ the term religious right. Language choice frequently defines where our thoughts and allegiances lie.

10. Some effort has been made to nullify insulting language and discourse communities through what is frequently termed political correctness. However, the language of political correctness is now its own discourse community. Those employing this language believe that words should exist without sexism or racism. By using politically correct speech, such members

actually are making statements that sexism and racism are not acceptable. Anti-politically correct discourse communities now battle it out with those who consider themselves politically correct. Thus, the two discourse communities are very much as Foucault described, fighting wars of words to express ideology.

True or False Statements

(b24) This passage mainly concentrates on linguistic aspect of discourse.

(b25) Discourse community, according to this passage, refers to people who stay together and share without exceptions the same values and norms.

(b26) It can be judged that wars must be fought between scholars.

(b27) Political correct discourse is really correct in the way that it is agreed by all people.

(b28) Discourse can be (a) weapon with which wars are fought.

(b29) "Flexibility" in the title can be replaced with the word "contradiction".

(b30) A single word, when it expresses viewpoint, can be called discourse.

(b31) The beginning sentence in Paragraph 1 intend to say that discourse is not easy to delimit.

(b32) Rhetoricians and philosophers often disagree with each other on the issue of discourse.

(b33) To nullify insulting language results from the study of language as discourse.

第二节　读、写、文本

导　读

后结构主义对结构主义观点的质疑使人们意识到符号意义产生的决定因素是读者而不是作者。读者的知识水平、个人经历以及社会背景等是决定意义的诸多因素，甚至阅读环境和阅读目的也都是重要因素。这样一来，作者说了什么、想说什么等传统阅读模式所追求的作者中心论被解构，作者只是发起符号活动(交际)的一方，其文本是交流平台，但这个平台是开放式的，读者进退自由、言论自由。不难看出，在后现代和后结构主义的视域中，读和写不仅是知识的交流而且是体现权利意识的过程。读者不再被作者的思想和意图所禁锢，而是处在平等甚至凌驾于作者之上的意义创造者。这种解构主义的阅读观对调动文学、文化批评中学生的主观能动性具有启发意义。

Passage: Reading, Writing and Text

(1) Reading

In the late 1960s and early 1970s, interest in the reading relationship shifted away from textual devices and the author's intention using them, toward the readers response. From this perspective, the author's intention is disavowed as the main influence on the reader, for most reader-response critics do not accept the idea that responses are author-driven. Instead, they view reading as a process of co-constructing meaning in which the reader processes information based on his/her pre-existing biases, expectations, and perceptions. Readers are presumed to maneuver with the protagonist notably in the interest of comprehending the meaning of the work. What this implies is that no single "correct" meaning can be conveyed by language and transmitted to all readers alike. Nonetheless, meaning is generally agreed to be constrained by a range of possibilities situated in the historical, ideological, and socio-cultural nexus where the individual engages with the written word. That is, the "normal" reader is assumed to be responding to something on the page, for words (unlike ink-blots) control the potential meanings available in a specific culture. "Reading" is the individually driven and culturally influenced process of interpretation that occurs regardless of the author's intention in "writing". The term does not refer to a finished and finite product, but to an activity that disseminates into an open set of diverse and opposed meanings.

(2) Writing

Writing is now paired with reading, for meaning emerges out of a co-constructive negotiation between author and reader. Social science writing is no longer dominated by the conventions of "realism" that require an objective narrative stance on the part of the author and that convey "a clear, unmediated record of a knowable world". The product-orientation has been under attack in the U.S. for approximately a generation, since the dissemination of French poststructuralism. Barthes (1974) challenged the notion of the written product, instead conceiving of writing (*ecriture*) as a process in which the author activates pre-existing language and literary conventions, and the readers interpret the marks-on-a-page in accordance with socially determined meanings. That is, the written word is not considered a finite object in a universe of fixed meanings (problems/solutions, causes/effects, questions/answers), but instead is seen as a mediated bundle of diverse meanings in a universe of particularized interpretations.

(3) Text

1. Nonetheless, "an open set of diverse meanings" requires faith in the possibility of "meaning". When we get to the term "text" as used by the deconstructive critics, the concept of meaning is discarded. "Text" refers to the manifestation of an open-ended, heterogeneous disruptive force of signification and erasure that transgresses all closure. It is a catch-all term for any and all phenomena—the world is a text and the written word's capacity to serve as a "representation" of things in the external world is an illusion; and language is a text that can only construct, reconstruct, and deconstruct itself. The written word as the locus of meaning is but a more sophisticated illusion, for when the claim that meaning is open-ended is taken to its logical conclusion, openness is infinite, not "ended" or endable.

2. Derrida insisted that text comprised an indeterminate cycle of questions rather than a neatly finite series of questions and answers. Although his own work actualized his theory, most of his American followers argue that a provisional stopping-point is a practical necessity, De Man, perhaps the most influential American methodologist, is comfortable with the acceptance of a finite set of possible (although contradictory) meanings available at any given time. This provisional finiteness represents a middle way, somewhere between Derrida's completely open text and prior criticism's rigidly closed box of meaning.

3. In sum, the term for research that one uses announces one's belief that it is one kind of work (representation, discourse, dialogue, writing, narrative, text) rather than another. "Reading" and "writing" return control to meaning co-constructed by author and audience; and "text" has been used so broadly that it can reference the absence of any decidable meaning as well as whatever meanings are present.

Exercises

A. Questions for Understanding

1. What do you find new about "reading"?
2. How do you like this "new way of reading"?

3. According to the section of "Reading" what factors determine meaning?

4. According to Barthes what is writing?

5. What does Paragraph 1 in the section of "Text" intend to say?

6. What is the different view on text between Derrida and his American followers such as De Man?

B. Gap Filling

Provide the missing words according to the paragraphs you have just read.

7. Nonetheless, "an open set of diverse meanings" requires ______ in thepossibility of "meaning". When we get to the term "text" as used by the deconstructive critics, the concept of meaning is ______. "Text" refers to "the ______ of an open-ended, heterogeneous ______ force of signification and ______ that ______ all closure". It is a ______ term for any and all phenomena—the world is a text and the written word's capacity to serve as a "representation" of things in the external world is an illusion; and language is a text that can only construct, reconstruct, and deconstruct itself. The written word as the locus of meaning is but a more sophisticated illusion, for when the claim that meaning is open-ended is taken to its logical conclusion, openness is infinite, not "ended" or ______. Derrida insisted that text comprised an indeterminate cycle of questions rather than a neatly finite series of questions and answers. Although his own work actualized his theory, most of his American followers argue that a ______ stopping-point is a practical necessity, De Man, perhaps the most influential American methodologist, is comfortable with the acceptance of a finite set of possible (although contradictory) meanings available at any given time. This provisional finiteness represents a ______ way, somewhere between Derrida's completely open text and prior criticism's rigidly closed box of meaning.

Supplementary Reading(5)

Passage A: Semiotics—Its Heterogeneity

1. If you go into a bookshop and ask an assistant where to find a book on semiotics, you are likely to meet with a blank look. Even worse, you might be asked to define what semiotics is—which would be a bit tricky if you were looking for a beginner's guide. It's worse still if you

do know a bit about semiotics, because it can be hard to offer a simple definition which is of much use in the bookshop. If you've ever been in such a situation, you'll probably agree that it's wise not to ask. Semiotics could be anywhere. The shortest definition is that it is the study of signs. But that doesn't leave enquirers much wiser. "What do you mean by a sign?" people usually ask next. The kinds of signs that are likely to spring immediately to mind are those which we routinely refer to as "signs" in everyday life, such as road signs, pub signs and star signs. If you were to agree with them that semiotics can include the study of all these and more, people will probably assume that semiotics is about "visual signs". You would confirm their hunch if you said that signs can also be drawings, paintings and photographs, and by now they'd be keen to direct you to the art and photography sections. But if you are thick-skinned and tell them that it also includes words, sounds and "body language", they may reasonably wonder what all these things have in common and how anyone could possibly study such disparate phenomena. If you get this far, they've probably already "read the signs" which suggest that you are either eccentric or insane and communication may have ceased. Beyond the most basic definition as "the study of signs", there is considerable variation among leading semioticians as to what semiotics involves.

2. One of the broadest definitions is that of Umberto Eco, who states that "semiotics is concerned with everything that can be taken as a sign" (Eco, 1976). Semiotics involves the study not only of what we refer to as "signs" in everyday speech, but of anything which "stands for" something else. In a semiotic sense, signs take the form of words, images, sounds, gestures and objects. Contemporary semioticians study signs not in isolation but as part of semiotic "sign-systems" (such as a medium or genre). They study how meanings are made and how reality is represented.

3. Theories of signs (or "symbols") appear throughout the history of philosophy from ancient times onwards (see Todorov, 1982), the first explicit reference to semiotics as a branch of philosophy appearing in John Locke's Essay Concerning Human Understanding (1690). However, the two primary traditions in contemporary semiotics stem respectively from the Swiss linguist Ferdinand de Saussure (1857-1913) and the American philosopher Charles Sanders Peirce (pronounced "purse") (1839-1914). Saussure's term sémiologie dates from a manuscript of 1894. The first edition of his *Course in General Linguistics*, published posthumously in 1916, contains the declaration that: It is...possible to conceive of a science which studies the role of signs as part of social life. It would form part of social psychology, and hence of general psychology.

4. Semiology (from the Greek se-meîon, "sign") investigates the nature of signs and the laws governing them. Since it does not yet exist, one cannot say for certain that it will exist. But it has a right to exist, a place ready for it in advance. Linguistics is only one branch of this general science. The laws which semiology will discover will be laws applicable in linguistics, and linguistics will thus be assigned to a clearly defined place in the field of human knowledge. (Saussure, 1983) While for the linguist Saussure "semiology" was "a science which studies the role of signs as part of social life", to the philosopher Charles Peirce the field of study which he called "semeiotic" (or "semiotic") was the "formal doctrine of signs", which was closely related to logic (Peirce, 1931). Working quite independently from Saussure across the Atlantic, Peirce borrowed his term from Locke, declaring that: Logic, in its general sense, is...only another name for semiotic (sémeiötiké), the quasi-necessary, or formal, doctrine of signs. By describing the doctrine as "quasi-necessary", or formal, I mean that we observe the characters of such signs as we know, and... by a process which I will not object to naming abstraction, we are led to statements, eminently fallible, and therefore in one sense by no means necessary, as to what must be the characters of all signs used by a "scientific" intelligence, that is to say, by an intelligence capable of learning by experience. (Peirce, 1931)

5. Peirce and Saussure are widely regarded as the co-founders of what is now more generally known as semiotics. They established two major theoretical traditions. Saussure's term "semiology" is sometimes used to refer to the Saussurean tradition while the term "semiotics" sometimes refers to the Peircean tradition. However, nowadays the term "semiotics" is widely used as an umbrella term to embrace the whole field (Nöth, 1990). We will outline and discuss both the Saussurean and Peircean models of the sign. Some commentators adopt Charles W. Morris's definition of semiotics (a reductive variant of Saussure's definition) as "the science of signs" (Morris, 1938). The term "science" is misleading. As yet, semiotics involves no widely agreed theoretical assumptions, models or empirical methodologies. Semiotics has tended to be largely theoretical, many of its theorists seeking to establish its scope and general principles. Peirce and Saussure, for instance, were both concerned with the fundamental definition of the sign. Peirce developed logical taxonomies of types of signs. Many subsequent semioticians have sought to identify and categorize the codes or conventions according to which signs are organized.

6. Clearly there is a need to establish a firm theoretical foundation for a subject which is currently characterized by a host of competing theoretical assumptions. As for methodologies, Saussure's theories constituted a starting point for the development of various structuralist

methodologies for analysing texts and social practices. For Roman Jakobson, semiotics "deals with those general principles which underlie the structure of all signs whatever and with the character of their utilization within messages, as well as with the specifics of the various sign systems and of the diverse messages using those different kinds of signs" (Jakobson, 1968). Structuralist methods have been very widely employed in the analysis of many cultural phenomena. However, they are not universally accepted: socially oriented theorists have criticized their exclusive focus on structure, and no alternative methodologies have as yet been widely adopted. Semiotics is not widely institutionalized as an academic discipline (although it does have its own associations, conferences and journals, and it exists as a department in a handful of universities). It is a field of study involving many different theoretical stances and methodological tools.

7. Although there are some self-styled "semioticians", those involved in semiotics include linguists, philosophers, psychologists, sociologists, anthropologists, literary, aesthetic and media theorists, psychoanalysts and educationalists. This book concentrates on structuralist semiotics (and its poststructuralist critiques). It is difficult to disentangle European semiotics from structuralism in its origins. Linguistic structuralism derived primarily from Saussure, Hjelmslev and Jakobson. It was Jakobson who first coined the term "structuralism" in 1929 (Jakobson, 1990). Structuralism is an analytical method which involves the application of the linguistic model to a much wider range of social phenomena. Jakobson wrote that "Language is ... a purely semiotic system ... The study of signs, however ... must take into consideration also applied semiotic structures, as for instance, architecture, dress, or cuisine ... any edifice is simultaneously some sort of refuge and a certain kind of message. Similarly, any garment responds to definitely utilitarian requirements and at the same time exhibits various semiotic properties" (1968). He identified "the cardinal functions of language" and argued that this should lead to "an analogous study of the other semiotic systems" (ibid.). Structuralists search for "deep structures" underlying the "surface features" of signsystems: Lévi-Strauss in myth, kinship rules and totemism; Lacan in the unconscious; Barthes and Greimas in the "grammar' of narrative. Julia Kristeva declared that "what semiotics has discovered ... is that the law governing or, if one prefers, the major constraint affecting any social practice lies in the fact that it signifies; i. e. that it is articulated like a language" (Kristeva, 1973). Saussure argued that "nothing is more appropriate than the study of languages to bring out the nature of the semiological problem" (Saussure, 1983).

8. Semiotics draws heavily on linguistic concepts, partly because of his influence, and also

because linguistics is a more established discipline than the study of other sign-systems. Saussure referred to language (his model being speech) as "the most important" of all of the systems of signs (Saussure, 1983). Many other theorists have regarded language as fundamental. Roman Jakobson insisted that "language is the central and most important among all human semiotic systems" (Jakobson, 1970). Émile Benveniste observed that "language is the interpreting system of all other systems, linguistic and non-linguistic" (Benveniste, 1969) while Claude Lévi-Strauss noted that "language is the semiotic system par excellence; it cannot but signify, and exists only through signification" (Lévi-Strauss, 1972). Language is almost invariably regarded as the most powerful communication system by far. One of the most powerful "design features" of language is called double articulation (or "duality of patterning"). Double articulation enables a semiotic code to form an infinite number of meaningful combinations using a small number of low-level units which in themselves are meaningless (e. g. phonemes in speech or graphemes in writing). The infinite use of finite elements is a feature which in relation to media in general has been referred to as "semiotic economy".

9. Traditional definitions ascribe double articulation only to human language, for which this is regarded as a key "design feature" (Hockett, 1958). Louis Hjelmslev regarded it as an essential and defining feature of language (Hjelmslev, 1961). Jakobson asserted that "language is the only system which is composed of elements which are signifiers and yet at the same time signify nothing" (Jakobson, 1976). Double articulation is seen as being largely responsible for the creative economy of language. The English language, for instance, has only about forty or fifty elements of second articulation (phonemes) but these can generate hundreds of thousands of words. Similarly, from a limited vocabulary we can generate an infinite number of sentences (subject to the constraint of syntax which governs structurally valid combinations). It is by combining words in multiple ways that we can seek to render the particularity of experience. If we had individual words to represent every particularity, we would have to have an infinite number of them, which would exceed our capability of learning, recalling and manipulating them.

10. Double articulation does not seem to occur in the natural communication systems of animals other than humans. A key semiotic debate is over whether or not semiotic systems such as photography, film or painting have double articulation. The philosopher Susanne Langer argued that while visual media such as photography, painting and drawing have lines, colours, shadings, shapes, proportions and so on which are "abstractable and combinatory", and which "are just as capable of *articulation*, i. e. of complex combination, as words", they have no

vocabulary of units with independent meanings (Langer, 1951):

> *A symbolism with so many elements, such myriad relationships, cannot be broken up into basic units. It is impossible to find the smallest independent symbol, and recognize its identity when the same unit is met in other contexts ... There is, of course, a technique of picturing objects, but the laws governing this technique cannot properly be called a "syntax", since there are no items that might be called, metaphorically, the "words" of portraiture.* (Langer, 1951)

11. Rather than dismissing "non-discursive" media for their limitations, however, Langer argues that they are more complex and subtle than verbal language and are "peculiarly well-suited to the expression of ideas that defy linguistic "projection". She argues that we should not seek to impose linguistic models upon other media since the laws that govern their articulation "are altogether different from the laws of syntax that govern language". Treating them in linguistic terms leads us to "misconceive" them: they resist "translation" (1983). Saussure saw linguistics as a branch of "semiology":

> *Linguistics is only one branch of this general science [of semiology]. The laws which semiology will discover will be laws applicable in linguistics ... As far as we are concerned ... the linguistic problem is first and foremost semiological ... If one wishes to discover the true nature of language systems, one must first consider what they have in common with all other systems of the same kind ... In this way, light will be thrown not only upon the linguistic problem. By considering rites, customs etc. as signs, it will be possible, we believe, to see them in a new perspective. The need will be felt to consider them as semiological phenomena and to explain them in terms of the laws of semiology.* (Saussure, 1983)

12. While Roland Barthes (1967) declared that "perhaps we must invert Saussure's formulation and assert that semiology is a branch of linguistics", most of those who call themselves semioticians at least implicitly accept Saussure's location of linguistics within semiotics. The linguist and semiotician Roman Jakobson was in no doubt that "language is a system of signs, and linguistics is part and parcel of the science of signs or semiotics" (Jakobson, 1949). However, even if we theoretically locate linguistics within semiotics it is difficult to avoid adopting the linguistic model in exploring other sign-systems. The American linguist Leonard Bloomfield asserted that "linguistics is the chief contributor to semiotics"

(Bloomfield, 1939). Jakobson defined semiotics as "the general science of signs which has as its basic discipline linguistics, the science of verbal signs" (Jakobson, 1963). Semioticians commonly refer to films, television and radio programmes, advertising posters and so on as "texts", and to "reading television" (Fiske and Hartley, 1978). Media such as television and film are regarded by some semioticians as being in some respects like languages. The issue tends to revolve around whether such media are closer to what we treat as reality in the everyday world of our own experience or whether they have more in common with a symbolic system like writing. However, there is a danger of trying to force all media into a linguistic framework. Contemporary "social semiotics" has moved beyond the structuralist focus on signifying systems as languages, seeking to explore the use of signs in specific social situations.

True or False Statements

(a30) "Semiotics could be anywhere" in Paragraph 1 means people study it everywhere.

(a31) You agree that semiotics is about "visual signs".

(a32) According to Eco (Paragraph 2) semiotics concerns itself with everything if it can be viewed as a sign.

(a33) Philosophy long concerns itself with semiotics. So do social psychology and general psychology.

(a34) Peirce and Saussure are both semioticians but differ from each other in their concerns.

(a35) According to Paragraph 8, Hjelmslev, Jakobson, Levi-Struauss, Lacan, Kristeva, Barthes and Greimas are "self-styled" semioticians, who study semiotics from non-semiotic fields.

(a36) Langer in Paragraphs 10-11 benefited a lot from linguistic model (double articulation) when she studied non-language signs.

(a37) Semiotics, according to scholars in Paragraph 11, develops on the basis of linguistics although the former includes the latter.

Passage B: Semiotics—Saussure, Peirce and Barthes

1. The Swiss linguist **Ferdinand de Saussure**① died in 1913 before putting into manuscript form the insights for which he is now chiefly known. *The Course in General Linguistics* was

① Ferdinand de Saussure：费迪南·索绪尔(1857—1913)，结构主义语言学家，著有《普通语言学教程》；瑞士人，被誉为“现代语言学之父”。(更多信息见上文)

subsequently compiled by several of Saussure's students from his lecture notes. That book not only reconceived linguistics along semiotic lines, but it called for the application of its semiotic principles to all aspects of culture: Language is a system of signs that express ideas, and is therefore comparable to a system of writing, the alphabet of deaf-mutes, symbolic rites, polite formulas, military signals, etc. But it is the most important of all these systems.

2. "A science that studies the life of signs within society is conceivable; it would be part of social psychology and consequently of general psychology; I shall call it semiology ..." Semiology would show what constitutes signs, what laws govern them. Since the science does not yet exist, no one can say what it would be; but it has a right to existence, a place staked out in advance. Linguistics is only a part of the general science of semiology; the laws discovered by semiology will be applicable to linguistics, and the latter will circumscribe a well-defined area within the mass of anthropological facts. (*Course in General Linguistics*)

3. Recent years have more than justified Saussure's prediction. Umberto Eco points out in *A Theory of Semiotics* that the present semiotic field consists of zoology, olfactory signs, tactile communication, paralinguistics, medicine, kinesics and proxemics, musical codes, formalized languages, written languages, natural languages, visual communication, systems of objects, plot structures, text theory, cultural codes, aesthetic texts, mass communication, and rhetoric—and one would of course want to add anthropology and psychoanalysis to this list,

4. Other important developments in the theory of signification were engineered by **Charles Sanders Peirce** (who started writing well before Saussure, but whose work was assimilated much later), by Roland Barthes, and by Jacques Derrida. Peirce increases the number of signifying relationships over those charted by Saussure, and makes the human subject their support. Peirce writes, "... the word or sign which man uses is the man himself ... the fact that every thought is a sign, taken in conjunction with the fact that life is a train of thought, proves that man is a sign ... the man and the ... sign are identical ... Thus my language is the sum total of myself; for the man is the thought." The point upon which Peirce here insists is that our access to and knowledge of ourselves is subject to the same semiotic restrictions as our access to and knowledge of the external world. In other words, we are cognitively available to ourselves and others only in the guise of signiflers, such as proper names and first-person pronouns, or visual images, and consequently are for all intents and purposes synonymous with those signiflers.

5. **Roland Barthes** demonstrates that signification cannot be divorced from the operations of myth or ideology, and that it thus always implies the larger cultural field. Derrida indicates that

certain privileged terms not acknowledged by Saussure function to anchor and restrain the play of signification. He also reveals the ideological basis of those terms, and in so doing attempts to liberate signification from their dominance. All three of these theoreticians agree that meaning is much more open-ended than Saussure would have us believe, and that it cannot be isolated from the symbolic order.

6. The above paragraphs mainly deal with the concept of semiology (semiotics) under which different branches and perceptions such Saussure's linguistic structuralism (linguistic as science), Eco's sociological perspective (hyperreality as social relation), Barthes' mythological conception (ideological reading of semiology), and Demda's introduction of deconstruction into the field all together make semiological study a world where different voices contend and bring it to full flowering. However one cannot ignore the American philosopher Peirce whose contribution to semiology lies in his invention of two interlocking triads. The first triad consists of what Peirce calls the "sign", the "interpretant" and the "object" upon whose interaction signification evolves. The second triad accounts for the different kinds of signs which human consciousness can interpret and accommodate. The differentiated signs are "icons", "indices" and"symbols". The iconic sign resembles its conceptual object in certain ways. It may share certain of the properties which that object possesses, or it may duplicate the principles according to which that object is organized. Photographs, paintings, sculptures, and cinematic images are obvious icons, but algebraic equations and graphs are also iconic. The indexical sign is defined by Peirce as "real thing or fact which is a sign of its object by virtue of being connected with it as a matter of fact and by also forcibly intruding upon the mind, quite regardless of its being interpreted as a sign". A weathervane, a pointing hand, according to Peirce, are two of many such examples. Peirce's final category, the symbol represents a general class of things, rather than a single, discrete object. It designates a sign whose relation to its conceptual object is entirely arbitrary. Natural languages and notional systems of sorts are preeminently symbolic.

True or False Statements

(b34) Saussure, although a linguist, is the first person who postulates the concept of semiology.

(b35) Upon Saussure's call other semioticians such as Peirce set to work on semiotic studies.

(b36) Despite their different areas of interests, these scholars agree with each other.

(b37) It seems that the Saussurean semiotic paradigm intends to reveal abstract things in its research.

(b38) It is obvious that semiology is a cacophony where different voices try to be heard.

(b39) According to this passage, Saussure, Peirce and Barthes are three semioticians famous for their different specialty in semiotics.

(b40) In the last paragraph the author indicates Peirce plays a very important role in the full flowering of semiotics.

(b41) In Peirce's second triad account symbol is more abstract than icons, indices.

(b42) From Paragraph 6 we know that semiotics is competing field of scholarship.

(b43) Symbolic language appears earlier than iconic language.

第三节　刻板印象

导　读

刻板印象(stereotype)，又称陈规，指在社会实践和社会活动过程中人们简单、机械地使用已有知识的文化现象。可以毫不夸张地说，刻板印象存在于知识的各个层面：性别、种族、阶级、历史、文化等。但是，在人们的知识水平达到一个新的高度之前，刻板印象的文化属性并没有引起人们的足够关注。比如，一提到继母，人们就想到冷漠、苛刻和尖酸等；黑人人种经常是艺术、体育、音乐等职业方面的天才。刻板印象显然是一种简单、有效的认知方式，但从文化研究的角度看，它也是传递价值观、施加权力的过程。对继母的看法负载了父权思想，而对黑人的认识有种族主义的嫌疑。我们学习刻板印象的主要目的在于，在殖民主义的过程中，殖民地的人民和文化都不可避免地遭受殖民主义和帝国主义文化的丑化和歪曲。再者，在当今全球化的进程中，发展中国家无法摆脱西方发达国家意识形态的制约。因此，学习刻板印象的目的，就是让学生增长抵抗新殖民主义(neo-colonialism)的意识，在国际文化交流中尽可能地少犯文化中心主义的错误。

Passage One: Stereotype—Definition, Characteristics and Meaning

1. A stereotype is a standardized conception or image of a specific groupof people or

objects. Stereotypes are "**mental cookie cutters**"①—they force a simple pattern upon a complex mass and assign a limited number of characteristics to all members of a group. While we commonly use the term as it is applied to human beings, it is quite possible to stereotype objects as well. In popular culture we can examine both types of stereotypes so that we often find people stereotyped around characteristics of age ("All teenagers love rock and roll and have no respect for theirelders."), *sex* ("Men want just one thing from a woman."), *race*("All Japanese look and think alike."), religion ("All Catholics love the Pope more than their country."), *vocation* ("All lawyers are greedy weasels.") and *nationality* ("All Germans are Nazi warmongers."). Objects can be stereotyped around characteristics of *places* ("All cities are corrupt and sinful." "Small towns are safe and clean." "In England, it rains all the time.") and *things* ("A good house has a large lawn, big garage, and at least two bathrooms."). Because objects are studied more rewardingly as icons, however, we will use stereotypes primarily as a tool to examine popular beliefs and values about people.

2. The standardized conception is held in common by the members of agroup. Popular stereotypes are images which are shared by those who hold a common cultural mindset—they are the way a culture, or significant sub-group within that culture, defines and labels a specific group of people.

3. Stereotypes are direct expressions of beliefs and values. A stereotype is a valuable tool in the analysis of popular culture because once the stereotype has been identified and defined, it automatically provides us with an important and revealing expression of otherwise hidden beliefs and values. This means that stereotypes are especially useful in tracing the evolution of popular thought—the way in which the beliefs and values associated with specific groups change over time. American attitudes toward Russians, for example, can be easily marked by the changing nature of the popular stereotype associated with them—from WWII ("fur-hatted vodka drinking comrades-in-arms") to Cold War ("Godless communists in an Evil Empire") to the break-up of the Soviet Union ("poor, hungry victims of a disorganized and self-defeating socialist system").

4. The term stereotype initially referred to a printing stamp which was used to make multiple copies from a single model or mold, but the great journalist and commentator Walter Lippmann adopted the term in his book *Public Opinion* (1922) as a means of describing the way society set about categorizing people— "stamping" human beings with a set of characteristics—

① mental cookie cutter：千篇一律的或俗套的思想（观点）。

as well. In his pioneering work, Lippmann identified four aspects of stereotypes. They are:

(1) Simple: certainly more simple than reality but also often capable of being summarized in only two to three sentences.

(2) Acquired secondhand: people acquire (and absorb) stereotypes from cultural mediators rather than from their own direct experience with the groups being stereotyped. The culture "distills" reality and then expresses its beliefs and values in stereotypical images which convince audiences of the "truth" of the stereotype by placing it in a carefully controlled context in which there is a measure of truth tothe image. Of course women *can and should be and are thin and beautiful*—there's Barbie! There's the *Sports Illustrated* swimsuit issue, and Jane Fonda's exercise tape is number one on the charts.

(3) Erroneous: *all* stereotypes are false. Some are less false than others, and (more importantly) some are less harmful than others. But allare rendered false by their very nature. They are attempts to claim that each individual human being in a certain group shares a set of common qualities. Since an individual is different from all other individuals by definition, stereotypes are a logical impossibility. Even countertypes are false when they are presented as the "new" truth about a group and escape this label only when they are presented as possibilities rather than actualities.

(4) Resistant to change: during the last twenty-five years the difficulties with racial and gender inequalities in American life have alerted most people to the tragic consequences lurking in beliefs about popular stereotypes. Yet, even after more than a quarter of a century, old stereotypes still stubbornly color our perceptions. During 1992, for example, two sensational rape trials dominated the headlines in the popular press: William Kennedy Smith was tried and found innocent of raping Patricia Bowman, and boxer Mike Tyson was convicted of raping Dessiree Washington. In both cases stereotypes assumed by both the prosecution and the defense dominated the public images of both the accusers and the accused.

5. Despite the fact that stereotyping is a natural method of classification and despite the fact that stereotyping has some useful functions under certain circumstances, all too often stereotypes are the festering rot in the American mindset. It is not very pleasant to study them and it is even less pleasant to study their horrific effects. But study them we must. Common stereotypes directly reflect our beliefs, and like other more pleasant beliefs, we must understand them if we are tounderstand ourselves.

Exercises

A. Questions for Understanding

1. Is stereotype a semiotic phenomenon or a cultural phenomenon? Why?

2. From the examples given in Paragraph 1, do you think that all stereotypes are false? How do you like Walter Lippmann's opinion on stereotypes?

3. According to point (3) in Paragraph 4, what leads to the conviction of Mike Tyson's guilt?

4. Can you think of a few of examples of the stereotyped Chinese or stereotyped foreigners?

5. What, according to this passage, might stereotype cast light on?

B. Gap Filling

Provide the missing words according to the paragraphs you have just read.

8. The standardized conception is held in ______ by the members of a group. Popular stereotypes are images which are shared by those who hold a common cultural ______ —they are the way a culture, or significant sub-group ______ that culture, defines and labels a specific group of people. Stereotypes are direct ______ of beliefs and values. A stereotype is a valuable ______ in the analysis of popular culture because once the stereotype has been identified and defined, it ______ provides us with an important and ______ expression of otherwise ______ beliefs and values. This means that stereotypes are especially useful in tracing the evolution of popular thought—the way in which the beliefs and values associated with specific groups change over time. American attitudes toward Russians, for example, can be easily marked by the changing nature of the popular stereotype associated with them—from WWII ("fur-hatted vodka drinking comrades-in-arms") to Cold War ("Godless communists in an Evil Empire") to the ______ of the Soviet Union("poor, hungry victims of a disorganized and self-defeating socialist ______").

Passage Two: Consequences of Stereotypes

1. The actions taken or facilitated by cultural stereotypes are not often so benign or neutral as may have been suggested thus far. Stereotypes are frequently negative, and because a culture

bases its actions upon beliefs and values which characterize the cultural mindset, negative stereotypes can be associated with actions of an exceedingly negative, harmful nature—ugly emotions and even worse behavior.

2. The American civil rights movements of the 1950s and 1960s dramatically demonstrated to the world that non-white American ethnic groups, in being considered inferior human beings by a large proportion of the white majority, had suffered through centuries of horrible social and economic victimization. Conversely, the narrow view of whites as a group of racist exploiters, termed "honkies" by some non-whites during the last quarter century had led to a hardening of racial resentments by both groups. It is clearer now than it once was that the oversimplification of characteristics of any race of people into a narrow, negative stereotype can have tragic consequences. Black Americans were enslaved through three-quarters of a century during which the United States Constitution guaranteed basic human rights. Characterizations of Orientals in popular books and movies of the 1920s and 1930s as vicious, rat-like sneaks, part of a world-wide "**yellow peril**"① may have unconsciously been one reason why more than 100, 000 Japanese Americans were incarcerated in American concentration camps during the Second World War and might even have strongly contributed to the causes that led to the outbreak of that war, Germans, believing Jews to be pollutants of the Aryan master race, stood by passively while the Nazis systematically butchered six million men, women and children.

3. A second danger of stereotyping is not quite as obvious as these actions because-it is often the result of popular stereotypes which are neutral or even somewhat positive in nature. Yet this danger is responsible for a great deal of frustration and unhappiness. Essentially, this second danger results from the fact that stereotypes are not merely descriptions of the way a culture views a specific group of people, but are also often prescriptions as well—thumbnail sketches of how a group of people is perceived and how members of that group perceive themselves. Stereotyping is, as we have seen, a natural ordering function of the human and social mind: stereotypes make reality easier to deal with because they simplify the complexities that make people unique, and this simplification reflects important beliefs and values as well. These two characteristics combined mean that a society has two powerful motives to encourage people to "live up to their stereotypes": to encourage them to act like the images a culture already has of

① yellow peril (yellow terror)：黄祸或黄色恐怖，种族主义术语。19世纪末华人工人不断输出，美国以及其他西方国家开始担忧华人的大量涌入会给他们带来威胁，因此产生了一种反华人、排斥华人，以及鄙视所有黄皮肤的亚洲人的思想。

them (popular culture is conservative) and to thereby fulfill their proper social roles. In other words, stereotypes encourage people to internalize a cultural image, as their goal—a task which may be convenient for the culture (and especially for the power structure status quo) but this proves to be both impossible and damaging to the individuals being asked to mold themselves in such a narrow manner.

4. As human beings, each of us has a seemingly infinite number of choices about what kind of person we want to be. In fact, most of us choose to be several kinds of persons—efficient at the office, sloppy around the house, formal with our boss, loose and vulgar with our friends warm and loving with our parents—we enjoy wearing different personalities for different occasions. If we accept someone else's stereotyped image of what we ought to be, even if the image is a positive one, we sadly, perhaps even tragically, limit the choices that are such a wonderful part of our humanity and confine ourselves to being narrow and standardized. We become less human and more like robots. For example, the current national stereotype of the attractive woman being pencil-thin and the fads that accompany this stereotype dramatically illustrates this danger. For the woman who comes to fully embrace this stereotype as valid and adopts it for herself, the symbol of her robotization is the self-destructive **anorexia-nervosa**①, and if accepted fanatically enough, it is the ultimate symbol of dehumanization and death.

Exercise

A. Questions for Understanding

1. What might a (negative) stereotype result in according to Paragraph 1?

2. According to Paragraph 2 who might easily stereotype whom? Why?

3. If you compare the Jews' history in Germany and that of the Asians in the United States, what conclusion can you draw about stereotype?

4. Judging from Paragraph 4 what philosophy do you think the author validates about human beings?

5. Does the author make a suggestion that people should choose to be a stereotyped person? Give your reason.

B. Gap Filling

Provide the missing words according to the paragraph you have just read.

---

① anorexia-nervosa:(医)神经性食欲缺乏。

9. As human beings, each of us has a seemingly ______ number of choices about what kind of person we want to be. In fact, most of us ______ to be several kinds of persons—efficient at the office, ______ around the house, formal with our boss, ______ and vulgar with our friends warm and loving with our parents—we enjoy ______ different personalities for different occasions. If we accept someone else'sstereotyped image of what we ought to be, even if the image is a positive one, we sadly, perhaps even tragically, limit the choices that are such a wonderful part of our ______ and ______ ourselves to being narrow and standardized. We become less human and more like robots. For example, the current national ______ of the attractive woman being ______ and the ______ that accompany this stereotype dramatically illustrates this danger. For the woman who comes to fully embrace this stereotype as valid and adopts it for herself, the symbol of her ______ is the self-destructive anorexia-nervosa, and if accepted fanatically enough, it is the ultimate symbol of dehumanization and death.

Supplementary Reading(6)

Passage A: Some Thoughts About Stereotype

1. In the story "The Myth of the Latin Woman", Judith Ortiz Cofer discusses how she was treated by various people due to their conception of her as a Latin woman. Her strong theme discusses various stereotypes that Latin women are subjected to such as they are being viewed as uneducated, hot tamale, and labeled as submissive workers. Judith Ortiz Cofer believes Latin women are stereotyped as sexual firebrand because of their dress. Clothing was always a big culture clash. She states that she learned to dress from her mother, "as young girls, it was our mother who had grown up on a tropical island, where the natural environment was a riot of primary colors, where showing your skin was one way to keep cool as well as to look sexy". In America, people think that Latin girls wear colorful clothes and show a lot of skin because they are prostitute or easy to get with. The author proves this is untrue after going to her first high school dance with a boy who tried to kiss her but she rejected.

2. In everyday use, the concept of the stereotype is used in various contexts: usually the word stereotype is used to refer to members of some kind of collective: firemen are courageous, blondes are less intelligent, Africans are poor, and the Latin girls are hot and so on. When a person makes inferences with a new person or about some social events, they use their existing

knowledge to reduce the uncertainty in the situation. The less one knows about the object, the more one uses stereotypical generalizations.

3. Americans are pushy and the English are reserved, right? Wrong, says a new study, which reveals there is no truth in this sort of cultural stereotypes. There was no correlation between perceived cultural characteristics and the actual traits. These stereotypes focus our attention on some certain features, which is not good at understanding one culture comprehensively. When we walk on the street, for instance, just to get to a certain address, we may not be able to tell how many barber shops we passed during our journey. However, if we walk on the same street to find one, our attention is tuned to see the barbershops' signs. Cultural stereotypes work in the same way: they focus our attention on certain features, and amplify them in our observation. In this way, we see what we are taught to see, and at the same time our observations also confirm the stereotypes.

4. In the article, the author mentions one facet of the myth of the Latin woman in the United States is the menial, the domestic. The myth of the Hispanic menial—the funny maid, mispronouncing words and cooking up a spicy storm in a shiny California kitchen—has been perpetuated by the media in the same way that "Mammy" from *Gone with the Wind* became America's idea of the black woman for generations. So when the author took her first public poetry reading at a restaurant in Miami, she was mistreated as a waitress because she was a Latin girl, and Latin girl are treated as uneducated.

5. The less we know about the other, the more we hang on stereotypes. If the stereotype is well-grounded and justifiable it may help to orient oneself in a certain situation. Stereotypes are only offensive when they are perceived as being negative. For example: How many times have you ever heard a black man stand up and angrily deny that all black men have huge penises? That statement is a stereotype, but I don't hear anyone complaining about it. There are other stereotypes that are accepted and even repeated by the very group being targeted. Chinese are hard workers, Swedish women are beautiful, Italian women are excellent cooks, black women are strong, bi-sexual women make better lovers and so on. But if it is unjust and loaded with negative emotions, it will harm the interaction without question, and also often results from, and leads to, prejudice. Some groups in society—such as blacks, women, Jews, gays and lesbians—have all experienced the effects of negative stereotyping and lack of positive images. The Americans looked down on the blacks. In the university classroom, the professor said, "the Black men's IQ is clearly lower than the White's ..." Among the 250 persons on the spot, Rice, the only black stood up excitedly, "This is no scientific basis. The Black do as hard as the

White. We can do what the white can." With father's studious edification, Rice becomes the first black female secretary of state in American, who is full of sense of calling to defend the color self-esteem. Her success is so inspiring to the people who are striving to eliminate the prejudice. When we break through the prejudice to love our own skin color, gender and so on, we should improve ourselves more hard, and show our ability to the world, to prove those stereotypes are so ridiculous.

6. Why we stereotype? The following three points are important. First, *the field of view*. From the time that we are very young children, human beings are constantly striving to process the world around us. We struggle to put things into some type of order, and to see the world in a way that makes sense to us. Imagine a preschooler playing with a set of blocks. He may put all of the blue blocks in one pile and the red ones in another. He may also sort the blocks by their shape or size. Throughout our lives, from the earliest years on, we classify people by these same sorts of criteria; boys and girls, adults and kids, fat and thin, tall and short. As we go through life, whether consciously or subconsciously, we are struggling to make sense of the people, places and things around us. The question is that most people's views are limited. We all know that the less variety of input that a person receives early in life, and the less experience they have with any other people group, the more likely they will be to develop a stereotype. Additionally, when a person with limited experience with any other group of people has a negative experience with that group first, they are far more likely to apply a stereotype to all people who fall into that group.

7. But why our views are so limited? As far as I am concerned, the education system and ourselves should pay the great responsibility. As for education, there are still some disadvantages in it. The main question is that people are always pursuing the marks, and always pursuing the knowledge utilitarian. Nearly every teacher and parent would say, "do your basic education and go to the best university". But what will they do after graduating from school? They Seldom give answers to this question. In some Chinese high schools, students study very crazily. They study more than twelve hours every day! They live in the school and never watch TV, read newspapers or play computer games. Students never really have a hobby. If you ask them about what are their hobbies, 99% of them will say, I like music, sports and reading. But most of them don't know the difference between jazz and blues. On the other side, the content of education is definitely imperfect, we should learn many things by ourselves if we want to understand the world deeply. In the history class, for instance, teacher taught us about Africa for its geographic position, climate condition, the poor conditions they face and so on. A picture in

the book describes many African children, some are as thin as rails, and some are big-stomached, not because good eating but no way to eat clean food. They impress me with the poverty only. The same as many others, for African, my initial impression comes from the wild animal and the virgin forest and grassland. They live in an "animal world". All things there seems linking with the original, barbarous, and mysterious. Later, in my mind, Africa has become a place with war, riot, and dirty and frightening infectious diseases. Then, I know that the mysterious pyramids of Egypt, gold and diamonds in South Africa and exotic tribal culture of Kan Bali ... If I don't read more about Africa myself, I still stereotype a poor place.

8. Second, *Media*. The media is the biggest stereotype of the world. And we as a nation we feed right into it. In the media it is common that a certain group is attached with a stereotype. The industry is under pressure to attract readers and viewers, which needs as wide an audience as possible to quickly understand information. In the article, through the media, advertisers in their special vocabulary have designated "sizzling" and "smoldering" as the adjectives of choice for describing not only the foods but also the women of the Latin America. Stereotypes act like codes that give audiences a quick, common understanding of a person or group of people—usually relating to their class, ethnicity or race, gender, sexual orientation, social role or occupation. By using stereotypes, a complex issue involving people with complex motives can be reduced to a simple conflict between "good guys" and "bad guys". This can happen when the media try to make real events appear more dramatic to appear audience.

9. Look at some of your movies that are out today. People believe what they see on television. And that is far away from the truth. In many shows and movies the male is the handsome hero and never makes mistakes, while the woman is the helpless, beautiful blonde who can only flutter her eye lashes, scream, apply make-up and kiss. In movies obese people are never seen without food in their hand or mouth and most of the time are disgusting and will give up anything for food. This is definitely a negative because weight isn't easily controlled for some people, sometimes it is because of their genes. Super models represent a stereotype of beauty in magazines that is super thin, this is negative because to be this type of beauty encourages young girls to be on diet and unhealthy. As far as I am concerned, they are obsessed with wealth, and lack of pure cultural communication. In order to seize the market, they tried everything to appear audience, including stereotyping, and the final purpose is making money.

10. Third, *culture differences*. All societies have cultures, and all societies overlap culture. Culture exists everywhere—in schools, in religious groups, in races, in neighborhoods and states, etc. Most people stereotype because they have failed to evaluate a culture within that

culture's scope. Misunderstanding is sure to result when one culture evaluates another by a foreign set of ideals. As the differences of natural environment, economic levels and national development history, each nation has its own unique accustomed lifestyle. For example: Chinese and Japanese use chopsticks to dine, Westerners use forks. Chinese people like to invite guests and give gifts, and the Westerners rarely entertain guests at home; Chinese people like to wear red setting, the color red is regarded as lucky. In the West, the red color is not ghillie.

11. I still remember the Arts Festival between Chinese and foreign students in our university. The French students performed the Chorus, they were good-looking, and their beautiful song was full of melody. Audiences were charmed with it, and confirmed their stereotype that French are nobly. Then another queue I forgot where they came from started to dance. I am not sure whether I could call it dance. They just wiggled their ass without any sense of beauty. So many people thought they were so rude. In fact, they just have the different ways to express the good mood; we should evaluate a culture within that culture's scope, not just another culture or our own preference. It doesn't need to go about all day comparing apples to oranges. Suppose I have squeezed both the apple and the orange. But instead of judging the orange by the apple, I simply look at the orange and say, "This orange squeezes extraordinarily well, as oranges go." I have appreciated the orange in its own scope and not discredited it for its lack of apple-ness.

12. Except the above main aspects, maybe, people stereotype other people because stereotypes exist. Do all black people like fried chicken and watermelon? Of course not. Are all white people horrible dancers? Of course not. But at one time or another there were enough people in a group with the same behaviors for it to become a defining characteristic of that group as a whole, which then trickled down to the individuals within that group. My point is that negative stereotypes exist for reasons. Only when we take the time to educate ourselves, to learn where these stereotypes come from, what the history behind them is, can we overcome them and move forward toward a progressively harmonious society.

13. While stereotypes will unfortunately continue to exist, the author signs that she is one of the lucky ones. There are thousands of Latinos without the privilege of an education or the entrees into society that she has. For them life is a constant struggle against the misconceptions perpetuated by the myth of the Latina. Her goal is to try to replace the old stereotypes with a much more interesting set of realities. And our goal is to erase some of these misconceived stereotyped preconceptions, by subjective; we must focus on open minds and develop a tolerance for understanding differences.

14. Everything has many sides, we must understand things wholly, and keep an open mind. In order to develop an open mind, we should read more about different cultures and understand about different races, ethnicities, religions and other groups to help know the truth about people who are different from us. We should make an effort to get to know people different from you. Looking for things in common with other people and celebrate the differences. We should learn from and appreciate something about everyone. Also, we should learn about other people and their culture. By learning about other people, our life will be greatly enriched and our appreciation for our own culture will deepen. Then, we should explore the unfamiliar. Attend an organization meeting, religious service or travel to a new region where you are in the minority. Experiences teach us more than any other activity and the more a person experiences and the more variety in those experiences, the more likely they will be to have an open mind. Everyone knows someone or has some experience traveling to, learning about or living in difficult cultures and it can be very revealing. Things can be done differently by others and seeing this helps us to realize that we don't have to do everything the same way as may have learned it or developed habits with.

15. Variety in our experiences quickly teaches us to explore life, to seek out new exciting things around us and to not limit to what is already known. Then we should develop a tolerance for understanding differences. Humankind is made up of various cultures and peoples, each of which has its own vision of life and a particular way of solving its problems and fulfilling its possibilities. No matter how great their dominion, all cultures have had to tolerate the existence of conceptions of life and the world that are different from their own. This makes us realize that there has never been a single worldview appropriate for everyone, and also that the differences among various cultures pertain to the functions each performs in the whole of humankind. Today close contact among the various peoples of the world and the capability of contemplating the earth as a whole help us to understand that cultures are interdependent. We also realize that if different visions of the world exist today, it is because none of them is integral. In order for a universal vision—one suited to all human beings—to evolve, each culture needs to consider not only its own interpretation of life, but also the interpretations of other cultures. If we develop a deep respect for what seems different to us, it will be easier for us to broaden our vision and understand the function of each individual, group, people and culture in the whole of humankind.

16. By being objective, media plays an important role. It not only entertains and offers news to people, but also transfers the stereotypes, beliefs and values of the society to reproduce

the existing order of social life. It should pay responsible for all of us: the news reports should be true and fair; the movies should not only emphasize the box office and please us, it should spread the true culture.

17. Through the text *The Myth of the Latin Woman: I Just Met a Girl Named Maria*, I have thought about it for a very long time, and looked up many materials. I have a deep understanding about stereotype. Stereotypes are pervasive in our society. We all stereotype and are all subject to being stereotyped by others. The stereotypes we use can be both positive and negative. We need to become aware of the stereotypes we have so we can see people for who they really are and understand the world objectively.

True or False Statements

(a38) Latin women like to show their skin because it is sexy, not to keep cool.

(a39) Latinos, Africans and Americans are all somehow stereotyped according to Paragraphs 2 and 3.

(a40) The barber example in Paragraph 3 shows stereotypes only focus on one aspect of a person or a thing in negligence of the rest.

(a41) In Paragraph 5 the author implies that stereotype sometimes can be positive.

(a42) Rice, the former secretary of the state of US, disagreed strongly with the professor in classroom and proved him wrong in real life.

(a43) The preschooler example in Paragraph 6 intends to say that stereotypes are learned.

(a44) The author in Paragraph 7 disagrees with the Chinese high school students because reading, music and sports can't be hobbies.

(a45) Cultural differences lead to stereotype.

(a46) In Paragraph 12 the author seems to say that stereotype is culturally inborn.

(a47) In Paragraph 14 the author suggests a dialectical attitude toward stereotype.

(a48) In Paragraph 15 the author advocates tolerance, respect and open-mindedness to overcome stereotypes.

(a49) The author used women as an example to critique stereotypes which pervade a society in all aspects.

第三章　后殖民主义

后殖民主义(postcolonialism)是一个备受争议的概念，同时也是一个极具号召力和影响力的概念。顾名思义，所谓“后”就是时间和空间上处在殖民主义之后的历史和文化，指第二次世界大战之后，前殖民地的国家和民族都相继获得了独立。然而，实际情况并非人们想象的那么简单。表面上看，入侵领土、征服异族、掠夺财物等殖民主义现象已不存在。但是，从殖民主义的掠夺本质来看，殖民主义并不会立刻消失。也正因为如此，后殖民主义的学者认为，在当今世界里，殖民主义通过变异，以一种不易察觉或者为人们所认同的方式继续存在着。所以，后殖民主义的另一层含义是，人们对殖民主义不再保持沉默，而是用一种质疑、解构、反抗的视角来重新审视已经定性的历史、文化、文学等殖民主义话语，以及抗阻在全球化过程中的新殖民主义(neo-colonialism)。

后殖民主义既然是指反抗殖民主义，它自然涉及很多内容。比如，族性(ethnicity)问题、民族主义、语言、教育、历史、表征(representation)、普遍性(universality)、不同性(difference)、生产(production)、空间(space)、他化(otherization)、多元化(plurality)、边缘化(marginalization)、身份(identity)以及女权和后现代主义等。在诸多后殖民主义的研究者中，爱德华·赛义德(Edward Said)、盖雅特丽·斯皮瓦克(Gayatri Spivak)、霍米·巴巴(Homi K. Bhabha)、贝尔·胡克斯(Bell Hooks)、弗兰茨·法侬(Fiwtz Fanon)等一批亚洲裔和非洲裔的学者最有影响。其中，赛义德的《东方主义》(*Orientalism*)一书具有里程碑的作用，开辟了后殖民研究理论上的新篇章。

后殖民主义(批评)和后现代主义有不少共同之处。比如，二者都关心权力问题，都具有反传统、反权威、反中心等解构主义特征。但是，后殖民主义关注的是西方(前殖民主义国家)和第三世界(前殖民地)国家之间的诸多关系，而后现代主义则主要是从西方内部来重新或以反传统的方式审视其社会关系；从后殖民主义的视角看，西方的价值观、文学以及各种版本的后现代主义都或多或少地表现出了民族文化中心主义(ethnocentrism)。西方的各种思想(亚里士多德、笛卡儿、康德、尼采、马克思、弗洛伊德等人的理论和学说)和文学(荷马、但丁、福楼拜、艾略特等人的作品)已经主导了世界文化，非西方的传统、文化和话语被边缘化或排斥。

第一节　殖民主义的定义

导　读

后殖民主义和殖民主义密不可分，学习后殖民主义首先要了解殖民主义。殖民主义的本性就是入侵、掠夺和屠杀，这似乎已经是不争的事实。但如果没有话语的传播，事实本身是不会被认识的。然而，话语并不是事实而只是工具，工具本身又负载文化价值观，因此，事实的真实性取决于由谁、用什么样的话语来表达事实。第三世界的人民饱受殖民主义的蹂躏和奴役，当然对殖民主义的本性有着切肤之痛的认识。但是，殖民地的人民往往没有话语权，而在殖民主义的话语中，殖民主义的侵略、掠夺和屠杀的本性总是被一种或另一种方式所掩盖或美化。以下这篇选文向读者阐明重新认识殖民主义的必要性。

Passage：Why Re-read Colonialism?

1. Colonialism and imperialism are often used interchangeably. The word colonialism is defined by OED as："a settlement in a new country. ... a body of people who settle in a new locality, forming a community subject to or connected with their parent state; the community so formed, consisting of the original settlers and their descendants and successors, as long as the connection with the parent state is kept up."

2. This definition, quite remarkably, avoids any reference to people other than the colonisers, people who might already have been living in those places where colonies were established. Hence it evacuates the word "colonialism" of any implication of an encounter between peoples, or of conquest and domination. There is no hint that the "new locality" may not be so "new" and that the process of "forming a community" might be somewhat unfair. Colonialism was not an identical process in different parts of the world but everywhere it locked the original inhabitants and the newcomers into the most complex and traumatic relationships in human history. For instance, "forming a community" in the new land necessarily meant unforming or re-forming the communities that existed there already, and involved a wide range of practices including trade, plunder, negotiation, warfare, genocide, enslavement and

rebellions. Such practices produced and were produced through a variety of writings—public and private records, letters, trade documents, government papers, fiction and scientific literature. These practices and writings are an important part of all that contemporary studies of colonialism and postcolonialism try to make sense of. In *The Tempest*, for example, Shakespeare's single major addition to the story he found in certain pamphlets about a shipwreck in the Bermudas was to make the island inhabited before Prospero's arrival. That single addition turned the adventure story into an allegory of the colonial encounter.

3. So colonialism can be denned as the *conquest and control* of other people's land and goods. But colonialism in this sense is not merely the expansion of various European powers into Asia, Africa or the Americas from the sixteenth century onwards; it has been a recurrent and widespread feature of human history. At its height in the second century AD, the Roman Empire stretched from Armenia to the Atlantic. Under Genghis Khan in the thirteenth century the Mongols conquered the Middle East as well as China. The Aztec Empire was established when, from the fourteenth to the sixteenth centuries, one of the various ethnic groups who settled in the valley of Mexico subjugated the others. Aztecs extracted tributes in services and goods from conquered regions, as did the Inca Empire which was the largest pre-industrial state in the Americas. In the fifteenth century too, various kingdoms in southern India came under the control of the Vijaynagara Empire, and the Ottoman Empire, which began as a minor Islamic principality in what is now western Turkey extended itself over most of Asia Minor and the Balkans. At the beginning of the eighteenth century, it still extended from the Mediterranean to the Indian Ocean, and the Chinese Empire was larger than anything Europe had seen. Modern European colonialism cannot be sealed off from these earlier histories of contact—the Crusades, or the Moorish invasion of Spain, the legendary exploits of Mongol rulers or the fabled wealth of the Incas or the Mughals were real or imagined fuel for the European journeys to different parts of the world. And yet, these newer European travellers ushered in new and different kinds of colonial practices which altered the whole globe in a way that these other colonialisms did not.

Exercises

A. Questions for Understanding

1. Why is OED's definition of "colonialism" quoted at the beginning?
2. According to Paragraph 2, what is wrong or improper with the quoted definition?
3. What does the example about *The Tempest* by Shakespeare intend to justify?

4. If you compare the old colonialism with the new European colonialism, what features can you find of the old colonialism?

5. Why is it necessary to redefine colonialism?

B. Gap Filling

Provide the missing words according to the paragraph you have just read.

10. This definition, quite remarkably, avoids any reference to people other than the ______, people who might already have been living in those places where ______ were established. Hence it ______ the word "colonialism" of any implication of an encounter between peoples, or of conquest and domination-There is no hint that the "new ______" may not be so "new" and that the process of "forming a community" might be somewhat unfair. Colonialism was not an identical process in different parts of the world but everywhere it ______ the original inhabitants and the newcomers into the most complex and ______ relationships in human history. For instance, "forming a community" in the new land necessarily meant ______ or re-forming the communities that existed there already, and involved a wide range of practices including trade, ______, negotiation, warfare, ______, enslavement and rebellions. Such practices produced and were produced through a variety of writings—public and private records, letters, trade documents, government papers, fiction and scientific literature. These practices and writings are an important part of all that contemporary studies of colonialism and ______ try to make sense of.

第二节　马克思列宁主义的殖民观

导　读

从《牛津英语词典》(OED)对殖民主义的定义不难看出，殖民主义的话语竭力掩盖其殖民主义的实质。只有以一种批判的眼光来分析和研究殖民主义才能客观评价殖民主义的思想和行为。在这方面，认识最深刻和最有影响力的人物是马克思和列宁。马克思不仅是社会主义国家的导师和奠基人，而且是意识形态和霸权等重要理论的创建者。文化研究中许多所谓“新马克思主义者”都得益于马克思主义的理论和观点。下面主要介绍的是马克思、列宁对殖民主义本质的认识以及列宁对帝国主义的界定。

Passage: Marxist and Leninist Views

(1) Marxist View

1. How do we think about these differences (between the old and new colonialisms)? Was it that Europeans established empires far away from their own shores? Were they more violent or more ruthless? Were they better organised? Or a superior race? All of these explanations have in fact been offered to account for the global power and drastic effects of European colonialisms. Marxist thinking on the subject locates a crucial distinction between the two: whereas earlier colonialisms were pre-capitalist, modern colonialism was established alongside capitalism in Western Europe. Modern colonialism did more than extract tribute, goods and wealth from the countries that it conquered—it restructured the economies of the latter, drawing them into a complex relationship with their own, so that there was a flow of human and natural resources between colonised and colonial countries. This flow worked in both directions—slaves and indentured Labour as well as raw materials were transported to manufacture goods in the metropolis, or in other locations for metropolitan consumption, but the colonies also provided captive markets for European goods. Thus slaves were moved from Africa to the Americas, and in the: West Indian plantations they produced sugar for consumption in Europe, and raw cotton was moved from India to be manufactured into cloth in England and then sold back to India: whose own cloth production suffered as a result. In whichever direction human beings and materials travelled, the profits always flowed back into the so-called mother country.

2. These flows of profits and people involved settlement and plantations as in the Americas, "trade" as in India, and enormous global shifts of populations. Both the colonised and the colonisers moved: the former not only as slaves but also as indentured labourers, domestic servants, travellers and traders, and the colonial masters as administrators, soldiers, merchants, settlers travellers, writers, domestic staff, missionaries, teachers and scientists. The essential point is that although European colonialisms involved a variety of techniques and patterns of domination, penetrating deep into some societies and involving a comparatively superficial contact with others, all of them produced the economic imbalance that was necessary for the growth of European capitalism and industry. Thus we could say that colonialism was the midwife that assisted at the birth of European capitalism, or that without colonial expansion the transition

to capitalism could not have taken place in Europe.

(2) Leninist View

3. In the early twentieth century, Lenin and Kautsky (among other writers) gave a new meaning to the word imperialism by linking it to a particular stage of the development of capitalism. In *Imperialism, the Highest Stage of Capitalism* (1947), Lenin argued that the growth of "finance-capitalism" and industry in the Western countries had created "Van enormous superabundance of capital". This money could not be profitably invested at home where labour was limited. The colonies lacked capital but were abundant in labour and human resources. Therefore it needed to move out and subordinate non-industrialised countries to sustain its own growth. Lenin thus predicted that in due course the rest of the world would be absorbed by European finance capitalists. This global system was called "imperialism" and constituted a particular stage of capitalist development—the "highest" in Lenin's understanding because rivalry between the various imperial wars would catalyse their destruction and the demise of capitalism. It is this Leninist definition that allows some people to argue that capitalism is the distinguishing feature between colonialism and imperialism.

4. Direct colonial rule is not necessary for imperialism in this sense, because the economic (and social) relations of dependency and control ensure both captive labour well as markets for European industry as well as goods. Sometimes the words "neo-imperialism" or neo-colonialism are used to describe these situations. In as much as the growth of European industry and finance-capital was achieved through colonial domination in the first place, we can also see that imperialism (in this sense) is the highest stage of colonialism. In the modern world then, we can distinguish between colonisation as the take over of territory, appropriation of material resources, exploitation of labour and interference with political and cultural structures of another territory or nation, and imperialism as a global system. However, there remains enormous ambiguity between the economic and political connotations of the word. If imperialism is defined as a political system in which an imperial centre governs colonised countries, then the granting of political independence signals the end of empire, the collapse of imperialism. However, if imperialism is primarily an economic system of penetration and control of markets, then political changes do not basically affect it, and may even redefine the term as in the case of "American imperialism" which wields enormous military and economic power across the globe but without direct political control. Thus, imperialism, colonialism and the differences between them are defined differently depending on their historical mutations. One useful way of distinguishing

between them might be not to separate them in temporal but in spatial terms and to think of imperialism or neo-imperialism as the phenomenon that originates in the metropolis, the process which leads to domination and control. Its result or what happens in the colonies as a consequence of imperial domination is colonialism or neo-colonialism. Thus the imperial country is the "metropole" from which power flows, and the colony or neo-colony is the place which it penetrates and controls. Imperialism can function without formal colonies (as in United States imperialism today) but colonialism cannot.

Exercises

A. Questions for Understanding

1. How does Marxist thinking differentiate the new colonialsm from the old one?
2. What do you think Marx examines in order to bring to the fore modern colonialism?
3. What is imperialism or capitalism? What marks off imperialism from colonialism?
4. Should imperialism be approached from political and economic aspects? Why?
5. Different as they are, what might be the essence both colonialism and imperialism share?

B. Gap Filling

Provide the missing words according to the paragraph you have just read.

11. However, there remains enormous ______ between the economic and political connotations of the word. If imperialism is defined as a political system in which an imperial centre governs colonised countries, then the ______ of political independence signals the end of empire, the collapse of imperialism. However, if ______ is primarily an economic system of ______ and control of markets, then ______ changes do not basically affect it, and may even redefine the term as in the case of "American imperialism" which ______ enormous military and economic power across the globe but without direct political control. Thus, imperialism, colonialism and the differences between them are defined differently depending on their historical mutations. One useful way of distinguishing between them might be to ______ separate them in temporal but in spatial terms and to think of imperialism or ______ as the ______ that originates in the metropolis, the process which leads to domination and control. Its result or what happens in the colonies as a consequence of imperial ______ is colonialism or ______. Thus the imperial country is the "______" from which power flows, and the colony or neo-colony is the place which it penetrates and controls. Imperialism can function without formal colonies (as in United

States imperialism today) but colonialism cannot.

第三节　后殖民主义及其批评

导　读

从内容上看，马克思和列宁的殖民主义观点（反对殖民主义）也属于后殖民主义的范畴，但是，作为一种理论，后殖民主义形成的年代要比马克思主义晚得多。许多学者都认为后殖民主义的形成以赛义德（Edward Said）的《东方主义》（*Orientalism*，1978）为标志。赛义德借助米歇尔·福柯（Michel Foucault）的话语理论，研究了在各种各样的西方著作中呈现出来的“东方”。东方在殖民主义的话语（《东方主义》）中并不是作为一种真实再现，而是西方人的一种“文化构想和话语实践”。另一方面，赛义德还引入了葛兰西的“文化霸权”概念，将政治学的视角引入文学和文化研究领域。总之，东方主义归根结底是一种西方人他化、异化东方人的理论、实践、心理和意识形态。毫无疑问，后殖民主义就是反对、揭露、颠覆和抗阻无处不在的东方主义，从中发现、恢复或建立真正的“自我”。

虽然反殖民主义和殖民主义共存，但是，世界范围内反殖民主义意识形态的形成以及抗阻殖民、关注自我成为一种体裁的文学或文化作品是近半个多世纪的事情。那么，后殖民主义在文学、文化领域究竟都涉及哪些具体问题？本节第二篇（Passage Two）有关后殖民主义文学批评的散论从一个侧面反映了后殖民主义的特征。

Passage One: Orientalism and *Orientalism*

1. The first Orientalists were 19th century scholars who translated the writings of "the Orient" into English, based on the assumption that a truly effective colonial conquest required knowledge of the conquered peoples. This idea of knowledge as power is present throughout Said's critique. By knowing the Orient, the West came to own it. The Orient became the studied, the seen, the observed, the object; Orientalist scholars were the students, the seers, the observers, the subject. The Orient was passive; the West was active.

2. One of the most significant constructions of Orientalist scholars is that of the Orient itself. What is considered the Orient is a vast region, one that spreads across a myriad of cultures and

countries. It includes most of Asia as well as the Middle East. The depiction of this single "Orient" which can be studied as a cohesive whole is one of the most powerful accomplishments of Orientalist scholars. It essentializes an image of a prototypical Oriental—a biological inferior that is culturally backward, peculiar, and unchanging—to be depicted in dominating and sexual terms. The discourse and visual imagery of Orientalism is laced with notions of power and superiority, formulated initially to facilitate a colonizing mission on the part of the West and perpetuated through a wide variety of discourses and policies. The language is critical to the construction. The feminine and weak Orient awaits the dominance of the West; it is a defenseless and unintelligent whole that exists for, and in terms of, its Western counterpart. The importance of such a construction is that it creates a single subject matter where none existed, a compilation of previously unspoken notions of the Other. Since the notion of the Orient is created by the Orientalist, it exists solely for him or her. Its identity is defined by the scholar who gives it life.

3. Said calls into question the underlying assumptions that from the foundation of Orientalist thinking. A rejection of Orientalism entails a rejection of biological generalizations cultural constructions, and racial and religious prejudices. It is a rejection of greed as a primary motivating factor in intellectual pursuit. It is an erasure of the line between "the West" and "the Other", Said argues for the use of "narrative" rather than "vision" in interpreting the geographical landscape known as the Orient, meaning that a historian and a scholar would turn not to a panoramic view of half of the globe, but rather to a focused and complex type of history that allows space for the dynamic variety of human experience. Rejection of Orientalist thinking does not entail a denial of the differences between "the West" and "the Orient", but rather an evaluation of such differences in a more critical and objective fashion.

4. *Orientalism*, published in 1978, is a critique of the academic field of Oriental Studies, which has been a scholarly pursuit at most of the prestigious European universities for several centuries. Oriental Studies is a composite area of scholarship comprising philology, linguistics, ethnography, and the interpretation of culture through the discovery, recovery, compilation, and translation of Oriental texts. Said makes it clear that he is not attempting to cover the whole area. His focus is on how English, French, and American scholars have approached the Arab societies of North Africa and the Middle East, He has nothing on the other areas that traditionally comprised the field such as Hebrew, Persian, Turkish, Indian and Far Eastern cultures, nor does he discuss the attitudes of German Russian, Italian, Spanish, or Portuguese Orientalists. The period he covers is more restricted than the scholarly field, too, extending only

from the late eighteenth century to the present, whereas European scholarship on the Orient dates back to the **High Middle Ages**①. Within his time frame, however, Said extends his examination beyond the works of recognized Orientalist academics to take in literature, journalism, travel books, and religious and philosophical studies to produce a broadly historical and anthropological perspective.

5. His book makes three major claims. The *first* is that Orientalism, although purporting to be an objective, disinterested, and rather esoteric field, in fact functioned to serve political ends. Orientalist scholarship provided the means through which Europeans could take over Oriental lands. Said is quite clear about the causal sequence: "Colonial rule was justified in advance by Orientalism, rather than after the fact." Imperial administrators like **Lord Curzon**②, a Viceroy of India, agreed that the products of this scholarship—our familiarity, not merely with the languages of the people of the East but with their customs, their feelings, their traditions, their history, and religion—had provided "the sole basis upon which we are likely to be able to maintain in the future the position we have won. In the late twentieth century, the field helps preserve American power in the Middle East and defends what Said calls "the Zionist invasion and colonization of Palestine"(Said, 1995) Today, however, there is much less interest in the traditional fields of philology and literature. American academic centers for Middle Eastern studies are more concerned with providing direct advice to the government on public policy.

6. His *second* claim is that Orientalism helped define Europe's self-image. "It has less to do with the Orient than it does with 'our' world." The construction of identity in every age and every society, Said maintains, involves establishing opposites and "Others". This happens because "the development and maintenance of every culture require the existence of another different and competing **alter ego**③. "Orientalism led the West to see Islamic culture as static in both time and place, as 'eternal, uniform, and incapable of defining itself', This gave Europe a sense of its own cultural and intellectual superiority. The West consequently saw itself as a dynamic, innovative, expanding culture, aswell as the spectator, the judge and Jury of every

① High Middle Ages：高中世纪，指公元1000—1300年这段时间，欧洲人口剧增，军事、宗教不断向外扩张和传播，经济和政治发生了巨变。欧洲中世纪的历史根据其发展特征可分为三段时间：早中世纪(Early Middle Ages：500—1000)、高中世纪和晚中世纪(Late Middle Ages：1300—1500)。

② (George Nathaniel) Curzon：柯曾(1859—1925)，英国驻印度总督(1898—1905)，任内整饬文官制度，保护印度艺术和文化遗产；后任外交大臣(1919—1924)，在解决中东问题、签订《洛桑条约》中曾起重要作用。

③ alter ego：第二个我，个性的另一面；知心朋友，极受信任的代理人。

facet of Oriental behavior." This became part of its imperial conceit.

7. *Thirdly*, Said argues that Orientalism has produced a false description of Arabs and Islamic culture. This happened primarily because of the essentialist nature of the enterprise—that is, the belief that it was possible to define the essential qualities of Arab peoples and Islamic culture. These qualities were seen in uniformly negative terms, he says. The Orient was defined as a place isolated from the mainstream of human progress in the sciences, arts, and commerce. Hence: "its sensuality, its tendency to despotism, its aberrant mentality, its habit of inaccuracy, its backwardness." Where this approach first goes wrong, Said says, is in its belief that there could be such a thing as *an* Islamic society, an Arab mind, *an* Oriental psyche. Where Orientalism goes even further astray, he claims, is its anachronistic assumption that Islam has possessed a unity since the seventh century, which can be read, via the *Koran*, into every facet of, say, modern Egyptian or Algerian society. The notion that Muslims suffer such a form of arrested development not only is false, he maintains, but also ignores more recent and important influences such as the experience of colonialism, imperialism, and, even, ordinary politics,

Exercises

A. Questions for Understanding

1. Why did the Orientalists translate the Oriental works in the early days?

2. How (Through which way or ways) do you think the Westerners knew the "Orientals"?

3. By "Orient" what did the Orientalists refer to? What's wrong with this geographical concept?

4. According to Said, what does it mean to reject Orientalism?

5. What does Said mean by "narrative" and "vision"?

6. According to Paragraph 4, do you think Orientalism only refers to the Orientalists' perception of people in the Arab societies of North Africa and the Middle East?

7. What are the three claims made by Said? How might they differ from one another?

8. What do you think might be the "correct" or expected way(s) Said suggests to construct the people and their land in the "Orient" ?

B. Gap Filling

Provide the missing words according to the paragraph you have just read.

12. Said calls into ______ the underlying assumptions that from the foundation of Orientalist

thinking. A rejection of Orientalism ______ a rejection of biological generalizations cultural constructions, and racial and religious prejudices. It is a rejection of greed as a primary ______ factor in intellectual pursuit. It is an erasure of the line between "the West" and "the Other", Said argues for the use of "narrative" rather than "vision" in interpreting the ______ landscape known as the Orient, meaning that a historian and a scholar would turn not to a ______ view of half of the globe, but rather to a focused and complex type of history that allows space for the ______ variety of human experience. ______ of Orientalist thinking does not entail a denial of the ______ between "the West" and "the Orient", but rather an ______ of such differences in a more critical and objective ______.

Passage Two: Postcolonialism in Literature

1. Colonialism and its effects can not be considered uniform: It was not practiced in the same way with identical results around the world. Nor did every region or nation follow the same process of decolonization at the same time and at the same rate. Nor did the various ethnic, political, gender, class, and religious groups experience colonization and decolonization in the same way and to the same extent. However, this (heterogeneity of "postcolonialism") does not negate its usefulness as a theoretical lens with which to look at literature and the World.

2. Postcolonial theory deals with the reading and writing of literature written in previously or currently colonized countries, or literature written in colonizing countries which deals with colonization or colonized peoples. It focuses particularly on the way in which literature by the colonizing culture distorts the experience and; realities, and inscribes the inferiority, of the colonized people on literature by colonized peoples which attempts to articulate their identity and reclaim their past in the face of that past's inevitable otherness. It can also deal with the way in which literature in colonizing countries appropriates the language, images, scenes, traditions and so forth of colonized countries.

3. Postcolonial theory is built in large part around the concept of **otherness**①. There are however problems with or complexities to the concept of otherness, for instance: otherness

① Otherness(other):"他性"或"他人意识"。在西方存在主义哲学看来,任何一个人的存在都是与他人的共存,既有"我"也就有"他"。但是在殖民主义话语和父权社会中,掌握话语权的"我"(殖民主义或父权)总是把"他"(被殖民者或父权社会里的女性)作为"我"的对立面而加以否定、排斥,使其永远都处于一个和"我"相对立的不利、边缘和从属的地位。所以,此处的 otherness 是一个具有特定意义的概念。

includes doubleness, both identity and difference, so that every other, every different than and excluded by is dialectically created and includes the values and meaning of the colonizing culture even as it rejects its power to define; the Western concept of the Oriental is based, on the Manichean allegory (seeing the world as divided into mutually excluding opposites) : if the West is ordered, rational, masculine, good, then the Orient is chaotic, irrational, feminine, evil. Simply to reverse this polarizing is to be complicit in its totalizing and identity-destroying power (all is reduced to a set of dichotomies, black or white, etc.); colonized peoples are highly diverse in their nature and in their traditions, and as beings in cultures they are both constructed and changing, so that while they may be "other" from the colonizers, they are also different one from another and from their own pasts, and should not be totalized or essentialized.

4. There are complexities and perplexities around the difficulty of conceiving how a colonized country can reclaim or reconstitute its identity in a language that is now but was not its own language, and genres which are now but were not the genres of the colonized. One result is that the literature may be written in the style of speech of the inhabitants of a particular colonized people or area, which language use does not read like Standard English and in which literature the standard literary allusions and common metaphors and symbols may be inappropriate and/or may be replaced by allusions and tropes which are alien to British culture and usage. It can become very difficult then for others to recognize or respect the work as literature.

5. The concept of **hybridity**①, an important concept in postcolonial theory, referring to the integration (or, mingling) of cultural signs and practices from the colonizing and the colonized cultures. The assimilation and adaptation of cultural practices, the cross-fertilization of cultures, can be seen as positive, enriching, and dynamic, as well as oppressive. "Hybridity" is also a useful concept for helping to break down the false sense that colonized cultures—or colonizing cultures for that matter—-are monolithic, or have essential, unchanging features.

6. To sum up (based on literary criticism), postcolonialism does the following things:

• To examine, question, and critique dominant. Western representations of race and cultural difference.

• To show how canonical literature as it is traditionally understood is silent on matters of colonization and imperialism and how that literature addresses issue of race and cultural

① hybridity：杂交文化，杂交。在殖民主义时期和后殖民主义时期是一直为学者们广泛关注的一个概念。殖民主义时期，殖民主义者为了保持对殖民地人民的优势和统治，始终宣扬和维护种族纯洁论；而后殖民主义时期，为了打破殖民主义的统治和奴役，把民族、文化融合看成世界多极、平等发展的趋势。所以，在"文化杂交"这个问题上，后殖民主义和殖民主义的观点是截然对立的。

difference.

- To foreground questions of cultural difference and diversity.
- To examine the natures of hybridity and otherness and to celebrate them as potential centers of cultural energy, plurality, and change.
- To recover marginalized voices and literatures both national and transnational that have been silenced and/or suppressed by colonial and neo-colonial domination.
- To study the ways in which nations reconstruct their political and cultural identity after independence from colonial domination.
- To study and eliminate the ways in which the Western industrialized powers continue to dominate the Third World even after the end of formal political colonialism.

Exercises

A. Questions for Understanding

1. What does the author intend to say about postcolonialism in Paragraph 1?
2. Whose literature will be the focus of postcolonialism?
3. What does Paragraph 3 try to tell the readers?
4. According to Paragraph 4 what problem or trouble may a colonized nation encounter in creating its own literature?
5. What can be seen from the term "hybridity" about postcolonialism?

B. Gap Filling

Provide the missing words according to the paragraphs you have just read.

13. Postcolonial theory is built in large part around the concept of ______. There are however problems with or ______ to the concept of otherness, for instance: otherness includes doubleness, both identity and difference, so that every other, every different than and ______ by is dialectically created and includes the values and meaning of the colonizing culture even as it rejects its power to define; the Western concept of the Oriental is based, on the Manichean allegory (seeing the world as divided into mutually excluding opposites): if the West is ordered, rational, masculine, good, then the ______ is chaotic, irrational, feminine, evil. Simply to reverse this ______ is to be complicit in its totalizing and identity-destroying power (all is reduced to a set of dichotomies, black or white, etc.); colonized peoples are highly diverse in their nature and in their ______, and as beings in ______ they are both constructed

and changing, so that while they may be "other" from the colonizers, they are also different one from another and from their own pasts, and should not be totalized or ______. There are complexities and perplexities around the difficulty of conceiving how a colonized country can ______ or reconstitute its identity in a language that is now but was not its own language, and ______ which are now but were not the genres of the colonized.

Supplementary Reading(7)

Passage A: Locating Postcolonialism

1. Post-colonialism loosely designates a set of theoretical approaches which focus on the direct effects and aftermaths of colonization. It also represents an attempt at transcending the historical definition of its primary object of study toward an extension of the historic and political notion of "colonizing" to other forms of human exploitation, normalization, repression and dependency. Post-colonialism forms a composite but powerful intellectual and critical movement which renews the perception and understanding of modern history, cultural studies, literary criticism, and political economy.

2. "Colonialism" is a term that critically refers to the political ideologies which legitimated the modern invasion, occupation and exploitation of inhabited lands by overwhelming outside military powers. For the local populations, it implied the forceful elimination of resistance, the imposition of alien rules, and the parasitic utilization of natural resources including manpower. This term appeared in the context of Marxism and became a cornerstone of the discourse of resistance during the 20th century. It was meant to counter the positive connotations attached to the use of "colonization"—understood as a legitimate "civilizing process" often reinforced by a religious agenda—by calling attention to its actual economic motivations and denouncing its ruthless oppression.

3. "Post-colonialism" appeared in the context of decolonization that marked the second half of the 20th century and has been appropriated by contemporary critical discourse in a wide range of domains mapped by at least half a dozen disciplines. However, in spite of some two decades of definitional debates, this term remains a fuzzy concept stretching from a strictly historical definition to the more encompassing and controversial sphere of its contemporary kin-terms similarly prefixed by a morpheme that indicates temporal succession while suggesting

transcending perspectives (post-structuralist, post-modern and the like).

4. Indeed, on the one hand, "post-colonial" may refer to the status of a land that is no longer colonized and has regained its political independence (e. g. post-colonial India). In this sense, "post-colonialism" will pertain to the set of features (economic, political, social, etc.) which characterizes these countries and the way in which they negotiate their colonial heritage, being understood that long periods of forced dependency necessarily had a profound impact on the social and cultural fabric of these societies (the post-colonial condition). It may also apply to the former colonizers in as much that both extended contacts with the alien societies they conquered, and the eventual loss of these profitable possessions, deeply influenced the course of their economic and cultural evolution.

5. On the other hand, "post-colonialism" may designate, and denounce, the new forms of economic and cultural oppression that have succeeded modern colonialism, sometimes called "neo-colonialism". The term tends to point out that cooperation, assistance, modernisation and the like are in fact new forms of political and cultural domination as pernicious as the former imperial colonialism or colonial imperialism were: the devaluation of autochthonous ways of life and their displacement by the ethos of dominant nations which are technologically more advanced. Obviously, these two senses are intimately linked but foreground different aspects of a single process: the cultural homogenization of ever larger areas of the globe.

6. This process raises several kinds of conceptual and pragmatic problems. One of the most challenging is to understand the historical conditions in which this new analytical tool emerged and how its epistemological impact transformed policies and practices not only in the academic agenda and beyond but also in the management of representation. Crucial questions in this respect bear upon the source of the authoritative voices, whether they originate among the former colonizers or the former colonized and using whose discourse, whether they use the rhetoric of atonement or the rhetoric of resentment, whether they Promote strategies of true empowerment or opportunistic strategies of protracted control.

7. Another important issue is the extent to which the contemporary notions of colonialism and post-colonialism can legitimately help conceptualize all past colonizations and their political, economical and cultural consequences. Are these notions valid epistemological tools to better understand the past? Do such conceptual extensions result in defusing the ethical questioning of modern European colonization? Does post-colonial discourse describe "normal" processes of cultural change through conquest and domination or does it engage human responsibility in the novel context of global awareness? Can multi-voiced reassessments of history impact upon the

present or is the critical discourse of post-colonialism a mere epiphenomenon that is a symptom of broader and deeper interacting forces?

8. Questions relating to colonial medicine and science more generally will constitute another point of focus. Indeed, colonial medicine may be used as a prism through which to examine a host of postcolonial topics: from social control to ways in which colonial medical frameworks were subverted, from the place of the body in the colonial project to the construction of a colonial discourse on tropical diseases and their causes, to forms of colonial knowledge. In short, by dissecting colonial medical discourses and practices, one can shed light on the political and ideological agenda of colonialism and its postcolonial legacies.

True or False Statements

(a50) The first paragraph tells the readers why there has appeared postcolonialism.

(a51) Postcolonialism intends not to reinterpret the old conceptions and notions about colonialism.

(a52) History and culture of the former colonized lands are particularly the center for postcolonialism to construct.

(a53) In the eyes of postcolonialists technological exportation can be a form of colonialism.

(a54) Science can also be loaded with colonialism.

(a55) The author's attitude toward colonialism in Paragraph 2 is not critical at all.

(a56) As readers we can see Paragraphs 3 and 4 have a very consistent continuity on the topic of postcolonialism.

(a57) The word "advanced" in Paragraph 5 means that colonization continues in a more acceptable form.

(a58) In Paragraph 6, through the statement "to understand historical conditions in which the new analytical tool emerged and how its epistemological impact transformed policies and practices in the management of representation", the author is discussing postcolonialism.

(a59) The author disagrees with what should postcolonialism do through raising several questions in Paragraph 7.

(a60) In the last paragraph the author extend the scope of postcolonialism to the field of medicine.

Passage B: ______

1. Many, many people have pointed out the dilemmas and complicities in the academic

institutionalization of radical movements and discourses. Like academic feminism, postcolonialism is rife with contradictions that reside in the often unquestioned and rarely contested hierarchies and relations of power in the university or college. Our analysis, often trenchant and astute, of cultural texts, seems so often not to pertain to our institutional texts, discourses, and processes: to our relationships with our colleagues, students, support staff, administrators and the like. In our institutional lives, we can clearly see and frequently encourage the replication of the very structures colonialism and imperialism were based on and thrived on.

2. One of the paths I have chosen in my travels through the universities I have worked in is anti-racism, specifically in my classrooms. Anti-racist pedagogy, whether classroom, collegial, or otherwise institutional, seems to me to be an essential component of the postcolonial, of postcolonial pedagogy. Yet—and this is where my profoundest uneasiness and conflict with postcolonialism lies—the project of anti-racism seems in many cases to be elided by, or anathema to, those of us who may do "postcolonialism". The project of theorizing our pedagogies seems to be marginal even to us, with the consequence that those people and bodies of people who evaluate the postcolonial academic's progress can say with complete sincerity, "what does anti-racist pedagogy have to do with your research into postcolonial literatures?" While it is easy to attribute this kind of comment to outsider ignorance, I suspect the fault lies equally with those of us who profess the postcolonial, without professing the role of race and racism, and without resisting the role of race and racism in our methods of teaching, the texts and subjects we choose, and so on. I have certainly argued elsewhere, and often enough, for us postcolonialists to scrutinize the place that pedagogy (postcolonial pedagogy) has in our theorizing of the postcolonial, and argued that we must also write about it, talk about it, deprivatize the almost pathological isolation in which we teach, interrogate for ourselves, colleagues, and students how we privilege and institutionalize certain knowledge; critique even the most trivial of our assumptions about good teaching, important teaching, and important learning.

3. The postcolonial academic, it seems to me, must work out her reasons for silence, for certain kinds of grading strategies and types of assignments, for certain modes of transmitting knowledge, for her defensiveness and ignorance on certain occasions, for her position on advocating for students and colleagues alike, her position on what constitutes academic freedom, "proper" scholarship, and the like. And quite simply, not enough of us do that well—unlearning colonialist, racist, nationalist attitudes is not a simple task, and is perhaps doubly complex for those of us who have a vested interest in doing postcolonial work, as if that

naturally exempts us from the real work required for that unlearning. It is as if we too have accepted that learning is based on a model of consumption, that to be a postcolonialist is to have instantly jumped from darkness to enlightenment without the long and difficult work—the research if you like—which is in fact required.

4. With this in mind, I wonder how many of us examine our students' progress through the academy as both allegories and histories of colonialism; in Canada, how the position of "international students" is racialized through that history, in terms of funding, our often-unexamined attitudes about them, **ESL**① examinations, their choice of research areas, even their freedom of movement from nation to nation. It is here that we tend, even as we profess the importance of history and of historicizing, to become resolutely ahistorical, and in the fine tradition of liberal individualism, see these events as individual cases, as problems with personality conflicts, and as aberrant; at any rate, as something in which we cannot intervene.

5. Postcolonial scholars, at all places in the academic hierarchies, must intervene, must take on the anti-oppression work that is, to my mind, an integral part of the postcolonial project. Such work discomfits and discomforts many of us, and involves indeed a certain amount of risk, a certain blurring and redefining of boundaries that many of us hold very dear to our sense of academic selfhood. As **Rey Chow**)② points out, very uncomfortably for me, the hold of white supremacy can be seen on both sides of the debates around "political correctness"—debates, again, that are easier sometimes to ignore than to contest. I suggest, too, that we intervene as postcolonial pedagogues by critiquing, for example, in our classrooms (and outside of them) the particularly entrenched ideologies of multiculturalism that, particularly in Canada where it is established as an official political discourse and policy, are so effective that any anti-racist work in the university classroom must involve a discussion and unpacking of multiculturalism as a form of racism. Both **Deepika Bahri**③ and **Kalpana Sesahdri-Crooks**④ discuss these issues in the US context, and their own critiques serve as useful starting points for positing a pedagogical strategy for a solid critique not only of multiculturalism, but many of the concomitant debates

① ESL：英语作为第二语言(English as second language)。

② Rey Chow：周蕾，布朗大学的Andrew Mellon人文学教授，华裔文化研究最重要的学者之一。研究领域：现代中国文学，当代女性主义理论，中国电影，后殖民理论，文化研究。

③ Deepika Bahri：迪皮卡·巴瑞，埃默里大学英语副教授，《亚洲研究》主任。主要研究领域：后殖民主义和多元文化研究。著有：*Native Intelligence: Aesthetics Politics and Post Colonial Literature* (2003)；合编：*Realms of Rhetoric*(2003)；*Between the Lines: South Asians and Postcoloniality* (1996).

④ Kalpana Sesahdri-Crooks：卡尔波拿·克鲁克斯，后殖民主义学者。著有：*Desiring Whiteness: A Lacanian Analysis of Race* (2000)。

about equity, affirmative action, representation in various cultural texts, academic freedom, and the like.

6. As many have suggested in these two issues on postcolonialism, the field, perhaps more accurately called now a discipline, can at times be (and is often perceived to be) monolithic and universalizing, recapitulating the very colonizing strategies it seeks to critique; certainly those of us who practice it are often guilty of not allowing for plurality and specificity, guilty, in the tradition of multiculturalism, of merely tolerating dissenting views while guarding our own postcolonial territory. Or, as with multiculturalism, there are many who dabble in the field, hungry for song-dance-food-costume, who create of postcolonialism a secondary specialization, without sufficient regard for theoretical, political, and cultural homework.

7. In an earlier paper, I suggested that part of a shift in thinking might be a rhetorical one. At what point did postcoloniality become the discipline of postcolonialism, an-ism that competes with others for attention and for validation? If postcoloniality, like postmodernity, is conceived of as a cultural condition, a state of being, then the other-isms—feminism, anti-racism, racism, and so on are very clearly strands within a larger cultural project, and not, more narrowly, only an intellectual one. Here, I may be being idealistic—predictable counterpoint to postcolonial discontentment and cynicism—what use, after all, in playing with the master's words in his house? As students of imperialism, however, we know that discursive resistance is real resistance, and that identity politics often circulate in and through our languages.

8. The field of the postcolonial is enormous and complicated, more than many of our other literary fields and specializations. It is of necessity political; and for myself the politics inherent in it must in part define it. As with other political debates within the academy, I fear that we postcolonialists permit ourselves to accept the politics of ignorance, and the perpetuation of ignorance-as-knowledge, especially in our classrooms, especially when the issues we face and debate are controversial and emotional. The first step in my postcolonial pedagogy is to own up to ignorance, to point out that the will to know is not conducive to understanding, in essence to humble myself and my students into recognizing how our ways of knowing, thinking, and reading are defined by their own limits. Easier said than done, when the discourses of freedom, individuality, and tolerance sustain a cultural ignorance that is sometimes astounding and always frightening. Easier said than done, when the enormity of the task of cultural critique works directly against the interests of our disciplinary areas and assumptions.

9. I hope to suggest what I see as the biggest hurdle to overcome in establishing postcolonial studies as a truly intellectual, liberatory project. The atomization of our academic practices, the

institutional imperative to elide what at times must be obvious to all of us—that the academy is based on relationships which are identical to and indeed aconsequence of the imperialist impulse—is what we must tackle in our postcolonial work, so that we can never deny the real impact of postcoloniality, never relegate it to a simple reading of texts, never find ourselves theorizing in the service of our vested interests, theorizing against those who challenge us, never deny that current social and institutional oppressions, and active resistance to them, has to be an integral part of what it means to be a postcolonial intellectual. Until this occurs, even for myself, my discontentment with the postcolonialism, even as I define myself and my intellectual activity around and through it, will remain profound.

True or False Statements

(b44) The title for this passage, if you are required to provide one, is "The Discontents of Postcolonialism".

(b45) In the first paragraph the author seems to approve of strucutures to institutionalization of radical movement and discourse despite its dilemmas and complexities.

(b46) The author must be a traveler because he said "one of the paths I have chosen in my travels".

(b47) In Paragraph 2 from the word "profess" we can infer that the author complained about those who do postcolonialism in theory but not in practice.

(b48) In Paragraph 4 the quote "I wonder how many of us examine our students' progress" means "few of us examine students' progress".

(b49) In Paragraph 5 the author means that there still prevails white supremacy among the scholars who do postcolonialism.

(b50) By "postcoloniality" in Paragraph 7 the author means postcolonialism hasn't yet gained its true recognition.

(b51) In paragraph 8 the author suggests a humble attitude toward postcolonial studies but it's difficult to do.

(b52) Colonialism never comes to an end and exists everywhere even in the classroom.

(b53) The author seems to complain that her/his colleagues don't have a sense of postcolonialism.

(b54) The author is a pedagogic postcolonialist.

(b55) The author intends to bring home the idea that postcolonialism must start with routinely activities of people.

第四章　种族、族性：全球化与身份

前面的章节已涉及身份、种族和族性有关的内容，因为种族主义、民族中心主义(ethnocentrism)和殖民主义都与对相关本体的理解和认识有关。从社会学的角度看，这些"自我中心主义"的实质就是人类集体身份的一种无节制的膨胀和扩张。后殖民主义使人们认识了殖民主义的掠夺本质，为抗阻、消灭殖民主义提供了有力的理论武器。同时后殖民主义也向人们证明解构殖民主义有关种族、族性等身份的必要性和重要性。在殖民主义形成的过程中，殖民地的人民不仅被剥夺了政治权、文化权，而且被剥夺了话语权。世界知识的构造、人类文化的形成无不被强大的殖民主义话语所控制。达尔文的进化论曾经风靡世界，被认为是人类进化的经典和权威，但又有多少人意识到"适者生存"这种格言式的论断可能以一种不知不觉的方式助长、滋生殖民主义、种族主义以及白人优越论。世界上的人种被习惯性地按肤色划分为白、黄、黑三种类型，但又有多少人思考过生物性只是人的一种属性，并不能决定人类后天获得的文化属性？在殖民主义和种族主义的话语中，黑人是处在社会底层的族群，那是因为黑色(作为白色的对立面)往往被丑化、异化或妖魔化。因为所谓"白"代表的是白人的品质和特征。道理很简单，殖民主义或种族主义者以自己的肤色作为标准，离白色越远(色质越重/浓)品质就越差；反之，颜色越轻(靠近白色)就越好(比如黄种人)，直到白色为最好。这种种族构建的结果是，白人至上、优越，而黑人或其他有色人种则是低下、卑劣。毫无疑问，种族(主义)依靠动物的物理或生物特征来传达文化价值观，而族性主要是各种文化层面的因素(语言、文化、婚姻、归属感、家庭、价值观、身份等)所构成的人的集体身份。在殖民主义和欧洲中心主义的话语中，它同样蕴涵不平等的意识。因此，构建平等、自由、多样的种族和族性身份首先要从建立公正、客观的身份意识开始。

世界经济的一体化是把双刃剑，它既给人类带来物质财富，同时又引起了不少无法回避的问题。比如环境和生态问题、国家资源的保护和利用问题以及与之紧密相连的经济和政治问题等。就人类的生存空间而言，历史所造成的许多问题并未真正得到解决，比如以上谈到的种族问题、殖民主义和下章(第五章)所要讨论的性别问题等，而地球村的出现一下子又把人类抛进了前所未有的困惑和矛盾当中：我(们)是谁？我们的历史、文化如何？本章将概要引入有关种族、族性和全球化等有关概念，以便学生对这些悬而未决而又无法回避的现实问题进行思考，从而开阔视野，增加人文素养。

第一节　身份、全球化

导　读

身份是人们认识自我、区分他人的一种心理或意识，并通过行为、活动、衣着或其他外延形式反映出来。身份作为文化现象由来已久，而作为学问为人们所关注却是近几十年的事情。根据社会学家的研究，身份在个体和集体两个层面上体现出来。一方面，维持身份、完善或改变身份成了人们追求自我价值、从事社会或生产活动一个不可或缺的动因。身份给人以归属感、安全感，同时又赋予人责任和义务。另一方面，身份使一个个体或群体区分于另一个个体或群体，社会因此而丰富，生活因此而多彩。从这一点来讲，身份又是标示差异和不同。身份的这两个特性既对立又统一，正像个体身份和集体身份对立统一一样，人的身份是由各种矛盾体构成的。性别是个体身份特征，而种族和族性却是集体身份特征。父权社会中，性别的构建使男人支配女人，种族的滥觞使白人优越于有色人。总之，身份的作用是，认同使人凝聚，排斥产生异化。但是，(经济)全球化的到来，给人们提出了许多前所未有的挑战，信息的爆炸、地域界线的打破和外来文化的冲击，都使人们很难操守原来固有的价值观和文化观。本节的第一篇文章讨论身份的起源和历史，第二篇文章讨论身份和全球化的关系。

Passage One: Identity

1. The study of identity owes its initial impetus to individual and collective identity crises set in motion by the nationalistic global war. Although **Emile Durkheim**[①], Sigmund Freud, and **George Mead**[②] provided important conceptual antecedents, the study of identity as a serious

① Emile Durkheim：埃米尔·迪尔凯姆(1858—1917)。到目前为止，最重要和多产的社会学家，由于采用实证主义的方法，被誉为把社会学科学化的人。迪尔凯姆强调社会事实中外在性和强制性的特征源于某种社会性因素。

② George (Herbert) Mead：乔治·赫伯特·米德(1863—1931)，美国社会学家、社会心理学家及哲学家，符号互动论的奠基人。

social science enterprise is largely a post-World War II development. Since its initial formulation in the writings of **Erik Erikson**① in the mid-1940s, the concept of identity has come into use by many scholars from various disciplines, methodological orientations, and even political leanings, **Andrew Weigert**② and his colleagues treat the concept as a bridge that links the psychological study of the individual and the sociological study of symbolic interaction. *At the micro level*, identity is the enduring source of human motivation and behavior, confirming what human beings imagine to be true about themselves, in their own eyes and in those of their significant others. The meaning of life is thus derived from individuals' interaction with significant others. *At the macro level*, identity is a deeper cultural code of personal meanings that relate the individual to the most general level of societal meanings.

2. Following Freud, psychologists have generally tended to study identity in terms of inner processes. The dynamic source of identity is attributed to a biopsychological drive in the individual self, not to a social system's need for stability and predictability, even if its enactment often meets societal needs for solidarity and collective action. Sociologists often conceptualize identity as shared beliefs and sentiments and also as enacted social roles and statuses that maintain the social order. It is what Durkheim called "collective conscience"—the glue, or organic solidarity, of dissimilar individuals of the same community which "connects successive generations with one another"—that sociological theorists are most concerned with. Political scientists have generally studied identity as a political resource in state forming, nation building and modernizing, and democratic political processes. Some of them have applied role theory, a variant and corollary of identity theory, in the study of comparative foreign policy. Most recently, identity theory has found its way into international relations theory. In a pioneering work, William Bloom addresses the long-standing theoretical problem of aggregating from individual attitudes to mass behavior by applying identity theory both to nation building and to international relations. Identity theory postulates that:

1) There is a universal human biopsychological need for a sense of identity/difference so that ambiguities and uncertainties can be minimized and human life rendered more meaningful and manageable.

---

① Erik Erikson：艾里克·艾里克森(1902—1994)，美国神经病学家，著名的发展心理学家和精神分析学家。他提出人格的社会心理发展理论，把心理的发展划分为八个阶段，指出每一阶段的特殊社会心理任务，并认为每一阶段都有一个特殊矛盾，矛盾的顺利解决是人格健康发展的前提。

② Andrew Weigert：安德鲁·维吉特，印第安纳圣母大学社会心理学教授。研究领域包括社会心理学、宗教、理论、环境和现代身份。

2) The construction of identity to realize this sense of identity/belonging begins with the establishment of the categories of self and other as mutually conflictive yet interdependent, each depending on and partaking of the other (for although identity begins in differentiation, it cannot be confirmed and legitimized without internalizing the mores, symbols, and behavioral patterns of significant others).

3) An identity is an ongoing negotiating process through the cycles of human life to enhance physical and psychological survival, security, and well-being, in the course of which the self attempts, especially in those problematic moments of ambiguity, to secure an identity that others do not bestow while others attempt to bestow an identity that the self does not appropriate.

4) Identity enactment is situation-specific; that is, threats to, and opportunities for the enhancement of, security function as catalysts for identity mobilization.

5) All identifications, from an individual nuclear family to the global system, are a series of relationships with positive or negative reference groups.

6) People with the same or shared identification generally tend to pool their resources to act in concert for the enhancement of their common identity.

Exercises

A. Questions for Understanding

1. Why does the writer make a mention of those scholars such as Freud and Erikson in Paragraph 1 ?

2. What are the two levels at which identity works as a source of human motivation? Can you elaborate it with your individual identity?

3. According to sociologists what role does identity play in a society?

4. Why do people have a biopsychological need?

5. Which one do you think might be the most important characteristic of identity according to the six theoretical postulations?

B. Gap Filling

Provide the missing words according to the paragraphs you have just read.

14. Identity theory postulates that:

1) There is a universal human ______ need for a sense of identity/difference so that

ambiguities and uncertainties can be minimized and human life rendered more meaningful and manageable.

2) The ______ of identity to realize this sense of identity/belonging begins with the establishment of the categories of self and other as mutually conflictive yet interdependent, each depending on and partaking of the other (for although identity begins in ______, it cannot be confirmed and legitimized without internalizing the mores, symbols, and behavioral patterns of significant others).

3) An identity is an ongoing ______ process through the cycles of human life to enhance physical and psychological ______, security, and well-being, in the course of which the self attempts, especially in those ______ moments of ambiguity, to secure an identity that others do not bestow while others attempt to bestow an identity that the self does not appropriate.

4) Identity ______ is situation-specific; that is, threats to, and opportunities for the enhancement of, security function as catalysts for identity ______.

5) All identifications, from an individual nuclear family to the global system, are a series of relationships with positive or negative ______.

6) People with the same or shared identification generally tend to pool their ______ to act in concert for the enhancement of their common identity.

Passage Two: Globalization and Identity

1. What globalization had definitely contributed to was the erosion of the "master identities" such as, for example, citizenship in the abstract meaning of membership in the territorially defined and state-governed society, and its replacement by an identity based on ethnicity, race, local community, language, and other "local" and culturally concrete forms. In other words, the trends towards unification that were exacerbating during the past decades in turn provoked the appreciation of the role and importance of the opposing trends towards the specific and the local.

2. One of the explanations of these contradicting tendencies may be as follows: though the process of globalization undermines the traditional perception of locality as a bounded space characterized by a framework of close relations based upon kinship ties and length of residency since it diminishes the intensity of day-to-day contacts and overall involvement into communal activities, it seems to have a different kind of influence on another dimension of "locality"—that is, various rituals, ceremonies and collective memories that bind the people together. As

Mike Featherstone argues, this is the primary factor that fosters the sustainability of the communal ties because it is the use of commemorative rituals and ceremonies that can be understood as batteries that store and recharge the sense of communality when one is apart from the regular calendar of ceremonies,

3. It can be concluded that the impact of globalization is contradictory: on the one hand it works towards the unification of the world but on the other, this proves to have a dubious effect on diminishing the local specificity and the tendencies towards the local, the cultural become more and more discernible and avowed. It might be pertinent, in this respect, to speak of the unification of the parameters of difference, or structuring and limitations of the dimensions of changeability. As Wilk puts it, nowadays we confront universal categories and standards by which all cultural differences can be defined, a phenomenon that could be categorized as structures of common difference that underpins but not imposes particular kinds of diversity and constraint.

4. Nevertheless, the effect of globalization on identity formation was considerable. One of its major contributions to the shifts in the way identity is perceived and theorized nowadays is highlighting the constructed character of many of the taken-for-granted assumptions about identity. One of the most striking examples is the one with the modem nation-states. With the erosion of the identity of a nation-state as an "enclave" within the world economy whose growth and development is determined, primarily, by its internal processes, the concept of "national identity" as of the "natural state of affairs" also starts to diffuse. Instead, constructed character of national identities becomes obvious as the issue of identity politics arises. Such "natural" assumptions about the nation-state on which it was actually built, become questioned, as:

- the nation as the "one people's" place, the idea of "folk" (in fact, there is hardly a state populated by "one people");
- the notion of the"ideological" coherence of one nation and its unifying into one totality on volunteer grounds (as far as many of modem nations are concerned, they were united during the long period of aggression and oppression of some national groups by the others);
- the assumption that the nation is based upon common and old traditions (it turns out that most of them are recent).

Besides, at present, national identity continues to be the object of governmental policy. Almost all totalitarian states face the predicament of maintaining an official version of its "national culture" while being confronted with globalization and diverse searches for cultural and local identities. The endeavours they make to protect and preserve their own local culture reveal two orientations: one is the state strategy which emphasizes creating and reinforcing an official version of ("national culture"; the other features the different and innovative efforts of many individuals and grassroots communities, who have taken into their own hands the mission of conserving traditional and local customs, cultures and diversity.

Exercises

A. Questions for Understanding

1. What seems to be a dialectical relationship between globalization and identity based on this passage you have just read?

2. What features the tendencies of identity development in the process of globalization?

3. What does Wilk intend to say about the impact of globalization in the matter of identity?

4. According to Paragraph 4 what contribution does globalization make to identity development?

5. Does the Chinese face a similar situation with regard to its collective identity? If so, what is it?

B. Gap Filling

Provide the missing words according to the paragraph (Passage One: Identity) you have just read.

15. Following Freud, ______ have generally tended to study identity in terms of ______ processes. The dynamic source of identity is attributed to a biopsychological drive in the individual self, not to a social system's need for stability and predictability, even if its enactment often meets societal needs for solidarity and collective action. Sociologists often conceptualize identity as shared beliefs and ______ and also as enacted social roles and statuses that ______ the social order. It is what Durkheim called "collective conscience"—the ______, or organic solidarity, of dissimilar individuals of the same community which "connects successive generations with one another"—that sociological theorists are most concerned with. Political scientists have generally studied identity as a political resource in ______ forming, nation building and modernizing, and democratic political processes. Some of them have applied role theory, a variant and ______ of identity theory, in the study of comparative foreign policy. Most recently, ______ theory has found its way into international relations theory. In a ______ work, William Bloom addresses the long-standing theoretical problem of aggregating from individual

attitudes to mass behavior by applying identity theory both to nation building and to ______ relations.

Supplementary Reading(8)

Passage A: Identity as Treasure

1. To begin, let me sketch the implicit (for it is usually implicit) reasoning behind the assumption that globalization destroys identities. Once upon a time, before the era of globalization, there existed local, autonomous, distinct and well-defined, robust and culturally sustaining connections between geographical place and cultural experience. These connections constituted one's—and one's community's—"cultural identity". This identity was something people simply "had" as an undisturbed existential possession, an inheritance, a benefit of traditional long dwelling, of continuity with the past. Identity, then, like language, was not just a description of cultural belonging; it was a sort of collective treasure of local communities. But it was also discovered to be something fragile that needed protecting and preserving, that could be lost. Into this world of manifold, discrete, but to various degrees vulnerable, cultural identities there suddenly burst (apparently around the middle of the 1980s) the corrosive power of globalization.

2. Globalization, so the story goes, has swept like a flood tide through the world's diverse cultures, destroying stable localities, displacing peoples, bringing a market-driven, "branded" homogenization of cultural experience, thus obliterating the differences between locality-defined cultures which had constituted our identities. Though globalization has been judged as involving a general process of loss of cultural diversity, some of course did better, some worse out of this process. Whilst those cultures in the mainstream of the flow of capitalism—those in the West and, specifically, the United States—saw a sort of standardized version of their cultures exported worldwide, it was the "weaker" cultures of the developing world that have been most threatened. Thus the economic vulnerability of these non-western cultures is assumed to be matched by a cultural vulnerability. Cultural identity is at risk everywhere with the depredations of globalization, but the developing world is particularly at risk.

3. This, then, is the story that implicates globalization in the destruction of cultural identity, and in the threat to that particular subset of cultural identity that we call "national

identity". But another, quite contradictory, story can be told: that globalization, far from destroying it, has been perhaps the most significant force in creating and proliferating cultural identity. This story involves a rather different understanding of the idea of identity than the somewhat reified understanding of an individual or collective possession. And it also involves a rather more complex understanding of the globalization process: one, at least, which allows for a degree of unpredictability in its consequences.

True or False Statements

(a61) Geographical place and cultural experience are believed to contribute to cultural identity before the age of globalization.

(a62) Identity is considered important for both individual and community.

(a63) In globalization Western countries have all-round advantageous position over those of the non-Western countries.

(a64) Globalization destroys the old traditional identities completely and replaces it with the new homogeneous ones.

(a65) Globalization puts cultural identity at risk because identity is a barrier to globalization.

Passage B: Globalization and the Politics of Identity

1. For a variety of reasons, globalization creates the conditions for localization, that is various kinds of attempts at creating bounded entities—countries (nationalism or separatism), faith systems (religious revitalization), cultures (linguistic or cultural movements) or interest groups (ethnicity). For this reason, a more apt term, coined by sociologist Roland Robertson, might be **glocalization**①. I shall now present some features that the "glocal" identity movements of the turn of the millennium seem to have in common.

2. First, identity politics always entails competition over scarce resources. Successful mobilisation on the basis of collective identities presupposes a widespread belief that resources are unequally distributed along group lines. "Resources" should be interpreted in the widest sense possible, and could in principle be taken to mean economic wealth or political power,

① glocalization：环-本化(环球本土化)，新词(由 global 和 localization 合并而成)，指经济在一体/全球化的过程中，发展中国家(弱小文化)有意识地发展保护本土文化而不被强大的(西方)霸权文化所吞噬或同化。

recognition or symbolic power—although what is usually primarily at stake are either economic or political resources. Secondly, modernisation and globalization actualize differences and trigger conflict. When formerly discrete groups are integrated into shared economic and political systems, inequalities are made visible, since direct comparison between the groups becomes possible. In a certain sense, ethnicity can be described as the process of making cultural differences comparable, and to that extent, it is a modern phenomenon boosted by the intensified contact entailed by globalization. You do not envy your neighbour if you are unaware of his existence.

3. Thirdly, similarity overrules equality ideologically. Ethnic nationalism, politicized religion and indigenous movements all depict the in-group as homogeneous, as people "of the same kind". Internal differences are glossed over, and for this reason, it can often be argued that identity politics serves the interests of the privileged segments of the group, even if the group as a whole is underprivileged, since it conceals internal class differences.

4. Fourthly, images of past suffering and injustice are invoked. To mention an example: the African American movement draws extensively on the history of slavery. Even spokesmen for clearly privileged groups, such as anti-immigrant politicians in Western Europe, may argue along these lines.

5. Fifthly, the political symbolism and rhetoric evokes personal experiences. This is perhaps the most important ideological feature of identity politics in general. Using myths, cultural symbols and kinship terminology in addressing their supporters, promoters of identity politics try to downplay the difference between personal experiences and group history.

6. Sixthly, first-comers are contrasted with invaders. Although this ideological feature is by no means universal in identity politics, it tends to be invoked whenever possible, and in the process, historical facts are frequently stretched.

7. Finally, the actual social complexity in society is reduced to a set of simple contrasts. As Adolf Hitler already wrote in ***Mein Kampf***①, the truly national leader concentrates the attention of his people on one enemy at the time. Since cross-cutting ties reduce the chances of violent conflict, the collective identity must be based on relatively unambiguous criteria (such as place, religion, mother-tongue, kinship). Again, internal differences are undercommunicated in the act of delineating boundaries towards the frequently demonised Other.

---

① *Mein Kampf*:《我的奋斗》(*My Struggle*), 阿道夫·希特勒著。通过这部自传性作品, 法西斯独裁者希特勒宣扬了纳粹思想及意识形态。

True or False Statements

(b56) "glocalization" is a word coined by a scientist called Roland Robertson.

(b57) That identity becomes politics results from the competition over things such as (scarce) resources which can prove who one is.

(b58) In Paragraph 3 the author indicates that similarity always results in good things.

(b59) Paragraph 4 indicates that history is part and parcel of identity.

(b60) In Paragraph 6 the sentence "first-comers are contrasted with invaders" is a human understanding of "invaders".

(b61) Globalization causes people to be more aware of their global identity.

(b62) Materials (natural resources) can extend identity.

(b63) Globalization exacerbates conflict because it makes known differences between cultures.

(b64) In this analysis the author manifests that globalization does more harm than good to people.

(b65) Hitler is quoted to show that the public may be manipulated by the power stratum with their attention diverted to less wanted things.

Passage C: Identity as Cultural Power

1. Our world and our lives are being shaped by the conflicting trends of globalization and identity. The primary opposition to the power of globalization lies in "the widespread surge of powerful expressions of collective identity that challenge globalization ... on behalf of cultural singularity and people's control over their lives and environment". Far from being the fragile flower that globalization tramples, identity is seen here as the upsurging power of local culture that offers (albeit multi-form, disorganized and sometimes politically reactionary) resistance to the centrifugal force of capitalist globalization.

2. This more robust view of the "power of identity" is one to which anyone surveying the dramatic rise of social movements based around identity positions (gender, sexuality, religion, ethnicity, nationality) might easily subscribe. So, recognizing the significant cultural sources of resistance to the power of globalization goes a long way towards getting this power in perspective. The impact of globalization thus becomes, more plausibly, a matter of the interplay of an institutional-technological impetus towards globality with counterpoised "localizing" forces. The drive towards "globality" combines a logic of capitalist expansion with development

of deterritorializing media and communications technologies. But this drive is opposed by various processes and practices expressing different orders of "locality". Amongst these we can count the cultural identity movements, but also less formally organized expressions of identity, for example, those involved in local consumption preferences. And, on quite another level, we have to add the considerable cultural effort exercised by nation-states in binding their populations into another cultural-political order of local identification.

3. This more complex formulation clearly implies that cultural identity is not likely to be the easy prey of globalization. This is because identity is not in fact merely some fragile communal-psychic attachment, but a considerable dimension of institutionalized social life in modernity. Particularly in the dominant form of national identity, it is the product of deliberate cultural construction and maintenance via both the regulatory and the socializing institutions of the state: in particular, the law, the education system and the media. The deterritorializing force of globalization thus meets a structured opposition in the form of what **Michael Billig**① has called "banal nationalism"—the everyday minute reinforcement; the continuous routinized flagging of national belonging, particularly through media discourse—sponsored by developed nation-states.

4. Of course this is not to deny that nation-states are, to varying degrees, compromised by globalization in their capacity to maintain exclusivity of identity attachments, just as they are in their capacity independently to regulate national economies within a global market. For example, the complexities and tensions introduced by the multiethnic constitution of societies arising from global population movements—a chronic feature of all modem nation-states—pose obvious problems for the continued cultural "binding" of twenty-first-century nations into coherent identity positions. This problem is, moreover more dramatic in its consequences for some nations of the developing world, where multiethnic composition arising from the crude territorial divisions of colonial occupation combines with comparatively weak state structures to produce a legacy of often bloody political instability and interethnic violence.

True or False Statements

(c1) In Paragraph 1 the author seems to tell readers that in the process of globalization, people's identity is also globalized.

(c2) In Paragraph 2 one can see people's power in defending their identity when globalized

① Michael Billig：米歇尔·比理格，英国 Loughborough 大学社会学教授，曾在美国等国任客座教授。开设有"组际关系"(Intergroup Relations)、"说服修辞"(Persuasion and Rhetoric)等课程。

despite the passivity they face in globalization.

(c3) In Paragraph 4 the author discusses the conflictive elements of collective identity of the multiethnic constitution of societies.

(c4) According to Paragraph 4, globalization doesn't pose obvious problems for the continued cultural "binding" of twenty-first-century nations into coherent identity positions.

(c5) To identify who you are is in a way to resist being assimilated by capitalism in globalization.

(c6) On the whole the author employs a postcolonial approach in dealing with the matter of identity.

(c7) Globalization is exercising power and the best way not to be globalized is to abruptly refuse globalization.

(c8) Globalization incurs more instability and clashes in a nation state.

(c9) This passage seems to say globalization causes more identity problems than unity.

第二节　种族与族性

导　读

种族和族性如同生理性别和文化性别(参见第五章)一样，是两个既互相联系又互相区别的概念。种族往往指的是一个族群在生物方面具有一些区别于其他族群的共同特征，比如肤色、体型、五官特征等。而族性则指具有相同生物性的一个族群因在同一个地域生活所形成或表现出的文化特征，比如，美国文化是由不同族性(文化群体)所构成的多元文化。众所周知，殖民主义、种族主义和种族中心论同体共生，互为依存。在历史问题尚未(远未)解决的今天，全球化又使这些问题复杂化、普遍化和变异。因此，研究这些问题就显得更迫在眉睫。

Passage One: Race and Ethnicity

1. Have you ever asked yourself what are the defining characteristics of being "white" or "black" in America today? Is it solely a matter of skin color? Are other factors important or

even more important? What makes someone "Hispanic" or "Latino". Is it language or country of origin or cultural traditions or family values or religion or skin color? Can you be"white" or "black" and Hispanic at the same time? Can you be a non-Spanish speaking member of one of Mexico's Indian communities and be Hispanic? The answers to these questions probably are not entirely clear to you nor are they to most Americans. It addition, the answers very likely will differ depending on the region of America in which you live.

2. The ways in which we personally acquire our own group identities are often complex. Similarly, the way we assign group identity to others is not always straight forward. Race and ethnic group labels in America are not clearly based on criteria that everyone understands, agrees with, and can easily use. As a result, someone else may label you in a way that you consider inaccurate and very offensive. To comprehend the human diversity of the United States or any other country, it is important to first understand the criteria commonly used for making group distinctions. These generally are based on cultural and/or biological factors; Americans tend to see each other in terms of age, economic class, religion, gender, ethnicity, and race. We are usually a member of a particular group for each of these criteria. Which of our group identities is most important varies with the social situation. In America today, gender, ethnicity, and race often have the most far ranging impacts on us as individuals.

3. *Ethnicity* refers to selected cultural and sometimes physical characteristics used to classify people into groups or categories considered to be significantly different from others. Commonly recognized American ethnic groups include American Indians, Latinos, Chinese, African Americans, European Americans, etc. In some cases, ethnicity involves merely a loose group identity with little or no cultural traditions in common. This is the case with many Irish and German Americans. In contrast, some ethnic groups are coherent subcultures with a shared language and body of tradition. Newly arrived immigrant groups often fit this pattern.

4. It is important not to confuse the term minority with ethnic group. Ethnic group may be either a minority or a majority in a population. Whether a group is a minority or a majority also is not an absolute fact but depends on the perspective. For instance, in some towns along the southern border of the U.S., people of Mexican ancestry are the overwhelming majority population and control most of the important social and political institutions but are still defined by state and national governments as a minority. In small homogenous societies, such as those of hunters and gatherers and pastoralists, there is essentially only one ethnic group and no minorities.

5. For many people, ethnic categorization implies a connection between biological

inheritance and culture. They believe that biological inheritance determines much of cultural identity. If this were true, for instance, African American cultural traits, such as "black English", would stem from genetic inheritance. We now know that this is not true—biological race and cultureare not the same thing. The pioneering English anthropologist Edward Tylor may have been the first scientist to understand this fact and to state it in print. In 1871, he wrote that cultural traits are entirely learned. Subsequently, a baby can be placed into another culture shortly after birth and can be thoroughly enculturated to that culture, regardless of their skin color, body shape, and other presumed racial features.

6. A *race* is a biological subspecies, or variety of a species, consisting of a more or less distinct population with anatomical traits that distinguish it clearly from other races. This biologist's definition does not fit the reality of human genetic variation today. We are an extremely homogenous species genetically. As a matter of fact, all humans today are 99. 9% genetically identical, and most of the variation that does occur is in the difference between males and females and our unique personal traits. This homogeneity is very unusual in the animal kingdom. Even our closest biological relatives, the chimpanzees have 2-3 times more genetic variation than people. Orangutans have 8-10 times more variation.

7. It is now clear that our human "races" are primarily cultural creations, not biological realities. The commonly held belief in the existence of human biological races is based on the false assumption that anatomical traits, such as skin color and specific facial characteristics, cluster together in single distinct groups of people. They do not. There are no clearly distinct "black", "white", or other races.

Exercises

A. Questions for Understanding

1. Why does the author raise so many questions at the very beginning of the passage?
2. According to Paragraph 2, why do people need to conceptualize "race" and "ethnicity"?
3. What makes ethnicity? Is such term as "Latino" or "Chinese" an ethnic concept or racial concept?
4. What do you think the identical genetic make-up of human beings may disprove?
5. In what way(s) is the assumption about race false?

B. Gap Filling

Provide the missing words according to the paragraphs you have just read.

16. Have you ever asked yourself what are the ______ characteristics of being "white" or "black" in America today? Is it solely a matter of skin color? The answers to these questions probably are not entirely clear to you nor are they to most Americans. In addition, the answers very likely will differ depending on the ______ of America in which you live. The ways in which we personally ______ our own group identities are often complex. Similarly, the way we ______ group identity to others is not always straight forward. Race and ethnic group labels in America are not clearly based on criteria that everyone understands, agrees with, and can easily use. As a result, someone else may ______ you in a way that you consider inaccurate and very ______. To comprehend the human ______ of the United States or any other country, it is important to first understand the criteria commonly used for making group distinctions. These generally are based on cultural and/or biological ______; Americans tend to see each other in terms of age, economic class, religion, gender, ethnicity, and race. We are usually a member of a particular group for each of these ______. Which of our group identities is most important varies with the social situation. In America today, gender, ______, and race often have the most far ranging impacts on us as individuals.

Passage Two: Social and Cultural Aspects of "Race" and "Ethnicity"

1. *Race* and *ethnicity* both represent social or cultural constructs for categorizing people based on perceived differences in biology (physical appearance) and behavior. Although popular connotations of race tend to be associated with biology and those of ethnicity with culture, the two concepts are not clearly distinct from one another.

2. While diverse definitions exist, ethnicity may be defined as the identification with population groups characterized by common ancestry, language and custom. Because of common origins and intermarriage, ethnic groups often share physical characteristics which also then become a part of their identification—by themselves and/or by others. However, populations with similar physical appearance may have different ethnic identities, and populations with different physical appearances may have a common ethnic identity.

3. Ethnic group unity needs to be reinforced by a constant emphasis on what traits set the members apart from others, rather than what they share in common with the outsiders. This is a universal means of boundary maintenance, or defense, between ethnic groups. Ethnic symbols are convenient markers for making "we-they" distinctions and are the focal points for racism and

other unpleasant manifestations of ethnocentrism. They also mask in-group differences. In the United States, for instance, they help propagate the myth that there is a single, coherent American Indian ethnic group. The same goes for Hispanics, European Americans, African Americans, Asian Americans, and Pacific Islanders.

4. Whether or not individuals in minority ethnic or "racial" groups prominently emphasize their ethnic symbols may vary with the situation. They may not emphasize them if they are trying to identify with or join the dominant culture in their society. That is to say, they may de-emphasize the things that make them different if they wish to assimilate into the dominant ethnic group. For instance, the children of many immigrants to the United States prefer to speak in the local colloquial dialect of English rather than in their parents' native language. Likewise, they choose to dress and act like other Americans in their schools. This has the effect of making them less different from their neighbors while estranging them from their parents.

5. *Assimilation* can be speeded up by marriage across ethnic or "racial" boundaries. As intermarriage becomes common, ethnic/racial differences often are progressively blurred. Not surprisingly, many ethnic/racial group organizations are opposed to intermarriage—they see it as a tool of ethnocide. The effect of intermarriage on reducing ethnic group identity can be seen in the reduction of discrimination against each of the European immigrant group in North America after several generations. In the case of Jews, discrimination lasted longer but has also reduced dramatically with the progressive increase in marriage to non-Jews. In the early 1960's, only 6% of American Jews married outsiders. By 1985, the rate had grown to nearly 25%. By the mid 1990's it was 52%. Over these four decades, discriminatory barriers to Jews largely disappeared. Of course, there were social changes in America that also contributed to the reduction in institutionalized discrimination.

Forms of Discrimination

6. Prejudice and discrimination based on presumed ethnic/racial differences are universal—they are found in various forms in all societies. Acts of prejudice range all the way from benign classification of people to cruel persecution. However, the term racism has come to be imprecisely applied to all of these behaviors. Kwame Appiah, a British and Ghanaian scholar of African American issues, has made a useful distinction between kinds of prejudicial behavior. He uses the term racialism for the more benign forms of discrimination such as categorizing people for reference purposes on the basis of age, gender, and ethnicity/race. He reserves the term racism for harmful discrimination such as not hiring someone because of their "race". This

distinction will be followed here.

7. We are all racialists. It is normal to categorize people in our daily lives based on a number of traits. It can be a useful aid in predicting behavior. For instance, when you are lost in a strange city, you very likely approach an adult rather than a young child for help because you surmise that the adult will know more. Similarly, when you want to take an out-of-town guest to a good traditional Mexican restaurant, you may ask a Mexican American friend for recommendations. However, when categorizing leads to behavior that harms another person, it becomes racism.

8. While racism is universal, its focus usually changes in the transition from small-scale societies to large-scale ones. The smallest societies are almost always biologically and culturally homogenous without ethnic group distinctions. In such societies, the target of racism is other societies. Strangers are often thought of as being not quite human. In contrast, large societies are often heterogeneous and have many ethnic groups. The targets of racism are mostly other ethnic groups within the same society. In Italy, for instance, Northern Italians often look down upon Southern Italians and stereotype them as being ignorant, dishonest, and lazy. Southern Italians often view Northern Italians as being impersonal, dull, and not trustworthy. A similar north-south stereotyping occurs in many parts of the world.

Exercises

A. Questions for Understanding

1. In terms of social/cultural construct what do you think race and ethnicity may share in common?

2. What might be the results of the racial and ethnic categorization?

3. What does one do when he/she wants to be assimilated into the dominant cultural group?

4. What do you think the author of this passage intends people to do in order to reduce racism?

5. Do you agree that racism or ethnocentrism is the intrinsic nature of culture? Who might benefit from this "theory" created?

B. Gap Filling

Provide the missing words according to the paragraphs you have just read.

17. It is normal to ______ people in our daily lives based on a number of traits. It can be a

useful aid in ______ behavior. For instance, when you are lost in a strange city, you very likely approach an adult ______ than a young child for help because you surmise that the adult will know more. Similarly, when you want to take an out-of-town ______ to a good traditional Mexican restaurant, you may ask a ______ American friend for recommendations. However, when categorizing leads to behavior that harms another person, it becomes ______. While racism is universal, its focus usually changes in the transition from small-scale societies to large-scale ones. The smallest societies are almost always ______ and culturally homogenous without ethnic group distinctions. In such societies, the target of racism is other societies. Strangers are often thought of as ______ not quite human. In contrast, large societies are often heterogeneous and have many ethnic groups. The ______ of racism are mostly other ethnic groups within the same society. In Italy, for instance, Northern Italians often look down upon Southern Italians and stereotype them as being ignorant, dishonest, and lazy. Southern Italians often view Northern Italians as being ______, dull, and not trustworthy. A similar north-south stereotyping occurs in many parts of the world.

Supplementary Reading(9)

Passage A: Difference Between Ethnicity and Race

1. Race is a classification system that is used by sociologists to categorize humans into large and distinct populations or groups. This is done on the basis of hereditary physical appearances, geographic ancestry, culture, history, language, ethnicity, and social status. Ethnicity, on the other hand, is a method of classification based upon a common trait of the population, such as a common heritage, a common culture, a shared language or dialect.

2. The terms ethnicity and race used to be easier to discern. However, due to the immigration and globalization the terms have become overlapped, to the extent that most people don't even know the meaning of the two terms. Not to mention that the term race has gotten a bad reputation due to its skewed connotation due to racism and terms such as white, black, etc. These terms do not refer to race.

3. Race is a classification system that is used by sociologists to categorize humans into large and distinct populations or groups. This is done on the basis of hereditary physical appearances, geographic ancestry, culture, history, language, ethnicity, and social status. The common

populace uses race to classify people on the basis of hereditary physical appearances, such as skin color. This has given rise to the incorrect terms such as whites or blacks.

4. Ethnicity, on the other hand, is a method of classification based upon a common trait of the population, such as a common heritage, a common culture, a shared language or dialect. Ethnicity may also be based on common ancestry and religion. Some ethnic groups may be marked by little more than a common name. However, ethnic groups have a consciousness of their common cultural bond. They develop because of their unique historical and social experiences. This becomes the basis for the group's ethnic identity.

5. The distinction between race and ethnicity is considered highly problematic. Essentially, the difference is that ethnicity is considered to be the cultural identity of a group, whereas race is the biological constitution of a group of people. For example if you consider the Caucasian race, i. e., whites, it incorporates people from many countries, such as Americans, Europeans, etc. Whereas you can breakdown the Caucasian race in ethnic groups, such as British, Scottish, Irish, French, Spanish, German, Slavic, etc. Even Americans can be further categorized into groups, such as a Northerner, Southerner, Mid-Western, Canadian, etc.

6. Each ethnic group is different form the other. They have different cultural practices, different society norms, different mannerisms, behaviors. They may or may not have different languages, dialects or accents. Each ethnic group has a different culture, tradition and customs. That which may be accepted in one ethnicity, may be taboo or frowned upon in another. Back in the day, it was easier to tell one's ethnicity. However, due to global conglomeration, people have become more open and knowledgeable about other ethnicities. This has offered more choice and change for people, such as borrowing styles and ideas from other cultures or ethnicities. This overlap of ethnicities has made it impossible to identify ethnicity based solely on distinctive features.

7. Essentially, one can be the same race with a different ethnicity. It can even be said that race is nature, whereas ethnicity is nurture. One can change their ethnicity, by moving to another geographical location and adopting their social customs. The person then becomes a part of that ethnic group. However, race is inherited. One cannot change their race, as it is the ancestry and heritage that the person belongs to. Still, one should note that no matter what race or ethnicity, humans are 99. 9% genetically similar. They are the same with just some minor differences. They may look different, have different cultures and customs, or they may follow different religions. However, the biggest difference that can exist between two human beings genetically is their gender.

8. Despite this fact, people have been treated differently throughout history due to their race and even ethnicity to some extent. A race is often labeled as inferior due to their biological or cultural characteristics. This often singles out people of that race for unfair treatment. Hence, racial groups are often defined not because of science or fact but because of opinion and social experience; because of how one group of people view the other. Hence, one can also claim that race is a socially constructed category, defined by how groups have been treated historically and socially.

True or False Statements

(a66) "Hereditary" differs from "heritage" because they refer to different categories of object.

(a67) Race is classification system used to refer to people while ethnicity is a method of classification used to refer to animals based upon common traits such as hereditary.

(a68) Paragraph 5 indicates that people can easily distinguish race and ethnicity.

(a69) In Paragraph 6 the author indicates that globalization broaden people's ethnic mind and vision.

(a70) Sometimes different ethnic groups can be of the same race and vice versa.

(a71) Paragraph 8 implies that both race and ethnicity can be constructed.

第五章　性　　别

性别是身份的重要标志，性别关系是文化研究的重要内容。自有人类以来就有男女性别的区分，男女两性间的“战争”似乎从来停止过。在人类文明走向21世纪、在人类社会普遍提倡建设和谐社会、谋求共同发展的今天，探讨性别问题就有了更为现实的意义。

在性别关系的理论中，最具标志性的成果是生理性别(sex)和文化性别(gender)的区分。这一区分改变了人们对于性别的传统观念，促使人们关注性别的社会属性，关注性别是如何被社会和文化建构的，关注影响性别身份形成的要素。性别研究的内容非常广泛，主要包括：生理性别和社会性别的关系，男性气质和女性气质如何定义和描述，社会性别到底是如何建构的，性别在文化中的再现，性别身份如何界定，如何理解违反社会普遍价值观念的各种性关系等。

性别研究中最为重要的内容当属女性主义。作为一个政治、社会和文化运动，女性主义持续时间之长、影响面之广是不言而喻的，其内部的多样性也是有目共睹的，它给人们观念上带来的改变是无法估计的。更为重要的是，女性主义呼唤的平等意识、关爱思想，让人们凭借更多的同情心学会同他人相处，由此引发的男性主义研究更是为人类文明的进步增添了一道亮丽的风景线。

性别研究是跨学科的，在西方主要大学和科研机构，从它的归属我们可以看出它的跨学科性质：人们可以把它归入文化研究范畴，也可以归入社会学、人类学、哲学、心理学，人们在研究文学、电影、翻译等领域的问题时也会运用性别研究的视角。

本章共分四节：第一节，“关于性别的基本概念”，介绍在研究性别问题时人们经常用到的一些术语。第二节，“特殊性别身份与同性恋”，介绍有悖人们认识常理的特殊性别身份和性别关系。第三节，“女性主义的发展历程”，介绍女性主义发展主要阶段的代表人物和主要观点。第四节，“性别与文化再现”，展现不同的性别概念和意识在文化中是如何被再现，又如何反过来继续影响并塑造社会和文化性别的。

第一节 关于性别的基本概念

导 读

谈论性别，首先要清楚两个基本概念：生理性别(sex)和社会性别(gender)。目前人们普遍接受的观点是：生理性别是与生俱来的，以生理特征为主要标志；而社会性别是受后天文化因素影响而形成的，具有社会属性。也有学者把这两个术语分别译为"性别"和"性属"。

一个人标志为男人(a man, a male)或女人(a woman, a female)主要依据生理特征。但在文化建构之下，一个男人也可能呈现一些女性气质(femininity)，相反，一个女人也可能呈现男性气质(masculinity)。与此相对应的形容词分别是：feminine 和 masculine。虽然这些特质(attributes)带有明显的二元对立(binary oppositions)倾向；但文化研究者并不致力于简单地区分一个人的性别，他们关注的是：哪些因素决定和影响了一个人的文化性别？一个人的生理性别为何与社会性别发生不统一的现象？生理性别和社会性别如何影响了两性关系、家庭关系以及社会关系？标志生理性别的"男人"和"女人"在社会性别化的过程中获得并承载了怎样的文化意义？

Passage One: Feminism and Cultural Studies

1. To discuss questions of sex and gender it is necessary to engage with a large body of feminist theory. It is impossible to conceive of a cultural studies that did not do so. However, while feminist thinking permeates cultural studies, not all forms of feminism are to be thought of as cultural studies. Nor are all zones of cultural studies concerned with questions of gender (though many feminists would argue that contemporary cultural studies is hindered by its production of **ungendered**① understandings of culture). Consequently, it is more important to explore those streams of thought within cultural studies that are concerned with sex, gender and feminism than to know the history, classification or analysis of the women's movement per se.

① ungendered，无社会性别特征的，不带社会性别符号的。

2. Franklin et al. (1991) have pointed to a number of similarities of concern between cultural studies and feminism. They draw attention to: the aspiration of feminism and cultural studies to connect with social and political movements **outside of the academy**①; a critical stance vis-a-vis more established **disciplines**② such as sociology and English literature; a mutual suspicion of and challenge to established ideas of "certain knowledge"; a wish to produce "knowledge" of and by "marginalized" and oppressed groups with the avowed intention of making a political intervention. In conclusion, cultural studies and feminism have shared a substantive interest in issues of power, representation, popular culture, **subjectivity**③, identities and consumption.

3. However, the relationship between feminism and cultural studies has not always been comfortable. Stuart Hall has described feminism as "A thief in the night, it broke in; interrupted, made an unseemly noise, seized the time, crapped on the table of cultural studies." That is, feminism was not always warmly welcomed, but had to "shout" loudly to make itself be heard. Thus feminists put questions of sexuality, gender, subjectivity and power at the heart of cultural studies. In doing so they displaced but did not abandon what had been the central issue of class. (Rewritten from Chris Barker, *Cultural Studies: Theory and Practice*, pp. 279-280)

Exercises

A. Questions for Understanding

1. What do many feminists complain about as to contemporary cultural studies?

2. According to Franklin et al., what are the similarities of concern between cultural studies and feminism?

3. Why do you think feminism is interested in "issues of power, representation, popular culture, subjectivity, identities and consumption"?

4. In what way does Stuart Hall compare feminism to a thief?

5. Why does feminism have to "shout" in order to be heard?

---

① outside of the academy：学院派之外的，非主流的。后现代社会的特征之一就是学院派和非学院派、主流与非主流之间的界限被打破，而文化学研究的重点恰恰是非主流的文化现象。

② discipline：学科。

③ subjectivity：主体性。与之相联系的另一个概念是 subject(主体)，是西方哲学思想中非常重要的概念。一般认为，在后现代语境下，随着解构理论的盛行，传统的主体概念已经衰落或被消解。

B. Gap Filling

Provide the missing words according to the paragraphs you have just read.

18. To discuss questions of sex and gender it is necessary to ______ with a large ______ of feminist theory. It is impossible to conceive of a cultural studies that did not do so. However, while feminist ______ permeates cultural studies, not all forms of feminism are to be thought of as cultural studies. Nor are all ______ of cultural studies concerned with questions of gender (though many feminists would argue that contemporary cultural studies is hindered by its production of ______ understandings of culture). Consequently, it is more important to ______ those streams of thought within cultural studies that are concerned with sex, gender and feminism than to know the history, classification or analysis of the women's movement ______. However, the relationship between feminism and cultural studies has not always been ______. Stuart Hall has described feminism as "A thief in the night, it broke in; interrupted, made an unseemly noise, seized the time, crapped on the table of cultural studies." That is, feminism was not always warmly welcomed, but had to "shout" loudly to make itself be heard. Thus feminists put questions of sexuality, gender, subjectivity and power at the ______ of cultural studies. In doing so they ______ but did not abandon what had been the central issue of class.

Passage Two: Sex-gender Distinction

1. Identification of oneself as male or female is a foundation stone of a self-identity that is widely held to be the outcome of particular bodies and their **attributes**①. Common sense encompasses a form of biological reductionism suggesting that the biochemical and genetic structures of human beings determine the behavior of men and women in quite definite and specific ways. Men are commonly held to be more "naturally" domineering, hierarchically oriented and power-hungry, while women are seen as nurturing, child rearing and domestically inclined. By contrast, many writers in cultural studies and other humanities have argued for the complete plasticity of sex and gender. That is, the influence of biology has been rejected in favour of understanding **masculinity and femininity**② as cultural constructions.

---

① attributes：特征；特点；特性。

② masculinity：男性气质；男性特征；男子气。与之相对的是 femininity。

2. The language of biology enables us to make behavioural and bodily predictions. At the same time, what it means to be gendered remains a cultural question. The language of culture helps to re-cast the way we talk about and **perform**① "sex" with the consequences that we deem to be good, that is, acceptance of a wider range of **sexualities**②. We may say that sex as biology and sex as the discursive-performative are different languages for different purposes. The problems felt by men trapped in women's bodies may be usefully approached using the predictions made available to us through the language of biochemistry and drug therapy. They may also be advanced through therapeutic talk and the re-description of self in the symbolic domain (including dress and bodily movement).

3. On the one hand, there is evidence that points to the predictability of a range of male and female capabilities and behaviour that derives from genetics. On the other hand, there are also clear indications that masculinity and femininity are changeable. We can make a distinction between identity as a social construction, a representation with which we emotionally identify, and those human capacities and behaviours that correlate highly with certain biochemical structures of the brain.

4. The sex-gender distinction is now itself the subject of criticism. It is argued that sexual identity is not a reflection of a natural state of being but a matter of representation. The distinction between sex as biology and gender as a cultural construction is broken down on the grounds that there is in principle no access to biological "truths" that lie outside of cultural discourses. Thus, there can be no biological "sex" which is not also cultural. **Sexed bodies**③ are always already represented as the production of regulatory discourses. In this view, the body does not disappear. It becomes a **variable**④ rather than a **constant**⑤. For poststructuralists, the cultural variations that exist between women (and between men) suggest that there is no universal cross-cultural category of "woman" (or "man") that is shared by all. Rather, there are multiple modes of femininity (and masculinity) which are enacted not only by different women, but, potentially, by the same woman under different circumstances. The claim is that sex and gender are infinitely malleable in principle, even though in practice they are moulded and regulated into specific forms under particular historical and cultural conditions. As such,

---

① 美国学者 Judith Butler 认为性别具有表现性(performativity)。

② sexuality：性；性行为；性征。

③ sexed bodies：有生理性别特征的身体。

④ variable：变量。

⑤ constant：常量。

"women are constantly confronted with the cultural task of finding out what it means to be a woman, of marking out the boundaries between the feminine and unfeminine". (Rewritten from Chris Barker, *Cultural Studies: Theory and Practice*, pp. 283-284, 289-290)

Exercises

A. Questions for Understanding

1. What does biological reductionism advocate?

2. In what ways do men and women behave differently according to biological reductionism?

3. According to the writer of the passage, what is the relationship between the language of biology and the language of culture?

4. What is the biggest problem in distinguishing sex and gender?

5. In what way does the writer say that the body has become "a variable"?

B. Gap Filling

Provide the missing words according to the paragraphs you have just read.

19. The language of biology enables us to make behavioral and bodily ______. At the same time, what it means to be gendered remains a cultural question. The language of culture helps to ______ the way we talk about and ______ "sex" with the consequences that we deem to be good, that is, acceptance of a wider range of sexualities. We may say that sex as biology and sex as the discursive-performative are different languages for different purposes. The problems felt by men ______ in women's bodies may be usefully approached using the predictions made available to us through the language of ______ and drug ______. They may also be advanced through therapeutic talk and the re-description of self in the symbolic domain (including dress and bodily movement). On the one hand, there is evidence that points to the predictability of a range of male and female capabilities and behaviour that ______ from genetics. On the other hand, there are also clear ______ that masculinity and femininity are changeable. We can make a distinction between identity as a social construction, a representation with which we emotionally identify, and those human capacities and ______ that correlate highly with certain biochemical ______ of the brain.

Passage Three: Biological and Cultural Attributes

1. Along the primrose path of childhood children learn something fundamental. At a most basic level they incorporate that Dads and Moms are designations with very different implications. Upon front, it is accepted that Dads are men and Moms are women; that Dads and Moms do different things at home and elsewhere. Simultaneously children learn that boys play rough and girls play nice and they usually like to do different things. Then kids learn that boys grow up to be Dads and girls grow up to be Moms.

2. Interestingly, this is the standard pattern children incorporate even when they know these rules have exceptions. They almost always know families where its Mom who is the outside-the-home money earner and Dad who stays home, and where boys are nice and quiet while girls are hellions. The basic stereotypes, however, seem somehow branded on their psyche in the everyday course of growing up. The input is from family, friends, media, religion and even politics. And most of middle-class society colludes, in turn, to transmit social and cultural normative expectations with essentially the same rules. With a certain degree of schooling and maturity children learn that the sexes to which we are referring are **male and female**①. It further comes to be understood that male and female are terms used to incorporate a whole catalog of physical and behavioral differences.

3. As a designation of male or female, *sex* with the child's increasing sophistication and learning becomes understood as a descriptive set of terms and meanings that encompass the most common biologically accepted attributes—physical differences—of males and females; the terms imply certain gonads, internal and external genitalia, sex chromosomes and genes, sex hormones and so on. The student learns that a male is an individual that has penis and scrotum, testes, and accessory glands (prostate, seminal vesicles, bulbo-urethral glands); a female is a person with ovaries, a uterus, ovarian tubes, a vagina and clitoris. An **intersexed**② individual is understood to have a mixture of these attributes. And these basic understandings hold for the term *sex* as they did for the terms *Dad* and *Mom* wide variations and departures from the basic

① male and female：雄性和雌性，这是两个生理意义上的术语。就人来讲，二者(雄性和雌性)的文化特征就是男性气质(masculinity)和女性气质(feminity)。

② intersexed 指具有男性和女性双重生理特征的双性人，或称阴阳人、雌雄同体，英语中也称 bisexual。

generalities can be known without nullifying the common wisdom.

4. The term *gender* first became familiar to most of us in language class when, for those of us with English as a common tongue, we learned that nouns such as table and chair could be either **masculine, feminine or neuter**①. Of what use are such distinctions still remains lost on linguists. Why languages as different as French and German need these artifices while English and most Australasian languages, for instance, can get along quite well without them is subject for thought. Many languages do not even have sex identifying pronouns. But understanding of gender or sex-typical behaviors (the older expression for gender specific traits) serves quite practical use. And no known language is without gender identifying nouns.

5. General usage of the term gender began in the late 1960s and 1970s, increasingly appearing in the professional **literature**② of the social sciences. The term came to serve a useful purpose in distinguishing those aspects of life that were more easily attributed or understood to be of social rather than biological origin.

6. Males and females, as biological entities, were accepted as essentially similar cross-culturally but men and women, by virtue of the multitude of different roles they played in diversified societies, were not so easily catalogued. These anthropological life-style differences came to be accepted as social and cultural constructs. Indeed, the terms sex and gender came, for most investigators, to signify and reify these different areas of consideration; sex would refer to biological traits while gender would refer to social/cultural ones. At least this was generally so among those investigators more sensitive to biological studies. Among those more aligned with sociological and anthropological thinking these differences did not appear so clear cut. For this latter group the terms sex and gender were often used interchangeably. (Rewritten from Milton Diamond, "Sex and Gender: Same or Different?")

Exercises

A. Questions for Understanding

1. What is the family stereotype that is "branded" on the psyche of little children?
2. What is the general principle of the designation of male or female?
3. According to the passage, how do most people learn about "gender"? What does the

① 这里的 masculine, feminine 和 neuter 指的是名词的属性——阳性、阴性和中性。例如在法语中，名词 vin(葡萄酒)是一个阳性名词，而 plume(羽毛)则是一个阴性名词。不同属性的名词前使用的形容词和代词也要有所区别。

② 这里 literature 的意思不是"文学"，而是"文献"。

word mean in that circumstance?

4. What does the word "gender" mean now in academia? When did the present usage come to be accepted?

5. Do scholars agree on the distinction of sex and gender?

B. Gap Filling

Provide the missing words according to the paragraph you have just read.

20. Interestingly, this is the standard pattern children incorporate even when they know these rules have ______. They almost always know families where its Mom who is the outside-the-home money earner and Dad who stays home, and where boys are nice and quiet while girls are hellions. The basic stereotypes, however, seem somehow branded on their ______ in the every day course of growing up. The ______ is from family, friends, media, religion and even politics. And most of middle-class society colludes, in turn, to transmit social and cultural ______ expectations with essentially the same rules. With a certain degree of schooling and maturity children learn that the sexes to which we are referring are male and female. It further comes to be understood that male and female are terms used to incorporate a whole catalog of physical and behavioral differences. As a ______ of male or female, sex with the child's increasing sophistication and learning becomes understood as a descriptive set of terms and meanings that ______ the most common biologically accepted attributes—physical differences—of males and females; the terms imply certain ______, internal and external genitalia, sex chromosomes and genes, sex hormones and so on. The student learns that a male is an individual that has penis and scrotum, testes, and accessory ______ prostate, seminal vesicles, bulbo-urethral glands); a female is a person with ovaries, a uterus, ovarian tubes, a vagina and clitoris. An ______ individual is understood to have a mixture of these attributes. And these basic understandings hold for the term sexas they did for the terms *Dad* and *Mom* wide variations and departures from the basic generalities can be known without ______ the common wisdom.

Supplementary Reading(10)

Passage A: Feministic Gender Controversy

1. Is there a "gender which persons are said to have, or is it an essential attribute that a person is said to be," as implied in the question "What gender are you"? When feminist

theorists claim that gender is the cultural interpretation of sex or that gender is culturally constructed, what is the manner or mechanism of this construction? If gender is constructed, could it be constructed differently, or does its constructedness imply some form of social determinism, foreclosing the possibility of agency and transformation? Does "construction" suggest that certain laws generate gender differences along universal axes of sexual difference? How and where does the construction of gender take place? What sense can we make of a construction that cannot assume a human constructor prior to that construction? On some accounts, the notion that gender is constructed suggests a certain determinism of gender meanings inscribed on anatomically differentiated bodies, where those bodies are understood as passive recipients of an inexorable cultural law. When the relevant "culture" that "constructs" gender is understood in terms of such a law or set of laws, then it seems that gender is as determined and fixed as it was under the biology-is-destiny formulation. In such a case, not biology, but culture, becomes destiny.

2. Simone de Beauvoir suggests in *The Second Sex* that "one is not born a woman, but, rather, becomes one". For Beauvoir, gender is "constructed", but implied in her formulation is an agent, a **cogito**①, who somehow takes on or appropriates that gender and could, in principle, take on some other gender. Is gender as variable and volitional as Beauvoir's account seems to suggest? Can "construction" in such a case be reduced to a form of choice? Beauvoir is clear that one "becomes" a woman, but always under a cultural compulsion to become one. And clearly, the compulsion does not come from "sex". There is nothing in her account that guarantees that the "one" who becomes a woman is necessarily female. If "the body is a situation," as she claims, there is no recourse to a body that has not always already been interpreted by cultural meanings; hence, sex could not qualify as a **prediscursive**② anatomical **facticity**③. Indeed, sex, by definition, will be shown to have been gender all along.

3. In a move that complicates the discussion further. Luce Irigaray argues that women constitute a paradox, if not a contradiction, within the discourse of identity itself. Women are the "sex" which is not "one". Within a language pervasively masculinist, a phallogocentric language, women constitute the unrepresentable. In other words, women represent the sex that cannot be thought, a linguistic absence and opacity. Within a language that rests on univocal signification,

---

① cogito：我思，笛卡儿(Rene Descartes)的"我思故我在"论点的简称；自我思想活动过程；意识。

② prediscursive：先于话语而存在的。此处意思是说所谓性别是由话语构建的，没有话语也就没有性别，更不用说性别先于话语而存在了。

③ facticity：真实性；确凿性。

the female sex constitutes the unconstrainable and undesignatable. In this sense, women are the sex which is not "one", but multiple. In opposition to Beauvoir, for whom women are designated as the Other, Irigaray argues that both the subject and the Other are masculine mainstays of a closed phallogocentric signifying economy that achieves its totalizing goal through the exclusion of the feminine altogether. For Beauvoir, women are the negative of men, the lack against which masculine identity differentiates itself; for Irigaray, that particular dialectic constitutes a system that excludes an entirely different economy of signification. Women are not only represented falsely within the Sartrian frame of signifying—subject and signified—Other, but the falsity of the signification points out the entire structure of representation as inadequate. The sex which is not one, then, provides a point of departure for a criticism of hegemonic Western representation and of the metaphysics of substance that structures the very notion of the subject.

4. The discursive construction of "the body" and its separation from "freedom" in Beauvoir fails to mark along the axis of gender the very mind-body distinction that is supposed to illuminate the persistence of gender asymmetry. Officially, Beauvoir contends that the female body is marked within masculinist discourse, whereby the masculine body, in its conflation with die universal, remains unmarked. Irigaray clearly suggests that both marker and marked are maintained within a masculinist mode of signification in which the female body is "marked off", as it were, from the domain of the signifiable. (From *Gender Trouble* by Judith Butler)

True or False Statements

(a72) Judith Butler at the beginning of this passage has raised a series of questions because she doesn't agree at all with feminists.

(a73) Simone de Beauvoir is quoted in the next paragraph because obviously her idea "one is not born a woman, but, rather, becomes one" is regarded as fresh and innovative by Judith Butler.

(a74) Sex or gender only makes sense on the basis of discourse.

(a75) Though Luce Irigaray disagrees with Simone de Beauvoir, they look at women's issues from a similar perspective.

(a76) The principal difference between the two feminist scholars lies in the symbolic order through which genders are supposed to be constructed.

(a77) We can see from their disagreement that de Beauvoir would propose a head-on competition with men in order to gain women's equality while Luce Irigaray would prefer to invent a totally new way of signification which exclusively belongs to women.

第二节　特殊性别身份与同性恋

导　读

区分生理性别的主要标志是生殖器官和染色体形态，但由于基因的变异使染色体和生殖器官出现不相符合的情况，也有生殖器官本身无法判断生理性别的情况发生。这种同时具有男性和女性生理特征的人被称作"双性人"(an intersex 或 a bisexual)。他们往往在成年后通过外科手术辅助服用荷尔蒙药物的方法确定性别。而通过手术强行改变生殖器官的人被称作"变性人"(a transsexual)。

关于两性关系的社会规范是异性恋(heterosexuality)。同性之间的关系被称作"同性恋"(homosexual)，男同性恋和女同性恋分别被称作 gay 和 lesbian。性别取向不确定的是"双性恋"(bisexuality)。在很长一段时间里，人们认为同性恋是病态行为，同性恋者受到广泛的歧视。由于艾滋病的蔓延，世人对同性恋增长了仇恨和恐惧。然而，随着人们认识的提高，性别观不断变化，同性恋人士在许多国家和地区得到越来越多的尊重。

Passage One: Non-heterosexuals

1. Let us see how these terms and concepts might involve a developing child. A mother of an 8-year-old **chromosomal XY male**① with ambiguous genitalia said to me:

2. "My child has questions on her gender. Oddly enough, we have raised her as a complete female child, to date ... she does not know of her condition. We thought best to wait, as a young child would never understand ... Increasingly over the years she has said things like I'm not a girl ... I'm a boy ... clothing desired is neutral ... teachers' complaints (they are unaware) is that she is very tomboyish ... All her friends are boys. At home it is her brothers she hangs out

① chromosomal XY male：染色体为 XY 的男性。通常人们认为，染色体是区分男性、女性的重要标志。男性的染色体为 XY，女性的染色体是 XX。文中提到的孩子虽然染色体是 XY，但其外生殖器官却没有标志为男性性征的阴茎。

with. And her strength … Wow I …"

3. The mother, at the child's birth, had been advised by her physician to raise the child as a girl due to its lack of a penis. This was a standard recommendation until just several years ago. The child's sex is male but it had **an imposed gender**① of girl. It had been raised since birth as a girl. Obviously here is a case where sex and gender are not in agreement.

4. The child knows it is being raised as a girl and encouraged by its parents and physicians to live as one. The child recognizes it is being seen and reacted to as a social girl. It is, thus aware of its (social) *gender* identity. Yet, although raised as a girl, the child manifests gender roles more typical of a boy. Further, despite its rearing and ignorance of its biology, the child has developed the (inner) *sexual* identity of a boy; i. e. the child feels at his core that he is a boy or should be a boy. This realization comes about by comparing his feelings, interests, attitudes and preferences with those of male and female peers and judging that his living as a boy is a better"fit" with the reality he sees and comes to know.

5. The child has male chromosomes (is an intersexed male **pseudoher-maphrodite**②) with the imposed gender of a girl. When the childmatures and becomes more aware of his history I predict he will likely come to live as a man or as close to a neuter gender as possible. He will come to recognize that he is intersexed and might or might not openly identify as such.

6. The mother asked if I thought it would be better to allow the child to switch to live as a boy or proceed with the **prepubertal**③ feminizing hormone administration advised by her physicians. My advice was to allow the child to live as a boy and foster typical male development. Despite the genital ambiguity such management would allow gender and sex to be better matched than is presently so. Genital reconstruction can occur later if desired.

7. An intersexed individual is one born with physical characteristics that are both male and female. For instance an individual can be XX in chromosomal configuration but have a male-like phallus; another individual might be XY in chromosomal make-up and not have a penis but have a vagina instead. The intersex person might have genitals that are ambiguous in character or they might appear typical.

8. Intersexed men and women might identify as female, male or intersexed and they might live ostensibly as women or men or in somesort of neuter manner. Intersexed children, while not

---

① an imposed gender：强加的性别身份。这个例子可以很好地说明生理性别(sex)和社会性别(gender)的区别。

② pseudoher-maphrodite：假性阴阳人。

③ prepubertal：前青春期的。

aware of their condition, might nevertheless manifest this neuter status choice of dress, hairstyle and comportment.

9. The variety of intersex conditions is so large that only broad generalizations can be made as to how any single individual's sexual identity and gender identity might compare. While some intersexed individuals can easily meld their biological incongruities with the way they are raised and with the life they lead, others find great difficulty in reconciling the disparities they see and feel with the social input that is thrust upon them. Even within a single category of intersex there is a great variation. It is for this reason that I believe it best that the child itself, particularly after puberty, has the final say in how he or she is allowed to live.

10. Before leaving this topic let me emphasize that at issue here is not whether a person, male for example, thinks he is masculine looking "enough" or macho behaving "enough" to satisfy his ego or some social stereotype. Most men wish that they could increase some aspect of their male selves. And the same can be said similarly for females. Most women would relish the ability to enhance some aspect of their feminine looks and modify some aspect of their behavior. But for the typical person there is little doubt of his or her basic male or female self and sexual identity despite any lack in wishes for socially preferred gender feature. (Rewritten from Milton Diamond, "Sexual Identity and Gender Identity are Different".)

Exercises

A. Questions for Understanding

1. Why did the physician advise the mother to raise the child as a girl despite the fact that the child has XY chromosome?

2. In what ways does the child manifest his gender role as a boy?

3. How do the suggestions given by the physician and by the writer of this essay differ concerning the future raising and development of the child?

4. How does the writer of the essay define "an intersex"? Do intersexed individuals share the same features?

5. According to the writer, what element plays the key role in a person's gender identity?

B. Gap Filling

Provide the missing words according to the paragraphs you have just read.

21. The mother, at the child's birth, had been advised by her physician to raise the child as

a girl due to its lack of a penis. This was a standard recommendation until just several years ago. The child's sex is male but it hadan ______ gender of girl. It had been raised since birth as a girl. Obviously here is a case where sex and gender are not in ______. The child knows it is being raised as a girl and encouraged by its parents and physicians to live as one. The child recognizes it is being seen and reacted to as a ______ girl. It is, thus aware of its (social) ______ identity. Yet, although raised as a girl, the child ______ gender roles more typical of a boy. Further, despite its ______ and ignorance of its biology, the child has developed the (inner) *sexual* identity of a boy; i. e. the child feels at his ______ that he is a boy or should be a boy. This ______ comes about by comparing his feelings, interests, attitudes and ______ with those of male and female ______ and judging that his living as a boy is a better "fit" with the reality he sees and comes to know.

Passage Two: Homosexuality

1. Same sex physical sexual activity, "homosexuality", can be historically documented. This activity is not disputed. It has been tolerated; but the meaning given to it has been culturally specific according to the individual society in which it takes place. The norm in all cultures and societies is opposite sex physical sexual activity, "heterosexuality", marriage and procreation. The idea of a "gay identity" (two adults in a homosexual relationship) is a modern Western cultural type of homosexuality. A "gay identity" also must be viewed in the social political context which gives it its name and form.

2. Furthermore it was not until near the end of the twentieth century that a "gay liberation" movement has emerged and made homosexuality a controversial issue. Most commonly seen is that reluctantly societies tolerated some adult male same-sex relations with even more acceptance of adult female same-sex relations. While they more generously approved sexual relations between men and boys with some qualifications: the practice was understood more or less as **a rite of passage**① which must end for the man in his late twenties and for the boy in early teens. In all the instances of "homosexuality" continuing on today, "homosexuality" is based on behaviors and same-sex physical sexual activity, today the emphasis is based on self-identification as being a "homosexual. This "homosexual" today is a pattern of essentially

① a rite of passage: 成长过程中的仪式。

exclusive adult same-sex relationships, that historically and culturally specific to **postmodern**① Western societies.

3. Today as we discuss the topic of homosexuality, we see a wide variety of expressions of it in the lives of people. So now the term "homosexualities" is often applied in the literature on this topic. When talking about types of "homosexualities" we must remember we are taking a "verb" and using it as a "noun"; using two different parts of speech to label the same idea. I want to frame the discussion this way, "who one is, a homosexual" and "what one does, homosexuality." Also as we discuss types of "homosexualities" today we are doing so from a framework of our "postmodern generation" and "Western cultural" lenses. There have become two sides in this discussion, with a moral line dividing them; a pro-gay side (those who support a homosexual identity, including individuals who accept this identity), and those who oppose this "homosexual or gay identity". So often objectivity has become the "**baby thrown out with the bath water**"②. Common sense has been replaced by blind passion. This objectivity has also been lost in the scientific community. Before accepting the outcome of a scientific project, we must determine, whether the scientists have a particular political/societal agenda. Is the scientist himself accepting a "gay identity"? This present discussion, types of homosexualities is coming from a sociological framework, looking for a scientific causation may be found within my discussion about scientific studies.

4. Various authors use several terms in speaking about types of "homosexualities". Sometimes you will see the terms **facultative**③ and **obligative**④ used describing homosexuality. The latter, *obligative*, *is* considered exclusive homosexuality, a condition in which a person can only bond or pair with a person, of the same sex. There is no option for bisexual or heterosexual bonding. *Facultative* homosexuality is a technical term for sexual orientation and sexual activity with persons of the same sex. This term does not exclude sexual relations with members of the opposite sex; it also may be referred to as bisexuality. The same-sex physical activity may be engaged in only for sexual release, power, or control, or in situations where there are no

① postmodern：后现代的。人们通常认为，后现代的出现是同晚期资本主义社会形态相联系的，但对此观点也有争议。一般来讲，后现代的主要特征是去中心化和多元化。

② 英语中有一句俗语："To throw out the baby with the bath water."意思是指过分激烈的改革、变革或行动，在扫除不必要的因素时把本来至关重要的东西也同时抛弃了。这里作者借用这句俗语指那些反对同性恋行为的人在驳斥同性恋关系的同时往往会摒弃两性关系的本质。

③ facultative：偶发同性恋，指在某一特定环境或情境下发生的同性恋关系。

④ obligative：完全同性恋，指具有排除其他性关系性质的同性恋倾向。

members of the opposite sex, such as in a prison.

5. Homosexuality today expressed in a gay and lesbian identity may possibly be viewed as another type of homosexuality. Just as the others are historically and culturally specific so is the modern gay and lesbian. Being a gay and lesbian is not **a unitary construct**① that is culturally transcendent across all societies today. A gay and lesbian is a social political identity limited to modern Western cultures, although this gay and lesbian identity is gradually being expressed and adopted in other parts of the world.

6. There is **a wealth of**② cross-cultural evidence that point to the existence of numerous patterns of homosexuality varying in origins, subjective states and manifest behaviors. But the **parameters**③ of the discussion are still best framed as *Who one is*, a homosexual or *What one does*, homosexuality. The support for the latter is the strongest.

7. The reality is that this "gay identity", a pattern of essentially exclusive male homosexuality familiar to us which has been exceedingly rare or unknown in cultures that required or expected all males to engage in homosexual activity. So I would argue this "gay identity" should be seen not as a type of homosexuality, but rather as a social movement, a political cause, a new form of gender identity, and a life-style. Therefore the psychosocial conditions of being gay today must be understood in their own place and historical time.

8. Being "gay" cannot be seen as **monolithic**④ and invariant identity label culturally valid for ancient and medieval societies. As has been repeatedly stated, historically as well as culturally the pattern was for heterosexuality, marriage, and procreation. Although there have been cases, which are exceptions to the norm, instances of adult same sex behavior are almost always tolerated, but looked down upon with disapproval.

Exercises

A. Questions for Understanding

1. Does homosexuality meet with prejudice in human history since the norm of sexual relations is heterosexuality?

2. Since when did homosexuality become a controversial issue?

---

① a unitary construct：一种单一的建构。
② a wealth of：大量。
③ parameters：参数；范式。
④ monolithic：完整而统一的。

3. How does the writer of this essay define "homosexualities"?
4. What are the differences between obligative homosexuality and facultative homosexuality?
5. Why does the writer believe that being a gay and a lesbian "is not a unitary construct"?
6. How does the writer view "gay identity"?

B. Gap Filling

Provide the missing words according to the paragraph you have just read.

22. Today as we discuss the topic of homosexuality, we see a wide variety of expressions of it in the lives of people. So now the term "homosexualities" is often applied in the literature on this topic. When talking about types of "homosexualities" we must remember we are taking a "verb" and using it as a "noun"; using two different parts of ______ to label the same idea. I want to ______ the discussion this way, "who one is, a homosexual" and "what one does, ______." Also as we discuss types of "homosexualities" today we are doing so from a framework of our "postmodern generation" and "Western cultural" ______. There have become two sides in this discussion, with a moral line dividing them; a ______ side (those who support a homosexual identity, including individuals who accept this identity), and those who ______ this "homosexual or gay identity". So often objectivity has become the "baby thrown out with the bath water". Common sense has been ______ by ______ passion. This ______ has also been lost in the scientific community. Before accepting the ______ of a scientific project, we must determine, whether the scientists have a particular political/societal ______. Is the scientist himself accepting a "gay identity"? This present discussion, types of homosexualities is coming from a sociological framework, looking for a scientific ______ may be found within my discussion about scientific studies.

Supplementary Reading(11)

Passage A: Queer Theory

1. Once the term "queer" was, at best, slang for homosexual, at worst, a term of homophobic abuse. In recent years "queer" has come to be used differently, sometimes as an umbrella term for a coalition of culturally marginal sexual self-identifications and at other times to describe a nascent theoretical model which has developed out of more traditional lesbian and

gay studies. The rapid development and consolidation of lesbian and gay studies in universities in the 1990s is paralleled by an increasing deployment of the term "queer". As queer is unaligned with any specific identity category, it has the potential to be annexed profitably to any number of discussions. In the history of disciplinary formations, lesbian and gay studies is itself a relatively recent construction, and queer theory can be seen as its latest institutional transformation.

2. Broadly speaking, queer describes those gestures or analytical models which dramatise incoherencies in the allegedly stable relations between chromosomal sex, gender and sexual desire. Resisting that model of stability—which claims heterosexuality as its origin, when it is more properly its effect—queer focuses on mismatches between sex, gender and desire. Institutionally, queer has been associated most prominently with lesbian and gay subjects, but its analytic framework also includes such topics as cross-dressing, **hermaphroditism**①, gender ambiguity and gender-corrective surgery. Whether as transvestite performance or academic deconstruction, queer locates and exploits the incoherencies in those three terms which stabilise heterosexuality. Demonstrating the impossibility of any "natural" sexuality, it calls into question even such apparently unproblematic terms as "man" and "woman".

3. The recent intervention of this confrontational word "queer" in altogether politer academic discourses suggests that traditional models have been ruptured. Yet its appearance also marks a continuity. Queer theory's debunking of stable sexes, genders and sexualities develops out of a specifically lesbian and gay reworking of the post-structuralist figuring of identity as a constellation of multiple and unstable positions. Queer is not always seen, however, as an acceptable elaboration of or shorthand for "lesbian and gay". Although many theorists welcome queer as "another" discursive horizon, another way of thinking the sexual, others question its efficacy. The most commonly voiced anxieties are provoked by such issues as whether a generic masculinity may be reinstalled at the heart of the ostensibly gender-neutral queer; whether queer's transcendent disregard for dominant systems of gender fails to consider the material conditions of the west in the late twentieth century; whether queer simply replicates, with a kind of historical amnesia, the stances and demands of an earlier gay liberation; and whether, because its constituency is almost unlimited, queer includes identificatory categories whose politics are less progressive than those of the lesbian and gay populations with which they are aligned.

---

① hermaphroditism：对雌雄同体、半阴阳、性别畸形的研究或学问。

4. Whatever ambivalences structure queer, there is no doubt that its recent redeployment is making a substantial impact on lesbian and gaystudies. Yet, almost as soon as queer established-market dominance as a diacritical term, and certainly before consolidating itself in any easy vernacular sense, some theorists are already suggesting that its moment had passed and that "queer politics may, by now, have outlived its political usefulness". Does queer become defunct the moment it is an intelligible and widely disseminated term? **Teresa de Lauretis**①, the theorist often credited with inaugurating the phrase "queer theory", abandoned it barely three years later, on the grounds that it had been taken over by those mainstream forces and institutions it was coined to resist.

5. In some quarters and in some enunciations, no doubt, queer does little more than function as shorthand for the unwieldy lesbian and gay, or offer itself as a new solidification of identity, by kitting out more fashionably an otherwise unreconstructed sexual essentialism. Certainly, sudden and often uncritical adoption has at times foreclosed what is potentially most significant—and necessary—about the term. Queer retains, however, a conceptually unique potential as a necessarily unfixed site of engagement and contestation. Admittedly not discernible in every mobilisation of queer, this constitutes an alternative to de Lauretis's narrative of disillusionment. Judith Butler does not try to anticipate exactly how queer will continue to challenge normative structures and discourses. On the contrary, she argues that what makes queer so efficacious is the way in which it understands the effects of its interventions are not singular and therefore cannot be anticipated in advance. Butler understands, as de Lauretis did when initially promoting queer over lesbian and gay, that the conservative effects of identity classifications lie in their ability to naturalise themselves as self-evident descriptive categories. She argues that if queer is to avoid simply replicating the normative claims of earlier lesbian and gay formations, it must be conceived as a category in constant formation.

6. In stressing the partial, flexible and responsive nature of queer, Butler offers a corrective to those naturalised and seemingly self-evident categories of identification that constitute traditional formations of identity politics. She specifies the ways in which the logic of identity politics—which is to gather together similar subjects so that they can achieve shared aims by mobilising a discourse—is far from natural or self-evident.

7. In the sense that Butler outlines the queer project—that is, to the extent that she argues

① Teresa de Lauretis：特瑞莎·劳瑞提斯，在意大利出生和接受高等教育，现为加利福尼亚大学心理历史教授；符号、女权等理论家，酷儿理论的创始人。

there can't be one—queer may be thought of as activating an identity politics so attuned to the constraining effects of naming, of delineating a foundational category which precedes and underwrites political intervention, that it may better be understood as promoting a non-identity—or even anti-identity—politics. If a potentially infinite coalition of sexual identities, practices, discourses and sites might be identified as queer, what it betokens is not so much liberal pluralism as a negotiation of the very concept of identity itself. For queer is, in part, a response to perceived limitations in the liberationist and identity-conscious politics of the gay and lesbian feminist movements. The rhetoric of both has been structured predominantly around self-recognition, community and shared identity; inevitably, if inadvertently, both movements have also resulted in exclusions, delegitimation, and a false sense of universality. The discursive proliferation of queer has been enabled in part by the knowledge that identities are fictitious—that is, produced by and productive of material effects but nevertheless arbitrary, contingent and ideologically motivated. Unlike those identity categories labelled lesbian or gay, queer has developed out of the theorising of often unexamined constraints in traditional identity politics. Consequently, queer has been produced largely outside the registers of recognition, truthfulness and self-identity.

8. Queer, then, is an identity category that has no interest in consolidating or even stabilizing itself. It maintains its critique of identity-focused movements by understanding that even the formation of its own coalitional and negotiated constituencies may well result in exclusionary and reifying effects far in excess of those intended.

9. Acknowledging the inevitable violence of identity politics and having no stake in its own hegemony, queer is less an identity than a critique of identity. But it is in no position to imagine itself outside that circuit of problems energised by identity politics. Instead of defending itself against those criticisms that its operations inevitably attract, queer allows such criticisms to shape its—for now unimaginable—future directions. "The term", writes Butler, "will be revised, dispelled, rendered obsolete to the extent that it yields to the demands which resist the term precisely because of the exclusions by which it is mobilized." The mobilisation of queer—no less than the critique of it—foregrounds the conditions of political representation: its intentions and effects, its resistance to and recovery by the existing networks of power.

10. For Halperin, as for Butler, queer is a way of pointing ahead without knowing for certain what to point at. "Queer"... does not designate a class of already objectified pathologies or perversions, writes Halperin: "rather, it describes a horizon of possibility whose precise extent and heterogeneous scope cannot in principle be delimited in advance". Queer is always an identity under construction, a site of permanent becoming: "utopic in its negativity, queer

theory curves endlessly toward a realization that its realization remains impossible". The extent to which different theorists have emphasized the unknown potential of queer suggests that its most enabling characteristic may well be its potential for looking forward without anticipating the future. Instead of theorising queer in terms of its opposition to identity politics, it is more accurate to represent it as ceaselessly interrogating both the preconditions of identity and its effects. Queer is not outside the magnetic field of identity. Like some postmodern architecture, it turns identity inside out, and displays its supports exoskeletally. If the dialogue between queer and more traditional identity formations is sometimes fraught—which it is—that is not because they have nothing in common. Rather, lesbian and gay faith in the authenticity or even political efficacy of identity categories and the queer suspension of all such classifications energise each other, offering in the 1990s—and who can say beyond? —the ambivalent reassurance of an unimaginable future.

True or False Statements

(a78)"Queer theory" is a newly emerged paradigm which looks at the gender issues from an antitraditional perspective.

(a79) The theory is queer because it never understands gender in the way the mainstays of a society do.

(a80)"Queer theory" must have originated from the challenge of the authority in a society. So it is a postmodern theory.

(a81) One's identity is never such a simple matter as people in the mundane may assume because it is always a politicizing issue that engages power struggle.

(a82)"Queer theory" intends to provide people with more freedom and alternatives for the way they live.

第三节 女性主义的发展历程

导 读

"女性主义"和"女权主义",英语都是 feminism,是我国学者根据 feminism 发展的不同历史阶段及其不同的内涵而采纳的不同译法。要明白为什么会有不同的译法,首先要了解女性主义发展的历程。

人们通常认为，女性主义的发展经历了三个主要阶段，也称三次浪潮。第一次浪潮发生在19世纪末20世纪初，一些学者开始注意到女性在社会中所处的从属地位，呼吁建立各种立法保障女性享受同男性一样的政治、经济、教育、文化等权利。第二次浪潮发生在20世纪六七十年代，此时的女性主义代表人物与其说是理论家不如说是社会活动家，她们兴建各种女性研究的课程，出版女性主义刊物，呼吁更多的女性意识到性别的社会属性。第三次浪潮发生在20世纪90年代，人们更加关注身为女性所具备的生理、心理、社会特质，试图在意识形态层面建立同男性/父系相匹配的理论系统。

应该看到的是，女性主义在世界范围内的发展是不平衡的。一些发达国家的女性主义理论家已经开始建立女性主义理论体系，而在一些欠发达的地区和国家，人们还在为女性争取同男性享受同等的社会权利而努力。此外，女性主义内部也有分歧，许多女性主义理论家提倡的观点大相径庭，有时甚至互相矛盾。这反映出人们为最终建立消除性别差异的理想社会而所作的不同尝试。

Passage One: The First Wave

1. Feminism in general has a long political history, developing as a substantial force, in America and Britain at least, throughout the 19th and early 20th centuries. Feminist criticism of the early period is more a reflex of "first-wave" preoccupations than a fully fledged theoretical discourse of its own. But two significant figures may be selected from among the many other feminists working and writing in this period; **Virginia Woolf**①—in **Mary Eagleton**②'s phrase, "the founding mother of the contemporary debate"—who "announces" many of the issues later feminist critics were to focus on and who herself becomes the terrain over which some debates have struggled; and **Sinione de Beauvoir**)③, with whose *The Second Sex* (1949), **Maggie Humm**④ suggests, the "first wave" may be said to end.

---

① Virginia Woolf：维吉尼亚·伍尔夫(1882—1941)，英国现代派小说家、散文家、女性主义理论家，以其意识流小说《达罗维夫人》(*Mrs. Dalloway*, 1925)、《到灯塔去》(*To the Lighthouse*, 1927)、《海浪》(*The Waves*, 1931)等著称于世。

② Mary Eagleton：玛丽·伊格尔顿，当代著名理论家，著有《女性主义文学理论》(*Feminist Literary Theory*)、《女性主义文学批评》(*Feminist Literary Criticism*)等著作。

③ Simone de Beauvoir：西蒙·德·波伏娃(1908—1986)，法国作家、哲学家、女性主义理论家。

④ Maggie Humm：玛吉·休姆，东伦敦大学女性研究学者，编著有《女性主义读本》(*Feminisms: A Reader*)、《当代女性主义文学批评手册》(*A Readers Guide to Contemporary Feminist Literary Criticism*)、《女性主义理论词典》(*Dictionary of Feminist Theory*)、《女性主义与电影》(*Feminism and Film*)、《女性主义批评实践》(*Practising Feminist Criticism*)等。

2. Virginia Woolf's fame conventionally rests on her own creative writing as a woman, and later feminist critics have analyzed her novels extensively from very different perspectives. But she also produced two key texts which are major contributions to feminist theory, *A Room of One's Own*, (1929) and *Three Guineas* (1938). Like other "first-wave" feminists, Woolf is principally concerned with women's material disadvantages compared to men. However, her general contribution to feminism is her recognition that gender identity is socially constructed and can be challenged and transformed, but apropos of feminist criticismshe also continually examined the problems facing women writers. She believed that women had always faced social and economic obstacles to their literary ambitions, and was herself conscious of the restricted education she had received (she was taught no Greek, for example, unlike her brothers). Rejecting a "feminist" consciousness, and wanting her femininity to be unconscious so that she might "escape from the confrontation with femaleness or maleness", she **appropriated**① the **Bloomsbury**② sexual ethic of "**androgyny**"③ and hoped to achieve a balance between a "male" self-realization and "female" self-annihilation.

3. One of Woolf's most interesting essays about women writers is "Professions for Women", in which she regards her own career as hindered in two ways. First, she was imprisoned and constrained by the dominant ideologies of womanhood. Second, the taboo about expressing female passion prevented her from "telling the truth about her own experiences as a body". This denial of female sexuality was never consciously subverted in Woolf's own work or life, in that she thought women wrote differently not because they were different psychologically from men but because their social positioning was different. Her attempts to write about the experiences of women, therefore, were aimed at discovering linguistic ways of describing the confined life of women, and she believed that when women finally achieved social and economic equality with men, there would be nothing to prevent them from freely developing their artistic talents.

4. Simone de Beauvoir—French feminist, lifelong partner of **Jean-Paul Sartre**④, pro-

---

① appropriate：挪用。

② Bloomsbury：指从1905年起，定期在艺术家维尼萨·贝尔(Vanessa Bell)和他妹妹维吉尼亚·伍尔夫位于布卢姆斯伯里的家中聚会的一群艺术家、作家和知识分子。他们的艺术品位、文学主张和崇尚的生活方式使这群知识分子成为英国历史上一道独特的风景线。

③ androgyny："雌雄同体"。这是布卢姆斯伯里团体的知识分子提倡的道德和美学准则。

④ Jean-Paul Sartre：让-保罗·萨特(1905—1980)，法国著名小说家、存在主义哲学家。他的主要哲学著作有《想象》《存在与虚无》《存在主义是一种人道主义》《辩证理性批判》和《方法论若干问题》，文学作品有中篇小说《恶心》、短篇小说集《墙》和长篇小说《自由之路》等。

abortion and women's-rights activist—marks the moment when "first-wave" feminism begins to slip over into the "second wave". While her hugely influential book *The Second Sex* is clearly preoccupied with the "materialism" of the first wave, it beckons to the second wave in its recognition of the vast difference between the interests of the two sexes and in its assault on men's biological and psychological, as well as economic, discrimination against women. The book established with great clarity the fundamental questions of modern feminism. When a woman tries to define herself, she starts by saying "I am a woman": no man would do so. This fact reveals the basic asymmetry between the terms "masculine" and "feminine": man defines the human, not woman, in an imbalancewhich goes back to the *Old Testament*, Being dispersed among men, women have no separate history, no natural solidarity; nor have they combined as other oppressed groups have. Woman is riveted into a lopsided relationship with man: he is the "One", she the "**Other**"①. Man's dominance has secured an ideological climate of compliance: "legislators, priests, philosophers, writers and scientists have striven to show that the subordinate position of woman is willed in heaven and advantageous on earth", and, *a la* Virginia Woolf, the assumption of women as ("Other" is further **internalized**② by women themselves.)

5. De Beauvoir's work carefully distinguishes between sex and gender, and sees an interaction between social and natural functions: "One is not born, but rather becomes, a woman; ... it is civilization as a whole that produces this creature ... Only the intervention of someone else can establish an individual as an *Other*." It is the systems of interpretation in relation to biology, psychology, reproduction, economics, etc., which constitute the (male) presence of that (someone else). Making the crucial distinction between "being female" and being constructed as "a woman", de Beauvoir can posit the destruction of patriarchy if women will only break out of their **objectification**③. In common with other "first-wave" feminists, she wants freedom from biological difference, and she shares with them a distrust of "femininity"—thus marking herself off from some contemporary feminists' celebration of the body and recognition of the importance of the unconscious. (Rewritten from Raman Seldon, Peter Widdowson, and Peter Brooker, A *Reader's Guide to Contemporary Literary Theory*, pp. 124-127)

---

① Other: "他者"。

② internalize: 内在化; 内化。

③ objectification: 客体化。

Exercises

A. Questions for Understanding

1. Why do you think Mary Eagleton describes Virginia Woolf as "the founding mother of the contemporary debate"?

2. What does the writer of the essay believe to be Virginia Woolf's general contribution to feminism?

3. Why does Virginia Woolf advocate "androgyny"? What does the term suggest?

4. In what ways does Virginia Woolf see her own profession as a woman writer be hindered?

5. In what sense does the writer of the essay say that Simone de Beauvoir's book "beckons to the second wave"?

6. What "basic asymmetry" between "masculine" and "feminine" does Simone de Beauvoir's book reveal?

7. What does Simone de Beauvoir's saying—"One is not born, but rather becomes, a woman"—imply?

8. How significant is the distinction between "being female" and being constructed as "a woman"?

B. Gap Filling

Provide the missing words according to the paragraph you have just read.

23. Simone de Beauvoir—French feminist, lifelong ______ of Jean-Paul Sartre, pro-abortion and women's-rights activist—marks the moment when "first-wave" feminism begins to slip over into the "second wave". While her ______ influential book *The Second Sex* is clearly ______ with the "materialism" of the first wave, it beckons to the second wave in its recognition of the vast difference between the interests of the two sexes and in its assault on men's biological and psychological, as well as economic, ______ against women. The book established with great clarity the fundamental questions of modern feminism. When a woman tries to define herself, she starts by saying "I am a woman": no man would do so. This fact reveals the basic ______ between the terms "masculine" and "feminine": man defines the human, not woman, in an ______ which goes back to the *Old Testament*, Being dispersed among men, women have no separate history, no natural ______; nor have they combined as

other oppressed groups have. Woman is ______ into a lopsided relationship with man: he is the "One", she the "Other". Man's dominance has secured an ______ climate of compliance: "legislators, priests, philosophers, writers and scientists have ______ to show that the subordinate position of woman is willed in heaven and advantageous on earth", and, *a la* Virginia Woolf, the assumption of women as ("Other" is further internalized by women themselves.)

Passage Two: The Second Wave

1. Second-wave feminism in the United Sates took its impetus from **the civil-rights, peace and other protest movements**①, and Kate Millet's radical feminism is of this order. First published in 1969, a year after Mary Ellmann's *Thinking About Women* and just before Germaine Greer's *The Female Eunuch*, Eva Figes's *Patriarchal Attitudes* and Shulamith Firestone's *The Dialect of Sex* (all in 1970), Millett's *Sexual Politics* at once marks the moment when second-wave feminism becomes a highly visible, self-aware and **activist**② movement, and when it itself became the ***cause-celebre***③ text of that moment. It has been—certainly in the significant legacy of its title—perhaps the best-known and most influential book of its period, and it remains a ferociously upbeat, comprehensive, witty and irreverent demolition-job on male culture; and this, perhaps, it is a monument to its moment.

2. Millett's argument—ranging over history, literature, psychoanalysis, sociology and other areas—is that **ideological indoctrination**④ as much as economic inequality is the cause of women's oppression, an argument which opened up second-wave thinking about **reproduction**⑤, sexuality and representation (especially verbal and visual "images of women", and particularly pornography). Millett's title *Sexual Politics*, announces her view of "patriarchy", which she sees as pervasive and which demands a systematic overview—as a political institution". Patriarchy subordinates the female to the male or treats the female as an

---

① 民权运动、反越战的示威游行等主要发生在20世纪60年代，成为第二次浪潮女性主义产生的重要社会背景。

② activist：行动主义者。

③ cause-celebre：轰动一时的；满城风雨的；有重大影响的。

④ ideological indoctrination：意识形态的教化作用。

⑤ reproduction：再生产；生育。

inferior male, and this power is exerted, directly or indirectly, in civil and domestic life to constrain women. Millett borrows from social science the important distinction between "sex" and "gender", where sex is determined biologically but "gender" is a psychological concept which refers to *culturally* acquired sexual identity, and she and other feminists have attacked social scientists who treat the culturally learned "female" characteristics (passive, etc.) as "natural". She recognizes that women as much as men perpetuate these attitudes, and the acting-out of these, sex-roles in the unequal and repressive relations of domination and subordination is what Millett calls "sexual politics".

3. *Sexual Politics* was a pioneering analysis of masculinist historical, social and literary images of women, and is a formative text in feminist literary criticism. Millett's privileging of literature as a source helped to establish writing, literary studies and criticism as domains especially appropriate for feminism. One crucial factor in the social construction of femininity is the way literary values and conventions have themselves been shaped by men, and women have often struggled to express their own concerns in what may well have been inappropriate forms. In narrative, for instance, the shaping conventions of adventure and romantic pursuit have a "male" impetus and purposiveness. Further, the male writer addresses his readers as if they are always men, while advertising provides obvious parallel examples in mass culture. However, as we have noted in relation to Woolf and de Beauvoir, it is also possible for the female reader to collude (unconsciously) in this patriarchal positioning and read "as a man". In order to resist this indoctrination of the female reader, Millett exposes the oppressive representations of sexuality to be found in male fiction. By deliberately foregrounding the view of a *female* reader, she highlights the male domination which pervades sexual description in the novels of D. H. Lawrence, Henry Miller, Norman Miller and Jean Genet, offering in the case of Lawrence, for example, often hilarious and devastatingly deflationary analyses of his **phallocracy**①.

4. Millett's book provided a powerful critique of patriarchal culture, but other feminist critics believe that her sole selection of male authors was too unrepresentative and that she does not sufficiently understand the subversive power of the imagination in fiction. It appears that, for Millett, male authors are compelled by their gender to reproduce the oppressive sexual politics of the real world in their fiction, an approach which would underestimate, say, James Joyce's treatment of female sexuality. Some feminists therefore have seen Millett as holding a one-

① phallocracy：男权中心主义；男权思想。

dimensional view of male domination, treating **sexist**① ideology as **a blanket oppression**② which all male writers inevitable promote. (Rewritten from Raman Seldon, Peter Widdowson, and Peter Brooker, *A Reader's Guide to Contemporary Literary Theory*, pp. 130-132)

Exercises

Questions for Understanding

1. How significant is the fact that Millett's book appeared against a wide background of social movements?

2. Why does the author of the passage think that Millett's book is a "demolition job"?

3. What is Millett's main argument in the book? What does the title of the book mean?

4. How does Millett distinguish "sex" and "gender"? How significant is such a distinction?

5. Why does the author of the essay believe that Millett's book is "a formative text in feminist literary criticism" (Paragraph 3)?

6. In what way does Millett cite the novels of D. H. Lawrence, Henry Miller, Norman Miller and Jean Genet in her book?

7. How well is Millett's book received among feminists?

B. Gap Filling

Provide the missing words according to the paragraphs you have just read.

24. However, as we have noted in relation to Woolf and de Beauvoir, it is also possible for the female reader to ______(unconsciously) in this patriarchal positioning and read "as a man". In order to resist this indoctrination of the female reader, Millett exposes the oppressive representations of sexuality to be found in male fiction. By deliberately ______ the view of a female reader, she highlights the male domination which pervades sexual description in the novels of D. H. Lawrence, Henry Miller, Norman Miller and Jean Genet, offering in the case of Lawrence, for example, often ______ and ______ deflationary analyses of his ______. Millett's book provided a powerful ______ of patriarchal culture, but other feminist critics believe that her sole selection of male authors was too unrepresentative and that she does not sufficiently understand the ______ power of the imagination in fiction. It appears that, for Millett, male authors are compelled by their gender to reproduce the oppressive sexual politics of

---

① sexist：性别主义。

② a blanket oppression：一种普遍的压迫现象。

the real world in their fiction, an ______ which would underestimate, say, James Joyce's treatment of female sexuality. Some feminists therefore have seen Millett as holding a ______ view of male domination, treating sexistideology as a ______ oppression which all male writers inevitable promote.

Supplementary Reading(12)

Passage A: Four Waves of Feminism

1. It is common to speak of three phases of modern feminism; however, there is little consensus as to how to characterize these three waves or what to do with women's movements before the late nineteenth century. Making the landscape even harder to navigate, a new silhouette is emerging on the horizon and taking the shape of a fourth wave of feminism.

2. Some thinkers have sought to locate the roots of feminism in ancient Greece with Sappho, or the medieval world with Hildegard of Bingen or Christine de Pisan. Certainly Olympes de Gouge, Mary Wollstonecraft and Jane Austen are foremothers of the modern women's movement. All of these people advocated for the dignity, intelligence, and basic human potential of the female sex. However, it was not until the late nineteenth century that the efforts for women's equal rights coalesced into a clearly identifiable and self-conscious movement, or rather a series of movements. The first wave of feminism took place in the late nineteenth and early twentieth centuries, emerging out of an environment of urban industrialism and liberal, socialist politics. The goal of this wave was to open up opportunities for women, with a focus on suffrage. The wave formally began at the Seneca Falls Convention in 1848 when three hundred men and women rallied to the cause of equality for women. Elizabeth Cady Stanton drafted the Seneca Falls Declaration outlining the new movement's ideology and political strategies.

3. In its early stages, feminism was interrelated with the temperance and abolitionist movements and gave voice to now-famous activists like the African-American Sojourner Truth (1883), who demanded: "Ain't I a woman?" Victorian America saw women acting in very "un-ladylike" ways (public speaking, demonstrating, stints in jail), which challenged the "cult of domesticity". Discussions about the vote and women's participation in politics led to an examination of the differences between men and women as they were then viewed. Some

claimed that women were morally superior to men, and so their presence in the civic sphere would improve public behavior and the political process.

4. The second wave began in the 1960s and continued into the 90s. This wave unfolded in the context of the anti-war and civil rights movements and the growing self-consciousness of a variety of minority groups around the world. The New Left was on the rise, and the voice of the second wave was increasingly radical. In this phase, sexuality and reproductive rights were dominant issues, and much of the movement's energy was focused on passing the *Equal Rights Amendment to the Constitution* guaranteeing social equality regardless of sex. This phase began with protests against the Miss America pageant in Atlantic City in 1968 and 1969. Feminists parodied what they held to be a degrading "cattle parade" that reduced women to objects of beauty dominated by a patriarchy that sought to keep them in the home or in dull, low-paying jobs. The radical New York group called the Redstockings staged a counter pageant in which they crowned a sheep as Miss America and threw "oppressive" feminine artifacts such as bras, girdles, high-heels, makeup and false eyelashes into the trashcan.

5. Because the second wave of feminism found voice amid so many other social movements, it was easily marginalized and viewed as less pressing than, for example, Black Power or efforts to end the war in Vietnam. Feminists reacted by forming women-only organizations (such as NOW) and "consciousness raising" groups. In publications like "The BITCH Manifesto" and "Sisterhood is Powerful", feminists advocated for their place in the sun. The second wave was increasingly theoretical, based on a fusion of neo-Marxism and psycho-analytical theory, and began to associate the subjugation of women with broader critiques of patriarchy, capitalism, normative heterosexuality, and the woman's role as wife and mother. Sex and gender were differentiated—the former being biological, and the later a social construct that varies culture-to-culture and over time.

6. Whereas the first wave of feminism was generally propelled by middle class, Western, white women, the second phase drew in women of color and developing nations, seeking sisterhood and solidarity, claiming "Women's struggle is class struggle." Feminists spoke of women as a social class and coined phrases such as "the personal is political" and "identity politics" in an effort to demonstrate that race, class, and gender oppression are all related. They initiated a concentrated effort to rid society top-to-bottom of sexism, from children's cartoons to the highest levels of government. One of the strains of this complex and diverse "wave" was the development of women-only spaces and the notion that women working together create a special dynamic that is not possible in mixed-groups, which would ultimately work for the betterment of

the entire planet. Women, due whether to their long "subjugation" or to their biology, were thought by some to be more humane, collaborative, inclusive, peaceful, nurturing, democratic, and holistic in their approach to problem solving than men. The term eco-feminism was coined to capture the sense that because of their biological connection to earth and lunar cycles, women were natural advocates of environmentalism.

7. The third wave of feminism began in the mid-90's and was informed by post-colonial and post-modern thinking. In this phase many constructs were destabilized, including the notions of "universal womanhood", body, gender, sexuality and heteronormativity. An aspect of third wave feminism that mystified the mothers of the earlier feminist movement was the readoption by young feminists of the very lip-stick, high-heels, and cleavage proudly exposed by low cut necklines that the first two phases of the movement identified with male oppression. Pink floor expressed this new position when she said that it's possible to have a push-up bra and a brain at the same time.

8. The "grrls" of the third wave stepped onto the stage as strong and empowered, eschewing victimization and defining feminine beauty for themselves as subjects, not as objects of a sexist patriarchy. They developed a rhetoric of mimicry, which appropriated derogatory terms like "slut" and "bitch" in order to subvert sexist culture and deprive it of verbal weapons. The web is an important tool of "girlie feminism". E-zines have provided "cybergrrls" and "netgrrls" another kind of women-only space. At the same time—rife with the irony of third-wave feminism because cyberspace is disembodied—it permits all users the opportunity to cross gender boundaries, and so the very notion of gender has been unbalanced in a way that encourages experimentation and creative thought.

9. This is in keeping with the third wave's celebration of ambiguity and refusal to think in terms of "us-them". Most third-wavers refuse to identify as "feminists" and reject the word that they find limiting and exclusionary. Grrl-feminism tends to be global, multi-cultural, and it shuns simple answers or artificial categories of identity, gender, and sexuality. Its transversal politics means that differences such as those of ethnicity, class, sexual orientation, etc. are celebrated and recognized as dynamic, situational, and provisional. Reality is conceived not so much in terms of fixed structures and power relations, but in terms of performance within contingencies. Third wave feminism breaks boundaries.

10. The fourth wave of feminism is still a captivating silhouette. A writer for *Elle Magazine* recently interviewed me about the waves of feminism and asked if the second and third waves may have "failed or dialed down" because the social and economic gains had been mostly

sparkle, little substance, and whether at some point women substituted equal rights for career and the atomic self. I replied that the second wave of feminism ought not be characterized as having failed, nor was glitter all that it generated. Quite the contrary; many goals of the second wave were met: more women in positions of leadership in higher education, business and politics; abortion rights; access to the pill that increased women's control over their bodies; more expression and acceptance of female sexuality; general public awareness of the concept of and need for the "rights of women" (though never fully achieved); a solid academic field in feminism, gender and sexuality studies; greater access to education; organizations and legislation for the protection of battered women; women's support groups and organizations (like NOW and AAUW); an industry in the publication of books by and about women/feminism; public forums for the discussion of women's rights; and a societal discourse at the popular level about women's suppression, efforts for reform, and a critique of patriarchy. So, in a sense, if the second wave seemed to have "dialed down", the lull was in many ways due more to the success of the movement than to any ineffectiveness. In addition to the sense that many women's needs had been met, feminism's perceived silence in the 1990s was a response to the successful backlash campaign by the conservative press and media, especially against the word feminism and its purported association with male-bashing and extremism.

11. However, the second wave only quieted down in the public forum; it did not disappear but retreated into the academic world where it is alive and well-incubating in the academy. Women's centers and women's/gender studies have become a staple of virtually all universities and most colleges in the US and Canada (and in many other nations around the word). Scholarship on women's studies, feminist studies, masculinity studies, and queer studies is prolific, institutionalized, and thriving in virtually all scholarly fields, including the sciences. Academic majors and minors in women's, feminist, masculinity and queer studies have produced thousands of students with degrees in the subjects. However, generally those programs have generated theorists rather than activists.

12. Returning to the question the *Elle Magazine* columnist asked about the third wave and the success or failure of its goals. It is hard to talk about the aims of the third wave because a characteristic of that wave is the rejection of communal, standardized objectives. The third wave does not acknowledge a collective "movement" and does not define itself as a group with common grievances. Third wave women and men are concerned about equal rights, but tend to think the genders have achieved parity or that society is well on its way to delivering it to them. The third wave pushed back against their "mothers" (with grudging gratitude) the way children

push away from their parents in order to achieve much needed independence. This wave supports equal rights, but does not have a term like feminism to articulate that notion. For third wavers, struggles are more individual: "We don't need feminism anymore."

13. But the times are changing, and a fourth wave is in the air. A few months ago, a high school student approached one of the staff of the Center for Gender Equity at Pacific University and revealed in a somewhat confessional tone, "I think I'm a feminist!" It was like she was coming out of the closet. Well, perhaps that is the way to view the fourth wave of feminism.

14. The aims of the second feminist movement were never cemented to the extent that they could survive the complacency of third wavers. The fourth wave of feminism is emerging because (mostly) young women and men realize that the third wave is either overly optimistic or hampered by blinders. Feminism is now moving from the academy and back into the realm of public discourse. Issues that were central to the earliest phases of the women's movement are receiving national and international attention by mainstream press and politicians: problems like sexual abuse, rape, violence against women, unequal pay, slut-shaming, the pressure on women to conform to a single and unrealistic body-type and the realization that gains in female representation in politics and business, for example, are very slight. It is no longer considered "extreme", nor is it considered the purview of rarified intellectuals to talk about societal abuse of women, rape on college campus, Title IX, homo and transphobia, unfair pay and work conditions, and the fact that the US has one of the worst records for legally-mandated parental leave and maternity benefits in the world.

15. Some people who wish to ride this new fourth wave have trouble with the word "feminism", not just because of its older connotations of radicalism, but because the word feels like it is underpinned by assumptions of a gender binary and an exclusionary subtext: "for women only." Many fourth wavers who are completely on-board with the movement's tenants find the term "feminism" sticking in their craws and worry that it is hard to get their message out with a label that raises hackles for a broader audience. Yet the word is winning the day. The generation now coming of age sees that we face serious problems because of the way society genders and is gendered, and we need a strong "in-your-face" word to combat those problems. Feminism no longer just refers to the struggles of women; it is a clarion call for gender equity.

16. The emerging fourth wavers are not just reincarnations of their second wave grandmothers; they bring to the discussion important perspectives taught by third wave feminism. They speak in terms of intersectionality whereby women's suppression can only fully be understood in a context of the marginalization of other groups and genders—feminism is part

of a larger consciousness of oppression along with racism, ageism, classism, and sexual orientation (no "ism" to go with that). Among the third wave's bequests is the importance of inclusion, an acceptance of the sexualized human body as non-threatening, and the role the internet can play in gender-bending and leveling hierarchies. Part of the reason a fourth wave can emerge is because these millennials' articulation of themselves as "feminists" is their own: not a hand-me-down from grandma. The beauty of the fourth wave is that there is a place in it for all—together. The academic and theoretical apparatus is extensive and well-honed in the academy, ready to support a new broad-based activism in the home, in the workplace, in the sphere of social media, and in the streets.

17. At this point we are still not sure how feminism will mutate. Will the fourth wave fully materialize and in what direction? There have always been many feminisms in the movement, not just one ideology, and there have always been tensions, points and counter-points. The political, social and intellectual feminist movements have always been chaotic, multivalenced, and disconcerting; and let's hope they continue to be so; it's a sign that they are thriving. (an online extraction by Martha Rampton)

True or False Statements

(a83) According to Paragraph 1 there may be a fifth wave of feminism under way.

(a84) Paragraph 2 uses a historical approach to study feminism.

(a85) According to Paragraph 3 early feminism generally strives for the improvement of women's physical conditions like abortion and domesticity.

(a86) "Cattle Parade" is a metaphor employed to oppose women who show their beauty.

(a87) Feminism trusts women more than men because of the "special dynamic" the former creates.

(a88) "Grrl" in Paragraph 8 is a rhetoric of mimicry by the third wave feminists in order to agree with the dominant society.

(a89) In Paragraphs 9 and 10 the author feels contented with the achievement of the previous waves because their goals and needs are met.

(a90) Paragraphs 12 and 13 only concentrate on the third wave of feminist issues.

(a91) Paragraphs 14 and 15 tell reader the reason why there is the fourth wave of feminist movement: satisfaction with the previous waves.

(a92) The author is satisfied with the fourth wave of feminism but not so sure where feminism will develop.

第四节　性别与文化再现

导　读

性别的文化再现(cultural representation)是文化研究的重要内容之一，它关注不同的性别在社会各文化形态——文学、电影、电视、广告、音乐、舞蹈等——被再现的形式以及这样的再现如何反过来继续塑造社会性别、如何影响两性关系。

在一些文化研究者看来，男性气质、女性气质这样的文化建构在很大程度上都是再现出来的。由于人们的性别意识和性别观念会随着再现活动传达到作品中，所以文化产品会携带性别态度。通过分析性别在文化产品中的再现，人们可以反观现实中产品的生产者所拥有的性别观念。一些女性主义者着力批评文化产品对女性的错误再现(misrepresentation)，他们主张，女性身体在文化中的再现表明女性已被商品化。

本节所选的两篇文章分析了电视作品对男性气质和女性气质的塑造，研究者发现文化产品往往呈现出鲜明的性别模式，对不同性别的再现反映出人们对于男女两性应承担的社会角色的期待。

Passage One: Femininity and Masculinity

1. For most writers within cultural studies, masculinity and femininity are not essential qualities of embodied subjects. Rather, they are understood to be matters of representation. Sexual identity is constituted by ways of speaking about the disciplining bodies. This theme of representation is a **trope**① of cultural studies that is also manifested in the study of gender within popular culture.

2. A good deal of feminist writing in the field of culture has been concerned with the representation of gender and of women in particular. As Evans (1997) comments, in the first place there was a concern to demonstrate that women had played a part in culture, and in

① trope：转义，修辞学的基本概念之一，指词或短语偏离原有字面意义以取得修辞效果。

literature in particular, in the face of their omission from the **canon**① of good works. This was coterminous with a concern for the kinds of representations of women which had been constructed; that is, "the thesis that gender politics were absolutely central to the very project of representation".

3. Early feminist studies made the realist **epistemological**② assumption that representation was a direct expression of social reality and/or a potential and actual distortion of that reality. That is, representations of women reflected male attitudes and constituted misrepresentations of "real" women. This is known as the "images of women perspective". However, later studies informed by **poststructuralism**③ regard all representations as cultural constructions and not as reflections of a real world. Consequently, concern centers on how representations signify in the context of social power with what consequences for gender relations. This exploration of "women as a sign" we may call the "politics of representation".

4. The concept of the stereotype occupies a prominent place within the images of women perspective. A stereotype involves the reduction of persons to a set of exaggerated, usually negative, character traits. Through the operation of power a stereotype marks the boundaries between the "normal" and the "abject". Krishnan and Dighe (1990) argue that affirmation and denial were two main themes evident in their study of the representation of women on Indian television. The affirmation they describe is of a limited definition of womanhood as passive and subordinate, that is, being tied to housework, husbands and children. The denial is of the creativity, activity and individuality of women, particularly in relation to work and the public sphere. They report that men in television fiction were the principal characters in much larger numbers than women (105 men to 55 women). Further, while men were represented in a range of occupations, most women (34) were depicted as housewives. Each of the principal characters was described on the basis of 88 polar opposite personality attributes and analysis revealed that the most common characteristics ascribed to men and women were as in the following table.

Table: Attributes of masculinity and femininity on Indian television

Male Characters	Female Characters
self-centered	sacrificing

① canon：文学经典；被公众接受和认可的文学传统。

② epistemological：基于认识论的。

③ poststructuralism：后结构主义，指利用结构主义的基本命题对符号、知识和主体性等哲学概念进行新的阐释的哲学立场，是后现代主义理论的核心。

续表

Male Characters	Female Characters
decisive	dependent
self-confident	anxious to please
seeing a place in the larger world	defining the world through family relations
relational and conniving	emotional and sentimental
dominant	subordinate
paternal	maternal

(Rewritten from Chris Barker, *Cultural Studies: Theory and Practice*, pp. 306-308)

Exercises

A. Questions for Understanding

1. To what degree do you agree with the observation that women are omitted from the literary canon?

2. In what ways do the early feminist studies about the cultural representation of gender differ from those of later theorists?

3. Why does the writer of the passage believe that the cultural representation of gender is "politics of representation"?

4. What are the stereotypes of male and female characters on Indian television based on the study of Krishnan and Dighe?

5. Do you see similar stereotypes on Chinese screen?

B. Gap Filling

Provide the missing words according to the paragraphs you have just read.

25. For most writers within cultural studies, masculinity and femininity are not ______ qualities of ______ subjects. Rather, they are understood to be matters of ______. Sexual identity is ______ by ways of speaking about the ______ bodies. This theme of representation is a ______ of cultural studies that is also manifested in the study of gender within popular culture. A good deal of feminist writing in the field of culture has been concerned with the ______ of gender and of women in particular. As Evans (1997) comments, in the first place there was a

concern to ______ that women had played a part in culture, and in literature in particular, in the face of their ______ from the canon of good works. This was ______ with a concern for the kinds of representations of women which had been constructed; that is, "the thesis that gender politics were absolutely central to the very project of representation".

Passage Two: Representation of Women in Popular Culture

1. A subject position is that perspective or set of regulated and regulatory discursive meanings from which the text or discourse makes sense. It is that subject with which we must identify in order for the discourse to be meaningful. In identifying with this subject position, the text subjects us to its rules; it seeks to construct us as a certain kind of subject or person. For example, in the context of advertising:

> *Addressing us in our private personae, ads sell w, as women, not just commodities but also personal relationships in which we are feminine; how we are/should be/can, be a certain feminine woman, whose attributes in relation to men and the family derive from the use of these commodities.... A woman is nothing more than the commodities she wears: the lipstick, the tights, the clothes and so on are "woman".*

Winship① is arguing that advertising constructs subject positions for women that place them in the patriarchal work of domesticity, child care, beautification and "catching men". Women are to be mothers, housewives, sexually attractive, and so forth. The issue is not whether such imagery is "true" or "false" but what kinds of people it seeks to construct and with what consequences.

2. Among the more powerful and influential representations of women within western culture is that of the "slender body". This discourse has become a disciplinary cultural norm. Slenderness and a concern with diet and self-monitoring are preoccupations of Western media culture with its interest in a "tighter, smoother, more constrained body profile". Consequently, adverts target bulge, fat or flab and the desirability of flat stomachs and cellulite management.

① 上段引文出自 J. Winship 所著 *Sexuality for Sale*。

As Bordo①(1993) argues, the slender body is a gendered body for the subject position of the slender body is female. Slenderness is a contemporary ideal for female attractiveness so that girls and women are culturally more prone to eating disorders than men.

3. Paradoxically, advertising culture offers us images of desirable foods while proposing that we eat low-calorie items and buy exercise equipment. In the face of this contradiction, the capacity for self-control and the containment of fat is posed in moral as well as physical terms. The choice to diet and exercise leading to the production of a firm body is a symbol not only of gendered identity but also of the "correct" attitude. The failure to exert such control, symbolically manifested in obesity and anorexia, is disciplined through, among other things, television talk shows that feature portrayals of "eating disorders" of the struggles of the obese to lose weight. "**The Oprah Winfrey Show**"②, for example, has placed the presenter's struggle with weight gain at the center of its strategy to humanize her. (Rewritten from Chris Barker, *Cultural Studies: Theory and Practice*, pp. 310-311)

Exercises

A. Questions for Understanding

1. According to the passage, what is a subject position?

2. Why does Winship say that "A woman is nothing more than the commodities she wears"?

3. In what way is the slender body a gendered body, according to Bordo?

4. What are the consequences of advertised slenderness?

5. How does "the capacity for self-control" become a moral issue in the context of contradictory advertisement?

B. Gap Filling

Provide the missing words according to the paragraphs you have just read.

26. Winship is arguing that advertising constructs subject positions for women that place them in the ______ work of domesticity, child care, ______ and "catching men". Women are to

① 观点出自 S. Bordo 所著 *Unbearable Weight: Feminism, Western Culture and the Body*。

② "The Oprah Winfrey Show"是美国著名脱口秀节目，1999 年开办以来逐渐成为最受观众喜爱的电视节目之一。Oprah Winfrey 是美国著名黑人主持人。

be mothers, housewives, sexually attractive, and so forth. The issue is not whether such ______ is "true" or "false" but what kinds of people it ______ to construct and with what consequences. Among the more powerful and influential representations of women within western culture is that of the "slender body". This discourse has become a ______ cultural ______. Slenderness and a concern with diet and ______ are preoccupations of Western media culture with its interest in a "tighter, smoother, more constrained body ______". Consequently, adverts target bulge, fat or flab and the desirability of flat stomachs and cellulite management. ______, advertising culture offers us images of desirable foods while proposing that we eat low-calorie items and buy exercise equipment. In the face of this contradiction, the capacity for self-control and the containment of fat is posed in moral as well as physical terms. The choice to ______ and exercise leading to the production of a firm body is a symbol not only of gendered identity but also of the "correct" attitude.

Supplementary Reading (13)

Passage A: How to Do Feminism

1. What feminisms and critical methodologies are on offer? What can be gleaned about the status or interests of fields of feminist thought crossing through the spaces of "West"? The Call for Papers highlighted notions of the West as a space dominated by masculinity, whiteness, antimodernity, and settler culture. Its point was to pose, as a question, the work of women writers as a gendered category of writers, and to ponder the possibilities of this writing as a site of literary and spatial intervention. They range in their sense of "women writers" and "feminism". Jennifer L. Lieberman, drawing from science and technology studies, puns on definitions of "power" to include electricity, and women's historical and imaginative role in producing it. Addressing late nineteenth-century and early twentieth-century works of Mary Hallock Foote and Honore Willsie Morrow, Lieberman's recovery project introduces gender and technology as topics of Western literary studies as she also shows, in the electric industry's promotional materials, the production of settler/indigenous women along lines of modern/primitive. The rest of the essays address texts and issues of the more contemporary period, from the Civil Rights era to the present. An interesting link between the essays has to do with texts that live out of novelistic bounds, so to speak. Hedrick points to online audiences and dynamic

interplay between young adult readerships and writers' relatively direct contact with them—a network for cultural production that allows an unexpected pedagogy about Greater Mexican regional differences and poverty. Wars and their aftermath, and the colonial legacy of Western space as continuing geography of war, provide the contexts out of which the last two essays are conceived.

2. Back to the question: what is gleaned from these essays about the fields of feminist thought crossing through the spaces of "West"? An important methodological gain to be had from engaging the above discussion is to put theoretical pressure on the category of "women's writing". What feminisms do various texts or critical perspectives invoke? Does "women's writing" of itself evidence feminist aims? It likely is helpful to speculate about these aims, the when, why, where, how, and who of them. Speculation forces the issue for critics to explicate their worries over accountability, worries that preoccupy this special issue, and that I see as productive, political, and feminist. Feminists have long taken the question of a researcher's location in research, one's positionality (not identity), to be a serious methodological demand. Feminists have taken issues of political alliance and solidarity seriously as well. If critics accept critiques of experience, meaning that experience is not knowable in a transparent way nor can it be read straightforwardly from a text , what then might be better moves for theorizing "women's writing"—for instance, as I note above, situated knowledges? Since the world at large demonstrates that women are not by definition feminists, and that feminism is a politics and vision and not a female body, how might we translate that knowing into our critical perspectives?

3. Moving to part two of methodological gains: what about the strong critical work of so many of the scholars mentioned here, what are their feminisms, do they do gender analysis, and how are these distinct analytic operations? One can make the category of gender work all day long, but is it linked to a social vision, a genealogy of thought? Is writing about race as a woman of color the same thing as a feminist critical race perspective? If scholars are not focused on feminist questions, take as an example a great, important text like John Beck's *Dirty Wars*, how might feminists' work with them bring forward the legacies of, for instance, feminist insights on militarism, political economy, environment, coloniality, and migration?

4. Closing here, I want to reflect on the prominence of the trope of frontier in these essays and the importance for feminist studies to persist in this consequential area of scholarship. Frontier zones and the frontier as a critical subject have become increasingly important in transnational, Western, borderlands, and Indigenous studies, and of course in settler colonial

theory. I have made mention already of the completely basic point about social reproduction, its centrality to theorizations of the frontier and settler imagination. Still, feminist trajectories of knowledge are very far from the center of intellectual authority. Scholarship in Native feminist theory and queer theory has led the way in thinking through the social links between heteronormative kinship, heteropatriarchy, and settler sovereignties. It leads the way in thinking beyond apology about the politics of solidarity, decolonial alliance, and accountability.

True or False Statements

(a93) It can be seen from the passage that the author is an authoritative person for feminist studies in English literature.

(a94) With regard to the feminist methods quite a few examples have been mentioned.

(a95) The author likes to raise questions in order to provoke thoughts on how to do feminism in literature.

(a96) In Paragraph 4 the author seems to be satisfied with what has already been achieved in certain areas of feminist studies because they have already gained the central position of intellectuality.

第六章　现代性与城市空间

文化研究归根结底是关于人的学问，无论是现代性还是城市空间都不例外。虽然现代性和城市空间是两个截然不同的概念，但两者在“人”这个主体者身上却紧密相连。前面几章分别从不同角度侧面涉及了人的主体意识，本章主要讨论“城市空间”：城市人口的居住环境和人与人之间的时空关系，也同样揭示人的主体意识；比如，人们的审美观、身份概念、意识形态、种族或族性意识以及现代化给人们所带来的危机感、异化感等都会在城市空间里留下烙印。城市空间是一个庞大而又复杂的概念，它既包含距离、空间、建筑、城市布局等地理、物理概念，又包含人们的空间意识、心理距离以及疆界(boundary)需求等非物质因素。但是，从总体上来说，构成城市空间的硬性成分/材料还是城市建筑。因此，城市建筑就成了解读城市空间的主要途径。

从历史演变和经济发展来看，城市化(urbanization)的出现和城市空间的发展都是现代化的产物。那么，城市和城市空间所表现出来的特征就不可避免地带有现代性(当然，现代性不仅仅表现在城市和城市空间这两个方面)。所以，研究城市空间从现代性开始既是一个主题性的选择，同时也是一个认识上的共识。基于此前提，本章第一部分介绍什么是“现代性”(尽管这是一个众说纷纭的概念) 以及现代性的特征和意义；第二部分讨论什么是城市空间。

第一节　现代性

导　读

齐格蒙·鲍曼(Zygmunt Bauman)说：“我们可以把现代性当作一个时期，在这一时期，人们反思世界的秩序、人类生存的秩序、人类自身的秩序，以及前面三方面的关联之秩序；现代性是一桩思的事情，是关切的事情，是意识到自身的实践，是一个逐渐自觉的实践意识，一种在假如它终止或仅仅衰落了的情况下对所留下的虚空所产生的隐忧。现代性的历史就是社会存在与其文化之间紧张的历史。现代存在迫使其文化站在自己的对立面。这种不和谐恰恰就是现代性所需要的和谐。”(Bauman, “Modernity and Ambivalence”, *Polity*, 1991)正如齐格蒙·鲍曼一样，许多学者和评论家，比如米歇尔·福柯(Michel Foucault)、亨利·列菲弗尔(Henri Lefebvre)等都是从形而上的角度研究现代性，即现代性是指人们思想和意识形态的一种变更，这种变更是建立在对现实和传统文化或价值观的否定或质疑之上的(现代性制造社会存在和其文化之间的紧张)。换句话说，现代性是指信仰的破碎以及发现现实的缺失。而以斯图亚特·霍尔(Stuart Hall)为代表的学者则从社会生产的角度思考现代性。他认为现代性是指资本主义社会的各种生产关系以及随之而产生的观念的更替。总之，现代性可简单地理解为以下两种意义。

一种是作为西方文明历史中某个阶段的现代性——它是科学和技术进步的产物，工业革命的产物，资本主义所引起的广泛的经济和社会变迁的产物。另一种是作为美学概念的现代性。关于第一种现代性，亦即现代性的资产阶级观念，从总体上看，它延续了现代思想史早期的卓越传统：进步的信念，坚信科学技术造福人类的可能性，对时间(可测量的时间，亦即可买卖的时间，因而像任何其他商品一样，可计算成货币的等价物)的关注，崇拜理性，限于抽象的人道主义体系内的自由理想，还有实用主义取向，以及对行动和成功的崇拜等——所有这一切在不同程度上都和渴望现代的斗争密切相关，它们作为中产阶级所确立的成功之文明中的核心价值观而充满活力。另一种现代性，亦即演变成先锋派的现代性，在其浪漫主义发轫之初，就倾向于一种激进的反资产阶级态度，它痛恨中产阶级的价值标准，并借助极其丰富的方式(从反叛、无政府主义和末世论，到贵族式的自我流亡)来表达自己的痛恨。所以，界定文化的现代性绝不是其积极的目标，而是它对资产阶级现代性的彻底拒绝，是其毁灭性的否定激情。

Passage One: Modernity

1. Modernity is simply the sense or the idea that the present is discontinuous with the past, that through a process of social and cultural change (either through improvement, that is, progress, or through decline) life in the present is fundamentally different from life in the past. This sense or idea as a world view contrasts with what I will call tradition, which is simply the sense that the present is continuous with the past, that the present in some way repeats the forms, behavior, and events of the past. The "crisis of modernity" is the sense that modernity is a problem, that traditional ways of life have been replaced with uncontrollable change and unmanageable alternatives. The crisis itself is merely the sense that the present is a transitional

point not focused on a clear goal in the future but simply changing through forces outside our control.

2. How do we experience modernity in twentieth-century America? First, we experience change as either progress or transition, that is, we view our historical situation and our lives **teleologically**①, that is, as deriving meaning and value in some unrealized future. We experience modernity as a proliferation of alternatives either in regard to lifestyle or historical possibilities; future directed behavior (as opposed to tradition) tends to accelerate the proliferation of alternatives. Traditional cultures see themselves as repeating a finite number of alternatives in the present; in modern cultures, the future opens up a vast field of historical and lifestyle choices. This proliferation of alternatives is a source of great anxiety and often results in cultural attempts to restrict alternatives in the face of this anxiety. Let's keep in mind that it is not the alternatives themselves which create this anxiety, it is the sense that the proliferation of alternatives has become unmanageable.

3. Modernity has created a world view in us that is primarily **abstract**②, that is, we experience the world as composed of discrete, fragmented, and separable units. Abstraction is a difficult word to define; for our purposes, it is the idea that areas of existence and culture can be separated from, that is abstracted out of, other areas of existence and culture. In addition, we form social groups that are largely based on abstractions (corporations, nations, economic classes, religious preferences, race (which is really an abstract rather than a physical or biological category), sexual preferences, etc.) rather than real or biological relationships; as a result, membership in social groups tends to be unstable and transitory as one can easily move between social groups. This, again, creates a high sense of anxiety and tension; this anxiety results, on the one hand, in attempts within these abstract groups to define themselves as real, that is, "not abstract", and on the other hand, in attempts to limit the possible social groups, that is, to manage the alternatives. In distinction to modernity, traditional cultures tend to experience the world as whole and integrated; separate areas of existence and culture are seen as integrally related to other areas of existence and culture. In addition, social groups are based on real, biological kinship ties, so that social relations tend to be stable and permanent.

---

① teleologically：用目的论的方法，目的论地（认为事物的产生和发展都是有目的的）。

② abstract：抽象的，概念的（与具体的事物或经验相对立）。指在现代社会中，人们习惯以抽象的而非具体的视角看问题。比如，人们说"富有的白人社会"时，并不具体到到底有多少钱/财富才算富有，肤色浅到什么程度才算白色；另外，该词此处还有"零碎的、分离的、不连贯的"的意思，明显指的是现代性的世界观和方法论。

4. Finally, we see ourselves as having lost tradition, that is, that our behavior patterns, our rituals, etc., are all new and innovative, that we are not repeating the past. But in fact, the experience of modernity is to live in traditional ways and to repeat tradition in unrecognizable forms. Modern cultures still perform traditional rituals, such as sports (which are originally religious rituals) or shamming rituals, yet the origin and original meaning of these rituals have passed out of the culture.

5. Modern cultures still repeat ways of thinking in the past—in fact, the bulk of modern culture is based on traditional ways of thinking repeated relatively unchanged—yet modern cultures tend to view these ways of thinking as innovations. Although we base our social groups on abstract categories, the structure and content of these social groups repeat the structure and content of kinship groups, in other words, we base our abstract social groups on principles derived from real, biological relationships; we do not, however, experience these social groups as real, biological relationships. So, in sum, modernity—the sense that the present is discontinuous with the past, is an illusion—and this illusion creates modernity itself. What has changed is social memory; we have disconnected most of our practices and ideas from our collective memory of their origins and meaning.

Exercises

A. Questions for Understanding

1. According to the passage you have just read, does "modernity" refer to a period of time in relation to the old mode of production in the past or mainly a conceptual word that marks a set of characteristics of a trend of thought?

2. What does the author mean by creating the phrase "crisis of modernity"?

3. Do people in modern society live in stability and security? Why or why not?

4. How does the author conceptualize "traditional culture"?

5. Judging from this passage, do you think the author is "modernist" or "conservative"?

B. Gap Filling

Provide the missing words according to the paragraphs you have just read.

27. Modernity is simply the sense or the idea that the present is ______ with the past, that through a process of social and cultural change (either through improvement, that is, progress, or through decline) life in the present is fundamentally different from life in the past. This sense

or idea as a world view contrasts with what I will call tradition, which is simply the sense that the present is continuous with the past, that the present in some way repeats the forms, behavior, and events of the past. The "crisis of modernity" is the sense that modernity is a ______, that traditional ways of life have been replaced with ______ change and unmanageable alternatives. The crisis itself is merely the sense that the present is a transitional point not focused on a clear goal in the future but simply changing through forces ______ our control. How do we ______ modernity in twentieth-century America? First, we experience change as either progress or transition, that is, we view our historical situation and our lives ______, that is, as deriving meaning and value in some ______ future. We experience modernity as a ______ of alternatives either in regard to lifestyle or historical possibilities; future directed behavior (as opposed to tradition) tends to accelerate the proliferation of alternatives. Traditional culturessee themselves as repeating a ______ number of alternatives in the present; in modern cultures, the future opens up a vast field of historical and lifestyle choices. This proliferation of alternatives is a source of great ______ and often results in cultural attempts to restrict alternatives in the face of this anxiety.

Passage Two: Contradiction of Modernity

1. There have been numerous ways of understanding what modernity is, particularly in the field of sociology, a wide variety of terms are used to describe the society, social life, driving force, symptomatic mentality, or some other defining aspects of modernity. They include: bureaucracy, disenchantment of the world, rationalization, secularization, alienation, commodification, decontextualization, individualism, subjectivism, linear progression, objectivism, universalism, reductionism, chaos, mass society, industrial society, homogenization, unification, hybridization, diversification, democratization, centralization, hierarchical, organization, mechanization, totalitarianism, and so on. Modernity may be considered "marked and defined by an obsession with 'evidence'", visuality, and visibility. Modernity is often characterized by comparing modem societies to premodern or postmodern ones; to an extent, it is reasonable to doubt the very possibility of a descriptive concept that can adequately capture diverse realities of societies of various historical contexts, especially non-European ones, let alone a three-stage model of social evolution from premodernity to postmodernity.

2. However, in terms of social structure, many of the defining events and characteristics

listed above stem from a transition from relatively isolated local communities to a more integrated large-scale society. Understood this way, modernization might be a general, abstract process which can be found in many different parts of histories, rather than a unique event in Europe. In general, large-scale integration involves: increased movement of goods, capital, people, and information among formerly separate areas, and increased influence that reaches beyond a local area; increased formalization of those mobile elements, development of "circuits" on which those elements and influences travel, and standardization of many aspects of the society in general that is conducive to the mobility; increased specialization of different segments of society, such as the division of labor, and interdependency among areas.

3. Seemingly contradictory characteristics ascribed to modernity are often different aspects of this process. For example, unique local culture is invaded and lost by the increased mobility of cultural elements, such as recipes, folktales, and hit songs, resulting in a cultural homogenization across localities, but the repertoire of available recipes and songs increases, within an area because of the increased interlocal movement, resulting in a diversification within each locality. (This is manifest especially in large metropolises where there are many mobile elements.) Centralized bureaucracy and hierarchical organization of governments and firms grows in scale and power in an unprecedented manner, leading some to lament the stifling, cold, rationalist or totalitarian nature of modern society. Yet individuals, often as replaceable components, may be able to move in those social subsystems, creating a sense of liberty, dynamic competition and individualism for others. This is especially the case when a modern society is compared with premodern societies, in which the family and social class one is born into shapes one's lifecourse to a greater extent.

4. These social changes are somewhat common to many different levels of social integration, and not limited to what happened to the West European societies in a specific time period. In other words, while modernity has been characterized in many seemingly contradictory ways, many of those characterizations can be reduced to a relatively simple set of concepts of social change. At the same time, however, such an understanding of modernity is certainly not satisfactory to many, because it fails to explain the global influence of West European and American societies since the Renaissance. Mere large-scale integration of local communities, seen in the Macedon of Alexander the Great or the Mongolia of the Khans, would not necessarily result in the same magnitude of influence as the West European modernization. What has made Western Europe so special?

5. There have been two major answers to this question. First, an internal factor is that only

in Europe, through the Renaissance humanists and early modern philosophers and scientists, rational thinking came to replace many intellectual activities that had been under heavy influence of convention, superstition, and religion. (This line of answer is most frequently associated with Max Weber, a sociologist who is known to have pursued the answer to the above question.) Second, an external factor triggering the later modernity is that colonization, starting as early as the Age of Discovery, created exploitative relations between European countries and their colonies. (This view has notably been explored by the world systems theory of **Immanuel Wallerstein**①.) It is also notable that such commonly-observed features of many modern societies as the nuclear family, slavery, gender roles, and nation states do not necessarily fit well with the idea of rational social organization in which components such as people are treated equally. While many of these features have been dissolving, histories seem to suggest those features may not be mere exceptions to the essential characteristics of modernization, but necessary parts of it.

Exercises

A. Questions for Understanding

1. What does the title of the passage mean?

2. If, according to the author in Paragraph 1, the societal development can be divided into three stages, what do you think are the major features of the middle phase?

3. According to Paragraph 2, does a modern society become more diffused or integrated? In what way?

4. What are the contradictions in a modern society? Give examples.

5. What does the author intend to manifest with the examples of Macedon of Alexander the Great and the Mongolia of the Khans?

B. Gap Filling

Provide the missing words according to the paragraph you have just read.

---

① Immanuel Wallerstein：伊曼纽尔·沃勒斯坦(1930—2019)，是西方"新马克思主义"学者的代表人物，世界体系理论的开拓者和创始人。"霸权"论是其世界体系理论的重要组成部分。沃勒斯坦从资本主义世界经济体的角度，详细探讨了霸权的含义和实质、霸权的模式和兴衰、霸权国家的相互比较及共同特点、国家机器在霸权进程中的作用等诸多问题，进而认为"霸权……在资本主义世界经济体的历史发展中扮演了意义重大的角色"。

28. Seemingly ______ characteristics ______ to modernity are often different aspects of this process. For example, unique local culture is invaded and lost by the increased mobility of cultural elements, such as recipes, folktales, and hit songs, resulting in a cultural homogenization across ______, but the ______ of available recipes and songs increases, within an area because of the increased ______ movement, resulting in a ______ within each locality. (This is manifest especially in large metropolises where there are many mobile elements.) Centralized ______ and hierarchical organization of governments and firms grows in scale and power in an ______ manner, leading some to lament the stifling, cold, rationalist or totalitarian nature of modern society. Yet individuals, often as ______ components, may be able to move in those social subsystems, creating a sense of liberty, dynamic competition and individualism for others. This is especially the case when a modern society is compared with ______ societies, in which the family and social class one is born into shapes one's lifecourse to a greater extent.

Supplementary Reading(14)

Passage A: Modernity and Ruins

1. Modernity is a complex and much contested idea, but in this context it means, above all, the abstraction of social and cultural practices from contexts of local particularity, and their institutionalization and regulation across time and space. The examples of such institutionalization that most readily spring to mind are the organization and policing of social territory (the nation-state, urbanism), or of production and consumption practices (industrialization, the capitalist economy). But modernity also institutionalizes and regulates cultural practices, including those by which we imagine attachment and belonging to a place or a community. The mode of such imagination it promotes is what we have come to know as "cultural identity"—self and communal definitions based around specific, usually politically infected, differentiations: gender, sexuality, class, religion, race and ethnicity, nationality. Some of these differentiations of course existed before the coming of modernity, some like nationality are specifically modern imaginings. Since the beginning of the industrial era our world has been facing what some historians call an ongoing "crisis of modernity". As fast as we adjust to new circumstances, the circumstances change again, and, the rate of change seems to be multiplying exponentially. Of all the demands imposed by twenty first century, perhaps the

toughest is the ability of people to not only manage change but to instigate it, control it and to be its master. Dealing with the ever increasing rate of change may be the century's most potentially overwhelming task. For example, how to deal with the crisis or discontents that appear in modem urbanspace? How to see the architectural ruins that feature modernity?

2. Modern architecture has failed to communicate with its users. Partly because it doesn't make effective links with the city and history; cheap prefabrication, lack of personal "defensible" space, and the alienating housing estate. Thus explosions became a frequent method of dealing with the failure of modernist building methods. But the 9 · 11 represents a watershed in world history in more ways than are obvious. The destruction of an architectural and symbolic icon of modernity has brought to a catastrophic climax a debate about the ways in which modernity, broadly conceived, seems to have invented, framed, and even produced ruins. The question whether international terrorism is a side-product of modernity or a historical development responding to, but independent of, modernity echoes discussions around a possible elective affinity between ruins and modernity. Indeed, ruins began to be perceived and preserved as ruins only during the Renaissance, when the awareness of historical discontinuities, the demise of ancient civilizations, raised the status of traces from the past. These traces—architectural remnants that had long lost their functionality and meaning—could be invested with various attributes, historical, aesthetic, political and otherwise. A desire for preservation in the interest of historical continuity barely concealed political exploitations of ruins as signs of past greatness that could be reappropriated. The ruin is a ruin precisely because it has lost the presence of meaning, while retaining its suggestiveness. It bespeaks a loss of something, while denying complete irretrievability of the absent object. It evokes an ambivalent break from and nostalgia for the past. More pointedly, it signals the imminent breakdown of meaning, and therefore fosters dizzying compensatory discursive activity.

3. Theoreticians of various stripes have considered the peculiar status of ruins in modern culture. **Georg Simmel**①thought that ruins embody the justice of destruction, the reintegration of human design into nature that counteracts human interventions and makes them right. For

① Georg Simmel：乔治·齐美尔(1858—1918)，又译格奥尔格·齐美尔或西美尔，德国著名的社会学家、理论文化研究者。齐美尔认为，文化的产生和发展过程处于精神活动的生命-形式二元互动过程之中，主观文化和客观文化是主体精神和客观精神产品的物化结果。在这双重结构中，他强调文化的“教化”作用和综合的特点。文化现代性发展的结果是客观文化急速膨胀和主观文化过度萎缩，主体的能动性由于个体能量的局限性而在迅速发展的文化面前只能感到压抑。

Theodor Adorno and **Max Horkheimer**①, the process of ruination is an intrinsic component of the dialectic whereby modernity undermines itself and lapses into mythology and self-destruction, **Walter Benjamin**② drew a parallel between the ruin in the realm of things and the allegory in the realm of thoughts, for both ruin and allegory speak of a disruption in the relationship between form and meaning, to the point that semiotics becomes a wasteland. **Lurii Lotman**③has considered the ways in which ruins serve the project of cultural self-fashioning. Sigmund Freud framed the unconscious as a sort of ruin that needs to be excavated. **W. G. Sebald**④ referred to ruins as a trope of the trauma of modernity in several of his essays and fiction pieces. This rich body of approaches to ruins illustrates vividly the extent to which the ruin is predicated on a particular gaze cast upon it. The beholder is the one who defines the ruin, and the ruin could not exist without such creative appropriation. The ruin, in many ways, is a trope of reflexivity, the reflexivity of a culture that interrogates its own becoming. As a result, the ruin is often the playground of specular strategies that tell us more about the identity of the beholder than that of the ruin or its original environment. Poised at the symbolic end of the project of modernity, we will ponder the ways in which the ruin intersects with the two major axes of modernity: the divide between the east and the west, which has produced distinct variants of modernity, and the asymmetry between hegemonic and subaltern cultures, which continues to produce more ruins. Organized in a series of case studies grouped thematically and geographically, people from a variety of disciplines, including architectural design, architectural history, cinema, classics, cultural history, cultural studies, anthropology, history, literary criticism, and sociology, as well as artists have taken their initiatives in studying ruins in the urban space, and their focus is interdisciplinary in method and global in reach.

True or False Statements

(a97) Modernity finds its way both in the global situation and the local communities in that

---

① Theodor Adorno, Max Horkheimer：西奥多·阿多诺，麦克斯·霍克海默，法兰克福学派的两位代表人物。法兰克福学派认为当代资本主义社会的主要冲突不再是阶级与阶级的冲突而是个人与社会的冲突。因此，当代社会革命的首要任务不再是阶级启蒙而是个体启蒙。

② Walter Benjamin：沃尔特·本雅明，德国文学批评家和哲学家，与法兰克福学派有着密切的联系，深受马克思主义的影响。

③ Lurii (Mikhailovich) Lotman：(米卡洛维奇)洛特曼(1922—1993)，苏联人，研究领域是符号学、文化文学研究。

④ W. G. Sebald：温弗里德·格奥尔格·泽巴尔德(Winfried Georg Sebald，1944—2001)，出生于德国巴伐利亚州阿尔格伊地区的维尔塔赫(Wertach，Allgau)，当今最有影响的德国作家之一。

the former promotes similarities while the latter protects its indigenous cultures.

(a98) Living in such a situation as modernity, people find it difficult to orient their goals and drives for life. So they begin to worry about their living space created by modern architecture.

(a99) The 9 · 11 tragedy appears to be a matter of terrorism, but it is rooted in the way people live—modernity.

(a100) Ruins in the metropolis are nothing but the demolitions and rebuilding because of the urgent need of the expanding urban space. Even if the ruin of the modern urban space, in the light of some scholars, can be a trope, what it signifies is simply that the Westerners are experiencing the spiritual wasteland, which has nothing to do with other people in the world.

第二节　城市空间

导　读

城市空间是指城市占有的地域空间，更多地属于地理概念而非行政概念，是以非农业用地和非农业经济活动为主体的建成区。城市作为一种聚落景观，是人类文化的体现。不同地域的文化、宗教和社会观念等，都会对城市地域形态和空间结构产生深刻影响。城市建筑景观和格局等往往反映出地域文化对城市的影响。此处(本节)城市空间的定义是：为容纳某些活动而特意形成的并且是易于进入的空间，而建筑的围合是其一条重要的判断标准。在城市建筑景观中，最明显的特征是建筑物的高低。美国纽约、芝加哥等大城市，市中心摩天大楼高耸入云，四周建筑物错落其间；欧洲城市则大不一样，由于城市发展历史悠久，城市格局与主体建筑风格已经形成，市中心高大楼群聚集在一起的情况比较少见；我国具有悠久历史的政治中心——北京，皇宫建筑群雄踞城市中心，其他重要建筑物则沿城市中轴线排列。然而，在大众文化逐渐成为现代城市生活主流的今天，“容纳某些活动而又容易进入”的城市空间(除自己的家之外)当属城市中的公共场所，比如广场、街道以及具有其他公共设施的空间。本节所选的两篇文章集中讨论了城市空间的几个基本概念。作者从城市街道的空间意义入手，通过分析两位著名社会学家（Henri Lefebvre 和 Richard Sennett)对微(细)分空间(differential space)、抽象空间(abstract space)、空间的内向性(spatial inwardness)或私人空间(private space)和空间的外向性(spatial outwardness)或公众空间(public space)的不同理解和定义，重点向人们阐释了城市空间的文化含义，对城市空间的文化研究有着重要的指导作用。

Passage One: Two Scholars on Modern Urban Space

1. If we go to other professions than architects and planners to search for a deeper understanding of the lack of street life in most parts of contemporary cities, there is generally not much interest in the question. In North America, if asked, many would blame it on poverty, drugs and crime, the homeless and the gangs: in short the undesirables. In North Western Europe the weather would get part of the blame, although this is only partly true, as is shown by the growth of downtown street-life here in the last decades. Many would also blame it on the car. Others would blame TV, the average American watching more than 30 hours a week, the Europeans not quite reaching this level yet, but catching up.

2. Only a few would see the lack of street-life as a symptom of deep structures of modern society. Two intellectuals that have done it since the end of the 1960s—are the French philosopher **Henri Lefebvre**① and the New York sociologist **Richard Sennett**②. Both struggle to get street life back not only in sheer defiance of deep social obstacles, but to get rid of the roots of these obstacles themselves. Together they show, that to get life back on the streets we have to deal with forces as strong as Capital, God and Enlightenment. Lefebvre and Sennett—put together here, as far as we know, for the first time in the diagram—see the problems of modern urban space on two different polar axes. Lefebvre focuses most heavily on the contradiction of abstract space versus differential space, Sennett most heavily on the contradiction of spatial inwardness versus spatial outwardness. These spatial contradictions, if crossed, can define different aspects of the city of interest, and state our problem of street-life in general terms.

3. According to Lefebvre we live in a capitalist society, that has a general tendency to turn

① Henri Lefebvre：亨利·列菲弗尔(1901—1991)，一位和20世纪一同降生的现代法国思想大师，在其60多年的创作生涯中，为后人留下了60多部著作、300余篇论文这样一笔丰厚的精神遗产，是西方学界公认的“日常生活批判理论之父”“现代法国辩证法之父”，区域社会学，特别是城市社会学理论的重要奠基人。

② Richard Sennett：理查德·塞内特，麻省理工学院社会学教授，著有《新资本主义文化》(*The Culture of the New Capitalism*, Yale, 2006)，《不平等时代的敬意》((*Respect in an Age of Inequality*, Penguin, 2003)和《性格的侵蚀》(*The Corrosion of Character*, Norton, 1998)。美国艺术和科学学院院士；英国皇家文学、艺术协会成员。

the formerly absolute space of nature and early human culture into abstract space. Capitalist space is produced as commodity and as distribution networks. Therefore, seen from an exchange point of view, it should be as "general" as possible. Industrialised mass housing and mass office building are other obvious examples. But over and over again, economic competition and political struggle create a contradictory space, adding new differences to the original differences of space given by nature and history that so far have not been completely "neutralised". In this way, according to Lefebvre, spaces of difference are produced to some extent, although the general tendency is the production of abstract space. Since the 1960s differential space is also to some extent produced as a result of the growing importance of leisure and non-labour—a tendency of growing importance that may lead to a paradigmatic change in the concept of space.

4. According to Sennett, we also live in a capitalist society, but as he does not believe in Lefebvre's political ideas of great political revolutions, Sennett has to focus differently in his spatial analyses. If the capitalist economic "mechanisms" cannot be basically changed within a reasonable time, or without too large human costs, then the struggle for a better city has to be primarily cultural—not primarily political-economical. This interpretation of the differences of Lefebvre's and Sennett's basic points of view has to be included in the understanding of why Sennett has to fight God and Enlightenment instead of Capitalism as such. That the struggle for a better city is in vain without a cultural perspective, is also Lefebvre's point of view, as he sees no attractive cultural quality in socialist city building so far, but the cultural perspective is not the starting point of his analyses.

5. The statement of God and Enlightenment as the main villains in Sennett's universe must be further explained though, if we are to understand him right. The God in question is the Christian God, and the problematic aspect of Enlightenment is its quest for a Grand Unity of everything. For Sennett, the common denominator of Christianity and Enlightenment is the perversion of the relation between inside and outside in a way that promotes inwardness and cripples outwardness. The problem of Christianity goes all the way back to the early middle ages, as expressed by Augustin's rejection of the worldly city in favour of the city of Heavens. The problem of secular Enlightenment, on the other hand, is its attempt to overcome contradictions by escaping them in the name of unity, or by trying to brutally enforce a non-contradictory unity. This, of course, is doomed to fail. Inwardness continues as a result. To Sennett, the inward-outward axis of orientation is related to the questions of relations between private and public life (and private and public space), as well as to the relations between the Self and the Others in more general terms. Sennett wants to turn people outward instead of

inward—towards the streets and the encounter of human differences—instead of towards the home and the psychoanalyses with or without professional help. You could say that Sennett thinks it is both necessary and possible to break out of the mutual contradiction and unity that is a driving engine in most of Woody Alien's films—the alienating metropolis and a growing need for psychoanalyses.

6. But to turn outward, Lefebvre would say, is extremely difficult in a society based on private ownership to capital and land, and in a society dominated by large corporations and public bureaucracy. In spite of that, Lefebvre would agree that every possibility to turn outward should be cared for. In the end of The Production of Space he actually mentionsthe possibility of a reformist strategy towards differential space and a new society.

Exercises

A. Questions for Understanding

1. Why does "street-life" decline? Why do scholars show interest in "street-life"?
2. Why does the author study Lefebvre and Sennett together?
3. Between Lefebvre and Sennett, who might be more a Marxist? Why?
4. Why does Sennett disapprove God and Enlightenment? In what way do you think God shares similarities with Enlightenment?
5. In what way does Lefebvre probably agree with Sennett?

B. Gap Filling

Provide the missing words according to the paragraphs you have just read.

29. Only a few would see the lack of ______ as a symptom of deep structures of modern society. Two intellectuals that have done it since the end of the 1960s—are the French philosopher Henri Lefebvre and the New York sociologist Richard Sennett. Both struggle to get street life back not only in sheer defiance of deep social ______, but to get rid of the roots of these obstacles themselves. Together they show, that to get life back on the streets we have to deal with forces as strong as Capital, God and ______. Lefebvre and Sennett—put together here, as far as we know, for the first time in the diagram—see the problems of modern urban space on two different polar axes. Lefebvre focuses most heavily on the contradiction of abstract space versus differential space, Sennett most heavily on the contradiction of spatial ______ versus spatial outwardness. These spatial ______, if crossed, can define different aspects of the

city of interest, and state our problem of street-life in general terms. According to Lefebvre we live in a ______ society, that has a general tendency to turn the formerly absolute space of nature and early human culture into ______ space. Capitalist space is produced as ______ and as distribution networks. Therefore, seen from an exchange point of view, it should be as "general" as possible. Industrialised mass ______ and mass office building are other obvious examples. But over and over again, economic competition and political struggle create a contradictory space, adding new differences to the ______ differences of space given by nature and history that so far have not been completely "neutralised".

Passage Two: Abstractness/Inwardness and Differential/Abstract Space

1. We will get back to Lefebvre's and Sennett's conceptions of the city to fight for, but before that let us look at the diagram.

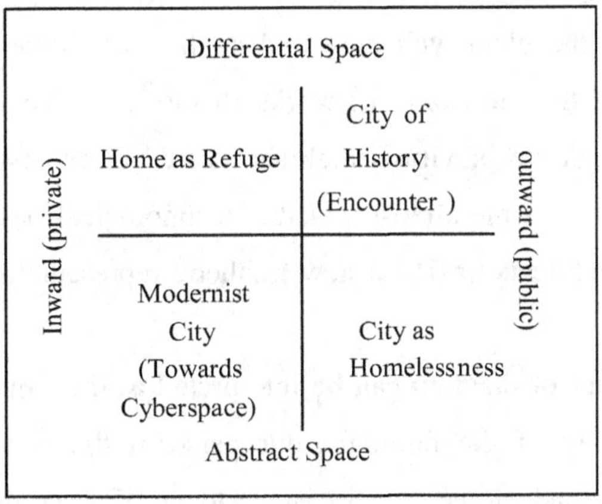

2. The Abstract Space/Differential Space dimension can be seen as an axis of spatial production, the Inward/Outward dimension as an axis of spatial orientation. The crossing gives us four quadrants: the first quadrant of the diagram can be interpreted as the "City of History" in a double sense—both as the historical pre-modernist city of streets and squares, which is as old as the preserved history of human societies (about 10, 000 years)—and as the city, where time makes a difference. This is the city of human encounter of other humans in real life, and the encounter of culture of different times.

3. The third quadrant—the diametrically opposite—can be interpreted as the "Modernist City". This is the city of advanced capitalism: an urban antispace of isolated and inwardly oriented built objects sprinkled in a technological landscape, interwoven with distance-keeping lawns to look at, simulating naturalness and simple countryside pleasures. Although this city is heavily focused on time—trying to catch up with time all the time—it kills time, as it can only develop through the destruction of history and through repetition. This is the reason, why Berman's book on modernity got its title from Marx's and Engels' *Communist Manifesto*: All that is solid melts into air. Modernity is the new as ever the same. In this "City of Modernity", there is not much encounter of real and different human beings. On the contrary it becomes increasingly clear, although Lefebvre and Sennett do not say much about it, that the ultimate "Modernist City" is an electronic network. Skyscraper areas are still being built in the image of downtown Chicago, Manhattan and **Le Corbusier's "Plan Voisin"**①, but the true modernist city of today is the electronic portable office of combined mobile-phones and portable computers, including portable fax-machines and networked modems, connected to satellite-based world wide services 24 hours a day. If you want to, you can even include global satellite navigation systems with a guarantied accuracy of 18 meters. If you have the right equipment, it does not matter where on the globe you are, and at the same time you can be sure that you cannot get lost, except in the electronic networks themselves. We now begin to see that the ultimate modern city is made up of virtual realities located in cyberspace: the antispace of real experiential space. Maybe, it is the almost invisible technological basis of this modern city that makes it so difficult for architects to find a new aesthetic representation of contemporary space, although they try so hard.

4. The second quadrant of diagram can be interpreted as the "Indoor Private Home" where we can escape to the safety of the familiar, our personal things and the shallow depths of spatially and socially contained intimacy. This is not to say that we do not need homes, or that the heavy focus on housing in the modernist city has been all wrong. On the contrary: the home is necessary for the development of individual human beings. At the same time though, it is to state that the home is a trap, if it is not complemented by a city of encounter. Today, the threat to the family is not located as much in the streets, as it is in homes of isolation. (In Denmark in

① Le Corbusier's "Plan Voisin": Le Corbusie, 勒·柯布西耶(1887—1965), 20世纪最著名的法国建筑大师、城市规划家、现代建筑激进分子，被称为"现代建筑的旗手"；Plan Voisin,(巴黎)规划图，1925年由柯布西耶设计，虽未实施，但其中钢筋水泥所构成的机械美对现代建筑风格影响深刻。

the 1990s most murders take place within the family, and if we look back we will see that in the period when we built the homes of the modern city, the number of people in Denmark with a psychiatric record grew to comprise 1/5 of the total population. This might be sheer coincidence, but there probably is some kind of relation between the different phenomena.)

5. The fourth quadrant can be interpreted as the "City of Homelessness"—in the double sense of an outside world that we do not care about, and a home for the really homeless—the backside of the coin of the modern City, exploding in the face of us all over the Western industrialised world, including in the Scandinavian welfare states. Why do abstractness and inwardness contradict urban possibilities and urban life? This should be a little clearer by now: abstract space is intended to generalise exchange value. As a consequence space is planned in a way that contradicts the promotion of difference. Town planning and building codes contribute to enforce homogeneity to a large extent. As for inwardness: as long as we focus too much on inwardness, people are separated from the differences of other people, and in the end they get alienated to themselves. We get lack of solidarity and psychological problems. If we do not experience ourselves in direct relation to others, the others get unreal to us and we get unreal ourselves too. It is a big problem, that our society has been extremely afraid of difference in real life. At the same time the large need for difference is shown by the obsessive focus on difference in entertainment and sports through various kinds of media.

6. Lefebvre wrote on "everyday-life" already in the 1950s. From 1968 to 1974 he took up questions of the city—not only in relation to different modes of production as seen from a Marxist"systemic" point of view, but also as an urban experience of humans living in the city—the city as lived space. He even claimed the city a human right. Later he had to focus on the role of the modern state. In his last book on the city—*The Production of Space*—Lefebvre heavily states the human need of difference as counter-weight to everyday routine, and the decisive role of difference in opening up new social and political opportunities. As capitalism creates contradictions in urban space, spaces of difference emerge, that can be transformed into counter-spaces of new human possibilities. If we cross-read his books on the city and on space thoroughly, we will find that the important qualities of differential space and counter-space have to do with aspects like: social and other human differences, the meeting of strangers, play and eroticism, human works as unique objects, possibilities for the unplanned, unpredictability, inter-change and inter-active communication, as well as the use of all senses. All this should be human rights in urban space, according to Lefebvre!

7. There is not much to learn about an urban design of difference in Lefebvre's books,

though. He also thinks that architects and especially urban planners normally do more harm than good. Sennett's characteristics of his urban spaces of interest resemble those of Lefebvre's in many ways—including the encounter of strangers—but Sennett explicitly mentions the street, as the most important general aspect of the city. When it comes to the question of urban design, Sennett is also as negative about the professionals involved, as is Lefebvre. Although, Sennett tries to find the keys to an urban design that makes a difference, he does not come up with very much of direct practical use either. He clearly is in favour of discontinuities and non-linearities in social space as well as in physical space, but nobody can learn how to build cities from his book.

Exercises

A. Questions for Understanding

1. What might be the supposed differences between the "City of History" and the "Modernist City"?

2. What can one enjoy at one's home according to Paragraph 4? Why does home become a trap for people?

3. Why do abstractness and inwardness hamper (contradict) urban possibilities and urban life?

4. From what perspective do you think that Lefebvre conduct his research on urban space? What impresses you most of his thoughts?

5. What does the last paragraph intend to say about the two scholars?

B. Gap Filling

Provide the missing words according to the paragraphs you have just read.

30. As capitalism creates contradictions in urban space, spaces of difference emerge, that can be transformed into ______ of new human possibilities. If we cross-read his books on the city and on space thoroughly, we will find that the important qualities of differential space and counter-space have to do with aspects like: social and other human differences, the meeting of strangers, play and ______, human works as ______ objects, possibilities for the ______, unpredictability, inter-change and inter-active communication, as well as the use of all senses. All this should be human rights in urban space, according to Lefebvre! There is not much to learn about an urban design of difference in Lefebvre's books, though. He also thinks that

architects and especially urban planners normally do more harm than good. Sennett's ______ of his urban spaces of interest ______ those of Lefebvre's in many ways—including the encounter of strangers—but Sennett explicitly mentions the street, as the ______ important general aspect of the city. When it comes to the ______ of urban design, Sennett is also as negative about the professionals involved, as is Lefebvre. Although, Sennett tries to find the keys to an urban design that makes a difference, he does not come up with very much of ______ practical use either. Heclearly is in favour of discontinuities and non-linearities in social space as well as in physical space, but nobody can ______ how to build cities from his book.

Supplementary Reading (15)

Passage B: Experiencing Place

1. Relph begins *Place and Placelessness* with a review of space and its relationship to place. He argues that space is not a void or an isometric plane or a kind of container that holds places. Instead, he contends that, to study the relationship of space to a more experientially-based understanding of place, then space too must be explored in terms of how people experience it. Although Relph says that there are countless types and intensities of spatial experience, he delineates a heuristic structure grounded in "a continuum that has direct experience at one extreme and abstract thought at the other..." (Relph, 1976: 9). On one hand, he identifies modes of spatial experience that are instinctive, bodily, and immediate—for example, what he calls pragmatic space, perceptual space, and existential space. On the other hand, he identifies modes of spatial experience that are more cerebral, ideal, and intangible—for example, planning space, cognitive space, and abstract space. Relph describes how each of these modes of space-as-experienced has varying intensities in everyday life. For example, existential space—the particular taken-for-granted environmental and spatial constitution of one's everyday world grounded in culture and social structure—can be experienced in a highly self-conscious way such as when one is overwhelmed by the beauty and sacredness of a Gothic cathedral; or in a tacit, unself-conscious way as one sits in the office day after day paying little attention to his or her surroundings. Although the spatial modes that Relph identifies may each play a particular role in everyday experience, Relph emphasizes that in reality these modes are not mutually exclusive but all part and parcel of human spatial experience as a lived, indivisible whole. For example,

he explains that cognitive conceptions of space understood through maps may help to form our perceptual knowledge, which in turn may color our day-to-day spatial encounters as we move through real-world places. Though a radical idea in the 1970s, Relph's conclusion that space is heterogeneous and infused with many different lived dimensions is largely taken for granted in geographical studies today as researchers speak of such spatial modes as sacred space, gendered space, commodified space, and the like.

2. One of Relph's central accomplishments in *Place and Placelessness* is his preserving an intimate conceptual engagement between space and place. Many geographers speak of both concepts but ultimately treat the two as separate or give few indications as to how they are related existentially and conceptually. For Relph, the unique quality of place is its power to order and to focus human intentions, experiences, and actions spatially. Relph thus sees space and place as dialectically structured in human environmental experience, since our understanding of space is related to the places we inhabit, which in turn derive meaning from their spatial context.

Depth of Place

3. A central reason for Relph's exhaustive study of place is his firmly held belief that such understanding might contribute to the maintenance and restoration of existing places and the making of new places. He argues that, without a thorough understanding of place as it has human significance, one would find it difficult to describe why a particular place is special and impossible to know how to repair existing places in need of mending. In short, before we can properly prescribe, we must first learn how to accurately describe—a central aim of phenomenological research.

4. In examining place in depth, Relph focuses on people's identity *of* and *with* place. By the identity *of* a place, he refers to its "persistent sameness and unity which allows that [place] to be differentiated from others" (Relph, 1976: 45). Relph describes this persistent identity in terms of three components: (1) the place's physical setting; (2) its activities, situations, and events; and (3) the individual and group meanings created through people's experiences and intentions in regard to that place.

5. Relph emphasizes, however, that place identity defined in this threefold way is not sufficiently pivotal or deep existentially because, most essentially, places are "significant centres of our immediate experiences of the world" (Relph, 1976: 141). If places are to be more thoroughly understood, one needs a language whereby we can identify particular place experiences in terms of the intensity of meaning and intention that a person and place hold for

each other. For Relph, the crux of this lived intensity is identity *with* place, which he defines through the concept of *insideness*—the degree of attachment, involvement, and concern that a person or group has for a particular place.

Insideness and Outsideness

6. Relph's elucidation of insideness is perhaps his most original contribution to the understanding of place because he effectively demonstrates that this concept is the core lived structure of place as it has meaning in human life. If a person feels inside a place, he or she is here rather than there, safe rather than threatened, enclosed rather than exposed, at ease rather than stressed. Relph suggests that the more profoundly inside a place a person feels, the stronger will be his or her identity with that place. On the other hand, a person can be separate or alienated from place, and this mode of place experience is what Relph calls *outsideness.* Here, people feel some sort of lived division or separation between themselves and world—for example, the feeling of homesickness in a new place. The crucial phenomenological point is that outsideness and insideness constitute a fundamental dialectic in human life and that, through varying combinations and intensities of out-sideness and insideness, different places take on different identities for different individuals and groups, with human experience taking on different qualities of feeling, meaning, ambience, and action.

7. The strongest sense of place experience is what Relph calls *existential insideness*—a situation of deep, unself-conscious immersion in place and the experience most people know when they are at home in their own community and region. The opposite of existential insideness is what he labels *existential outsideness*—a sense of strangeness and alienation, such as that often felt by newcomers to a place or by people who, having been away from their birth place, return to feel strangers because the place is no longer what it was when they knew it earlier.

8. In his book, Relph discusses seven modes of insideness and outsideness (no doubt there are more) grounded in various levels of experiential involvement and meaning. The value of these modes, particularly for self-awareness, is that they apply to specific place experiences yet provide a conceptual structure in which to understand those experiences in broader, more explicit terms.

True or False Statements

(b66) According to Relph, place is human knowledge.

(b67) To make place analyzable Relph has put it in different types.

(b68) It can be seen that in Relph's understanding place is the same as space.

(b69) It can be concluded that Relph's insideness and outsideness coincidentally correspond to Lefebvre's inwardness and outwardness.

(b70) "The depth of place" refers to physical dimension which can be mended when necessary.

(b71) It's safe to say that the depth of place must relate to the its insideness and not its outsideness.

(b72) Human consciousness must play a crucial role in making the placeness of place.

Passage C: Place and Space

Place and the Media

1. Before the modern period, everything that could be reached was in a place. This is what globalization theorists refer to when they claim that in pre-modern times the experience of place overlapped with the experience of time and space. In pre-modern times, everything, including time and space, was in one's place, because one had no knowledge of anything beyond one's own immediate experience. Although the use of place and space is often overlapping and confusing, it is important to try to distinguish between the two. If people's experience of time, place and space has fundamentally changed, what then is actually changing? To answer this question it is important to differentiate place from space. For Giddens (1990), place is best conceptualized by means of the idea of locale, which refers to the physical settings of social activity as situated geographically. Place compared with space is something familiar and concrete ("there is no place like home").

2. Relph writes that "to be human is to live in a world that is filled with significant places and to have and to know your place" (1976). Space is often understood as something bigger than place, often even as something empty. The shrinking of space is equivalent to the shrinking of distance in purely geographical terms. Space is thought to be out there, outside the borders of place. It can also be unknown and unconquered, an open space. In contrast to place, space used to be something that could not be reached, because it was outside the experience of place. Place has often been "naturalized"—taken for something that is more "real" than space. When one refers to place, one refers, although not often consciously, to such phenomena as roots, belonging, interpersonal relationships and face-to-face communication.

3. Mattelart (2000) observes that place is triply symbolic because it relates to identity, relationships and history. It symbolizes the relationship of each of its occupants with her/himself, with the other occupants, and with their common history. Obviously, the underlying thought here is that it is something small rather than big, close rather than distant. More often the use of the term "place" refers to villages, neighbourhoods and communities where people know each other and have interpersonal communication without recourse to media and communications. This is, of course, still how many people live most of their lives: they belong to a community, whether it is their neighbourhood, their workplace or the place they spend their free time.

4. Harvey (1993) refers to the importance of place in the formation of identities, because place is a fundamental means by which people make sense of the world and through which they act. Crang (1998) points out that people do not simply locate themselves, they define themselves through a sense of place. He writes:

> *Places provide an anchor of shared experiences between people and continuity over time. Spaces become places as they become "time thickened". They have a past and a future that bind people together round them. The lived connection binds people and places together. It enables people to define themselves and to share experiences with others and form themselves into communities.* (1998: 103)

5. In defining places, one often gets the impression that media and communication are not a part of these. The significance of place is clearly seen in many writers' work, most notably in Heidegger's famous phrase that "place is the locale of the truth of being". Heidegger made very few references in his writings to the media, and was disturbed and even terrified at the distancelessness which space-time compression introduced. As Harvey (1993) observes, Heidegger refused to see mediated social relationships with others as in any way expressive of any kind of authenticity. Heidegger is not alone. Many theorists see media and communications as bringing fundamental change to places. For example, Giddens writes:

> *In pre-modern societies, space and place largely coincide, since the spatial dimensions of social life are, for most of the population, and even in most respects, dominated by "presence"—by localised activities. The advent of modernity increasingly tears away from place by fostering relations between "absent" others, locationally distant from any given situation of*

face-to-face interaction. In conditions of modernity, place becomes increasingly phantasmagoric: that is to say, locales are thoroughly penetrated and shaped in terms of social influences quite distant from them. (1990)

6. Although Giddens acknowledges the changing nature of relationships between places, and thus indirectly inside places, he sees places becoming "phantasmagoric", which could mean "a shifting series or succession of phantasms or imaginary figures, as seen in a dream or fevered condition, as called up by the imagination, or as created by literary description". Many time-space theorists see media and communications as things that are unreal and that threaten even the authenticity of places. Relph (1976) makes a distinction between authentic and non-authentic attitudes to places. He writes:

An authentic attitude to place is thus understood to be a direct and genuine experience of the entire complex of the identity of places—not mediated and distorted through a series of quite arbitrary social andintellectual fashions about how the experience should be, nor following stereotyped conventions. It comes from a full awareness of places for what they are as products of man's intentions and the meaningful settings for human activities, or from a profound and unselfconscious identity with place. (1976)

7. Relph uses the concept of placelessness to describe the lookalike landscapes that result from improved communications, increased mobility and imitation. He points out the role of media and communications in this process by writing that "mass communication appears to result in a growing uniformity of landscape and a lessening of places by encouraging and transmitting general and standardized tastes and fashions" (1976). According to Relph (1976), among the processes that encourage placelessness are: (1) mass communication and modes of diffusion of mass attitudes and kitsch fashions; and (2) mass culture of dictated and standardized values, maintained by but also making possible mass communication.

Space and the Media

8. In contrast to place, space is a much more abstract term; but at the same time it is related to place. Massey writes that "social relations always have a spatial form and a spatial content... Given that it is a construction of space, a place is formed out of the particular set of social relations which interact at a particular location" (1994). De Certeau observes that "space

is a practiced place thus the street geometrically defined by urban planning is transformed into a space by walkers" (1984) is often quoted when people want to understand the difference between place and space. As Lie (2002) observes, in an interpretive sense, this quotation summarizes the difference between space and place. It means that space is a lived place; thus, through (inter) action and communication, places are transformed into spaces and become spaces of communication. Further, he writes that:

> *... places are fixed and stable. Borders of places are set and can precisely be determined. Borders of spaces are flexible and are constructed in a symbolic, interpretative way. Thus, "walking in the city" transforms the place into space. Moreover, "watching television in the home" can for instance also be seen as practiced or lived place. This is not only the case because the home is a geographical defined setting, but also because the television text itself—in De Certeau's words (in the context of a written text) "a place constituted by a system of signs" (De Certeau, 1984: 117)—is by the act of watching transformed into space. Such, by the act of consumption and interpretation, created spaces of communication can be geographical and physical, as well as non-physical and non-geographical.*

9. This is a very different view of the difference between place and space. They are not contradictory, but transitory and as a result often overlapping. Thus the difference between place and space should not be seen in a clear-cut way where place represents everything that is good and worth protecting threatened by space which seeks to transform it into non-authentic place (space). What we actually see is that place and space are becoming closer to each other, becoming *splace*, largely because of media and communications. Media and communications transform place and space, not only by connecting places with each other and shortening the distance between them, but by creating new spaces within and outside places where former rules and norms do not necessarily hold. Space could also be seen as something liberating, with elusive boundaries and with new possibilities, but spaces can also become restrictive, closed and hierarchical. Spaces like places are not free of power, and struggles are fought over who is taking control over them. We have talked about time, place and space in a rather abstract way, almost entirely without the people who live in places, transform places, move from one place to another, discover new places, and combine places with others, thus creating new combinations of places and spaces. All this occurs through time, in time and sometimes on time. While doing all this, people contribute to globalization in which time, place and space are becoming more

interrelated because of media and communications.

True or False Statements

Place and the Media

(c10) The first paragraph in the passage deals with the concept of "space".

(c11) Paragraphs 4 and 5, however, discuss how place get involved in physical dimension.

(c12) "Phantasmagoric" in Paragraph 6 means "place" can come into people's mind.

(c13) Heidegger and his like must feel very unaccustomed in the world where hyperreality dominates.

(c14) "Placelessness" is caused by mass media in communication.

Space and the Media

(c15) "Space" contains more human intervention.

(c16) The word "*splace*" in Paragraph 9 suggests the complexity of space.

(c17) It's not so interesting to study space as to study place for modern scholars because the former is more elusive to define.

(c18) Neither place nor space can get out of power's restrain because it's human's understanding of it.

(c19) Obviously "space" suggests more factors intertwined while place seems a more static concept.

Passage D: Hyperreality

1. Holography, the latest technical miracle of laser rays, was invented back in the '50's by Dennis Gabor; it achieves a full-color photographic representation that is more than three-dimensional. You look into a magic box and a miniature train or horse appears; as you shift your gaze you can see those parts of the object that you were prevented from glimpsing by the laws of perspective. If the box is circular you can see the object from all sides. If the object was filmed, thanks to various devices, in motion, then it moves before your eyes, or else you move, and as you change position, you can see the girl wink or the fisherman drain the can of beer in his hand. It isn't cinema, but rather a kind of virtual object in three dimensions that exists even where you don't see it, and if you move you can see it there, too.

2. Holography isn't a toy: NASA has studied it and employed it in space exploration. It is

used in medicine to achieve realistic depictions of anatomical changes; it has applications in aerial cartography, and in many industries for the study of physical processes. But it is now being taken up by artists who formerly might have been photorealists, and it satisfies the most ambitious ambitions of photorealism. In San Francisco, at the door of the Museum of Witchcraft, the biggest hologram ever made is on display: of the Devil, with a very beautiful witch. Holography could prosper only in America, a country obsessed with realism, where, if a reconstruction is to be credible, it must be absolutely iconic, a perfect likeness, a "real" copy of the reality being represented.

3. Cultivated Europeans and Europeanized Americans think of the United States as the home of the glass-and-steel skyscraper and of abstract expressionism. But the United States is also the home of Superman, the superhuman comic-strip hero who has been in existence since 1938. Every now and then Superman feels a need to be alone with his memories, and he flies off to an inaccessible mountain range where, in the heart of the rock, protected by a huge steel door, is the Fortress of Solitude.

4. Here Superman keeps his robots, completely faithful copies of himself, miracles of electronic technology, which from time to time he sends out into the world to fulfill a pardonable desire for ubiquity. And the robots are incredible, because their resemblance to reality is absolute; they are not mechanical men, all cogs and beeps, but perfect "copies" of human beings, with skin, voice, movements, and the ability to make decisions. For Superman the fortress is a museum of memories: Everything that has happened in his adventurous life is recorded here in perfect copies or preserved in a miniaturized form of the original. Thus he keeps the city of Kandor, a survival from the destruction of the planet Krypton, under a glass bell of the sort familiar from your great-aunt's Victorian parlor. Here, on a reduced scale, are Kandor's buildings, highways, men, and women. Superman's scrupulousness in preserving all the mementoes of his past recalls those private museums, or Wunderkammer, so frequent in German baroque civilization, which originated in the treasure chambers of medieval lords and perhaps, before that, with Roman and Hellenistic collections. In those old collections a unicorn's horn would be found next to the copy of a Greek statue, and, later, among mechanical crèches and wondrous automata, cocks of precious metal that sang, clocks with a procession of little figures that paraded at noon.

5. But at first Superman's fussiness seemed incredible because, we thought, in our day a Wunderkammer would no longer fascinate anybody. Postinformal art hadn't yet adopted practices such as Arman's crammed assemblage of watchcases arranged in a glass case, or Spoerri's

fragments of everyday life (a dinner table after an untidy meal, an unmade bed), or the postconceptual exercises of an artist like Annette Messanger, who accumulates memories of her childhood in neurotically archivistic notebooks which she exhibits as works of art.

6. The most incredible thing was that, to record some past events, Superman reproduced them in the form of life-size wax statues, rather macabre, very Musée Grévin. Naturally the statues of the photorealists had not yet come on the scene, but even when they did it was normal to think of their creators as bizarre avant-garde artists, who had developed as a reaction to the civilization of the abstract or to the Pop aberration. To the reader of "Superman" it seemed that his museographical quirks had no real connection with American taste and mentality. And yet in America there are many Fortresses of Solitude, with their wax statues, their automata, their collections of inconsequential wonders. You have only to go beyond the Museum of Modern Art and the art galleries, and you enter another universe, the preserve of the average family, the tourist, the politician.

7. The most amazing Fortress of Solitude was erected in Austin, Texas, by President Lyndon Johnson, during his own lifetime, as monument, pyramid, personal mausoleum. I'm not referring to the immense imperial-modern-style construction or to the forty-thousand red containers that hold all the documents of his political life, or to the half million documentary photographs, the portraits, the voice of Mrs. Johnson narrating her late husband's life for visitors. No, I am referring to the mass of souvenirs of the Man's scholastic career, the honeymoon snapshots, the nonstop series of films that tell visitors of the presidential couple's foreign trips, and the wax statues that wear the wedding dresses of the daughters Luci and Lynda, the full-scale reproduction of the Oval Office, the red shoes of the ballerina Maria Tallchief, the pianist Van Cliburn's autograph on a piece of music, the plumed hat worn by Carol Channing in Hello, Dolly! (all mementoes justified by the fact that the artists in question performed at the White House), and the gifts proffered by envoys of various countries, an Indian feather headdress, testimonial panels in the form of ten-gallon hats, doilies embroidered with the American flag, a sword given by the king of Thailand, and the moon rock brought back by the astronauts. The Lyndon B. Johnson Library is a true Fortress of Solitude: a *Wunderkammer*, an ingenious example of narrative art, wax museum, cave of robots. And it suggests that there is a constant in the average American imagination and taste, for which the past must be preserved and celebrated in full-scale authentic copy; a philosophy of immortality as duplication. It dominates the relation with the self, with the past, not infrequently with the present, always with History and, even, with the European tradition.

8. Constructing a full-scale model of the Oval Office (using the same materials, the same colors, but with everything obviously more polished, shinier, protected against deterioration) means that for historical information to be absorbed, it has to assume the aspect of a reincarnation. To speak of things that one wants to connote as real, these things must seem real. The "completely real" becomes identified with the "completely fake". Absolute unreality is offered as real presence. The aim of the reconstructed Oval Office is to supply a "sign" that will then be forgotten as such: The sign aims to be the thing, to abolish the distinction of the reference, the mechanism of replacement. Not the image of the thing, but its plaster cast. Its double, in other words. From Eco's *Travel in Hyperreality*, 1991)

True or False Statements

(d1) Holograph is a combination of the real and the unreal by modern technology.

(d2) NASA and medicine used holograph because it is virtual.

(d3) In Paragraph 2 the author said that the Americans obsessed with realism but people in other parts of the world didn't.

(d4) According to Paragraph 3 the Americans actually preferred unreal things.

(d5) Superman's robot is a copy of the copy the Americans copy.

(d6) According to Paragraph 5 Europeans don't like to relive their memories.

(d7) Paragraph 7 suggests that we can see the real from the unreal such as the average Americans and politicians.

(d8) According to Paragraph 7 people can see the Fortress of Solitude of the average Americans' psychological need.

(d9) In the last paragraph the author praises this form of new culture.

Bibliography

陈文华. 文化学概论[M]. 上海：上海文艺出版社，2001.

[英]多米尼克·斯特里纳蒂. 通俗文化理论导论[M]. 阎嘉，译. 周宪，许钧，主编. 北京：商务印书馆，2001.

胡文仲. 文化与交际[M]. 北京：外语教学与研究出版社，1997.

金元浦. 文化研究：理论与实践[M]. 开封：河南大学出版社，2004.

[美]彼默，瓦纳. 全球环境中的跨文化沟通[M]. 北京：清华大学出版社，2003.

周宪. 视觉文化的转向[M]. 北京：北京大学出版社，2008.

Barker, Chris. *Cultural Studies: Theory and Practice* [M]. London: Sage Publications Ltd., 2000.

Butler, Judith. *Gender Trouble: Feminism and Subversion of Identity*[M]. London: Routledge, 1990.

Barthes, Roland. *S/Z*[M]. Trans. R. Howard. Oxford: Blackwell, 1974.

Barthes, Roland. *The Fashion System* [M]. Trans. Matthew Ward and Richard Howard. London: Jonathan Cape, 1985.

Benveniste, Émile. The Semiology of Language[A]. In Innis Robert E. (ed.). *Semiotics, an Introductory Reader*[M]. Bloomington: Indiana University Press, 1986: 228-246.

Bloomfield, Leonard. *Linguistic Aspects of Science*[M]. Chicago, IL: University of Chicago Press, 1939.

Cohen, Anthony P. (ed.) *Signifying Identity*[M]. London: Routledge, 2000.

Crang, M. Places of Practice and the Practice of Science[J]. *Environment and Planning A.*, 1998, 30 (11): 1971-1974.

Saussure, Ferdinand. *Course in General Linguistics* [M]. Trans. R. Harris. London: Duckworth, 1983.

De Saussure, Ferdinand. *Course in General Linguistics*[M]. Trans. by Wade Baskin. New York: McGraw-Hill, 1966.

Diamond, Milton. Sex and Gender: Same or Different? [EB/OL]. http: //www. Hawaii.

edu/PCSS/online_artcls/intersex/sexual_I_G_web. html, n. p.

De Certeau, M. *The Practice of Everyday Life*[M]. Berkeley, CA: University of California Press, 1984.

Eco, Umberto. *A Theory of Semiotics*[M]. Bloomington: Indiana University Press, 1976.

Fiske, John. Popular Culture[A]. In Frank Lentricchia & Thomas Mclaughlin (eds.). *Critical Terms for Literary Study*[M]. Chicago: University of Chicago Press, 1995.

Fiske, John and John Hartley. *Reading Television*[M]. London: Methuen, 1978.

Giddens, Antony. *The Consequences of Modernity*[M]. Stanford University Press, Stanford, California, 1990.

Greenblatt, Stephen. Culture[A]. In Frank Lentricchia & Thomas Mclaughlin (eds.). *Critical Terms for Literary Study*[M]. Chicago: University of Chicago Press, 1995.

Hjelmslev, L. Prolegomena to a Theory of Language[M]. Trans. F. J.

Whitfield, Madison. WI: University of Wisconsin Press, 1961.

Hockett, Charles F. *A Course in Modern Linguistics*[M]. New York: Macmillan, 1958.

Houston, Larry. *Identity a "Homosexual"* [EB/OL]. http://www. banap. net/spip. php? article64, n. p; and http://www. banap. net/spip. php? articles94, n. p.

Jakobson, Roman. Current Issues of General Linguistics[A]. In Linda R. Waugh and Monique Monville-Burston (eds). *On Language*[M]. Cambridge, MA: Harvard University Press, Cambridge, MA. 1990.

Jakobson, Roman. *Essais de linguistique générale*[M]. Paris: Éditions de Minuit, 1963.

Jakobson, Roman. The Poetry of Grammar and the Grammar of of Poetry[J]. *Lingua*, 1968 (21): 597-609.

Jakobson, Roman. Linguistics in Relation to Other Sciences [A]. In Linda R. Waugh and Monique Monville-Burston (eds). *On Language* [M]. Cambridge, MA: Harvard University Press, 1990.

Jakobson, Roman. The Concept of Phoneme[A]. In Linda R. Waugh and Monique Monville-Burston (eds). *On Language*[M]. Cambridge, MA: Harvard University Press, 1990.

Jakobson, Roman. Quest for the Essence of Language [A]. In L. R Waugh, M Monville-Burston (eds.). *On Language*[M]. Harvard University Press, Cambridge, MA, 1990.

Kristeva, Julia. The System and the Speaking Subject [J]. *Times Literary Supplement*, 1973 (10): 1249.

Langer, Susanne K. *Philosophy in a New Key: A Study in the Symbolism of Reason, Rite and Art*[M]. New York: Mentor, 1951.

Locke, John. *An Essay Concerning Human Understanding*[M]. London and New York, 1960.

Lévi-Strauss, Claude. *Structural Anthropology* [M]. Trans. Claire Jacobson and Brooke Grundfest Schoepf. Harmondsworth: Penguin, 1972.

Loomba, Ania. *Colonialism/Postcolonalism*[M]. London: Routledge, 1998.

Mao Sihui. Cultures Translated and Appropriated: Rethinking Ethnicity, Nationscape and Cultural Identity[A]. *Translation Quarterly*, 2000, 16 &17.

Morris, C. *Foundations of the Theory of Signs* [M]. Chicago: University of Chicago Press, 1938.

Peirce, C. S. *Collected Papers of Charles Sanders Peirce*[M]. Cambridge, MA: The Belknap Press of Harvard University Press, 1974.

Relph, E. *Place and Placelessness*[M]. London: Pion, 1976.

Said, E. *Orientalism: Western Conceptions of the Orient*[M]. Harmondsworth, Penguin, 1995.

Selden, Raman. Peter Widdowsin & Peter Brooker (eds.). *A Reader's Guide to Contemporary Theory*[M]. London: Prentice Hall, 1997.

Silver, Kaja. *The Subject of Semiotics*[M]. London: Oxford University Press, 1983.

Todorov, Tzvetan. *Theories of the Symbol*[M]. Trans. Catherine Porter Ithaca, NY: Cornell University Press, 1982.

http://www. hawaii. edu/PCSS/online_artcls/intersex/sexual,, I_G _web. html.

http://www. hawaii. edu/PCSS/online_artcls/intersex/sexual,, I G_web. html.

http://www. banap. net/spip. php? article64 and http://www. banap. net/spip. php? article94.

http://www. riccibase. com/docflle/cw04. htm.

http://www. osi. hu/mp/program_uk/yorkcori^papers2001/Globalization and Identity, m.

http://www. wacc. org. uk/wacc/publications/media _ development/2006 _ 1/globalization _ national_culture_and, th_search_for_identity_a_chmese_dilemma.

http://plato. stanfo rd. edu/entries/globalization/#l.

http://www. wisegeek. corn/what-is-discourse, htm.

http://www. hydra, umn. edu/demda/sign-play. html.

http://csmt. uchicago. edu/glossaiy2004/discourse. htm.

http://www. lib. latrobe. edu-au/AHR/copyright. html.

http://anthro. palomar. edu/ethmcity/ethmc_l. htm.

http://wwv. zisi. net/htm/ztlw2/whyj/2005-07-20-34086-htm.

http://hjem. get2net. dk/gronlund/Life_and_complexity. html.

Appendix I

Answer Sheet for Supplementary Reading

Please copy out "T" (for true) or "F" (for false) in each circle from the supplementary passages you have chosen to read as homework.

Passages A (1-100)

1 ○	2 ○	3 ○	4 ○	5 ○	6 ○	7 ○	8 ○	9 ○	10 ○
11 ○	12 ○	13 ○	14 ○	15 ○	16 ○	17 ○	8 ○	19 ○	20 ○
21 ○	22 ○	23 ○	24 ○	25 ○	26 ○	27 ○	28 ○	29 ○	30 ○
31 ○	32 ○	33 ○	34 ○	35 ○	36 ○	37 ○	38 ○	39 ○	40 ○
41 ○	42 ○	43 ○	44 ○	45 ○	46 ○	47 ○	48 ○	49 ○	50 ○
51 ○	52 ○	53 ○	54 ○	55 ○	56 ○	57 ○	58 ○	59 ○	60 ○
61 ○	62 ○	63 ○	64 ○	65 ○	66 ○	67 ○	68 ○	69 ○	70 ○
71 ○	72 ○	73 ○	74 ○	75 ○	76 ○	77 ○	78 ○	79 ○	80 ○
81 ○	82 ○	83 ○	84 ○	85 ○	86 ○	87 ○	88 ○	89 ○	90 ○
91 ○	92 ○	93 ○	94 ○	95 ○	96 ○	97 ○	98 ○	99 ○	100 ○

Appendix Ⅱ

Answer Sheet for Supplementary Reading

Please copy out "T" (for true) or "F" (for false) in each circle from the supplementary passages you have chosen to read as homework.

Passages B (1-72)

1○	2○	3○	4○	5○	6○	7○	8○	9○	10○
11○	12○	13○	14○	15○	16○	17○	8○	19○	20○
21○	22○	23○	24○	25○	26○	27○	28○	29○	30○
31○	32○	33○	34○	35○	36○	37○	38○	39○	40○
41○	42○	43○	44○	45○	46○	47○	48○	49○	50○
51○	52○	53○	54○	55○	56○	57○	58○	59○	60○
61○	62○	63○	64○	65○	66○	67○	68○	69○	70○
71○	72○								

Passages C (1-19)

1○	2○	3○	4○	5○	6○	7○	8○	9○	10○
11○	12○	13○	14○	15○	16○	17○	8○	19○	

Passage D (1-9)

1○	2○	3○	4○	5○	6○	7○	8○	9○	